The design of educational exhibits

Second edition

compiled by
R. S. Miles* in collaboration with
M. B. Alt, D. C. Gosling,
B. N. Lewis and **A. F. Tout**

* British Museum (Natural History)
  London

London
UNWIN HYMAN
Boston   Sydney   Wellington

Published by the Academic Division of
Unwin Hyman Ltd
15-17 Broadwick Street, London W1V 1FP

Allen & Unwin Inc.,
8 Winchester Place, Winchester, Mass. 01890, USA

Allen & Unwin (Australia) Ltd,
8 Napier Street, North Sydney, NSW 2060, Australia

Allen & Unwin (New Zealand) Ltd in association with
the Port Nicholson Press Ltd,
60 Cambridge Terrace, Wellington, New Zealand

First published in 1982
Second edition, 1988

British Library Cataloguing in Publication Data

Miles, R. S.
    The design of educational exhibits. —
    2nd rev. ed
1. Exhibitions   2. Museum techniques
I. Title
069.5′5   AM151
ISBN 0-04-445078-8

Library of Congress Cataloging-in-Publication Data

Miles, Roger S.
    The design of educational exhibits/compiled by R. S. Miles in
    collaboration with M. B. Alt . . . (et al.). —2nd rev. ed.
Bibliography: p.
Includes index.
ISBN 0-04-445078-8 (pbk.: alk. paper)
1. Museums—Educational aspects. 2. Museum techniques.
3. Exhibitions.   I. Title.
AM7.M55   1988
069.5—dc19

Set in 10 on 11 point Times by Fotographics (Bedford) Ltd
and printed in Great Britain by The Oxford University Press, Oxford

Preface to first edition

We have written this book to help others engaged in the business of planning, designing, producing, evaluating and updating educational exhibitions. It is the sort of book we looked for some 10 years ago, but did not find, when starting work on a major new exhibition programme in the British Museum (Natural History) and needing guidance on what to think about and what to do. In the intervening years we have found that a lot of relevant knowledge does in fact exist, and would assist the systematic production of exhibitions of almost any kind. However, it does not, for the most part, exist in organised form or in the primary museum literature. Much of it comes from 'foreign' fields such as cybernetics, psychology, educational science and information design. But even where knowledge exists within the museum profession, it is rarely written down, so there is the problem of its repeated loss and rediscovery, with the side-effect that many exhibition failures are failures of knowledge rather than failures of individuals. Then again, published articles on exhibitions are, with one or two notable exceptions, too often anecdotal; they offer little in the way of practical advice and rarely draw conclusions that might be helpful to others. We hope, therefore, that this book will be the first step towards filling a real gap in the literature concerning exhibition design.

The scope and contents of this book were decided by the five authors in consultation with one another, each of whom then drafted one or more chapters. Although the five points of view do not always agree with one another, they are to a large extent reconcilable. M. B. Alt wrote Chapter 16; D. C. Gosling Chapters 7, 8, 9, 10 and 11; B. N. Lewis Chapter 3 and with M. B. Alt Chapter 15; R. S. Miles Chapters 1 and 2; and A. F. Tout Chapters 4, 5, 6, 12 13, 14 and 17. R. S. Miles edited the final drafts, assisted by B. N. Lewis, and saw the entire work through the press.

The views expressed in this book stem largely from our work in the British Museum (Natural History), but they are our views and do not necessarily, in all respects, reflect the attitudes or policy of the Museum. They have in fact been explicitly broadened to illuminate recurring problems of mounting educational exhibitions of virtually any sort. Throughout the book 'we' refers to the authors, unless the context clearly implies otherwise; 'he', 'his', 'himself' are used for both genders to avoid circumlocutions. Words printed in bold type are defined in the Glossary.

We are grateful to Kim Dennis-Bryan for her assistance throughout the production of this book, to Monica Bending for typing the manuscript and for unflagging help and encouragement in enumerable ways, and also to Ruth Withington for typing. We should like to thank Drs Howard Brunton, Giles Clarke, Michael Hills and Steven Griggs, and Rosalyn Rubenstein, for commenting on portions of the draft text, and other colleagues who have assisted in various ways. The photographs were taken by David Morbey.

R. S. MILES
London, March 1982

Preface to second edition

The scope and aims remain the same as in the first edition. However, in preparing this new edition I have taken the opportunity to clarify the text where this seemed possible, and to update it and the bibliography where this seemed necessary. Alan Tout has added a short section to Chapter 4, and he assisted with the revision of Chapters 7 and 8. Chapter 9 has been largely rewritten by the two of us to include developments in computer and videodisc exhibits, and new thinking on the relationship between media and modes. We are indebted to Naomi Lake for her word processing and to David Morbey for his photography.

Sadly our co-author Professor Brian Lewis died shortly after work started on this edition. He was the original inspiration behind the book, and a wise and gentle friend who, in addition to his own contributions, illuminated many of the problems that arose during its writing. This new edition is dedicated to his memory.

R. S. MILES
London, November 1986

Acknowledgements

We would like to thank the following organisations and individuals for permission to reproduce illustrations:

H. Bayer (1.7); University of Reading (1.8); Figure 2.3 reprinted with permission from *Curator*, vol. 19, 1976, copyright © The American Museum of Natural History; Figure 3.1 reprinted from *Educational technology in curriculum development* (D. Rowntree), 1974, with the permission of Harper & Row; Figure 4.1 reprinted from *Mathematics in management* (A. Battersby), p. 53, 1975, with the permission of Penguin Books; M. Neurath (9.14).

Contents

Preface to first edition	*page* vii
Preface to second edition	ix
Acknowledgements	x

1 Introduction — 1
Background — 1
Museums and educational exhibits — 2
The design tradition — 3
Objects, ideas and exhibits — 8
A second look at objects — 10

2 The general framework — 11
Stages of the operation — 11
Learning from experience — 14

3 Psychological and educational aspects of exhibition design — 20
The *prima-facie* case — 20
The empirical and theoretical case — 21
Improvability and its limitations — 22
The psychology of the exhibition visitor — 22
The lure of novelty — 24
The problem of attention — 24
Balancing reward and effort — 26
Some difficulties of empathy — 26
Techniques of effective teaching — 27
Subject-matter, content and structure — 28
Assessing suitability — 30
Order and format — 31
The problem of success — 32
Student success and difficulty — 33
Overarching principles — 33
Ways of knowing — 34
Some physical convincers — 37
General comment — 38

4 Planning the work — 39
Critical path analysis — 39
The secondment problem — 41
The exhibition brief — 43
Cost control — 45

5 The exhibition team — 46
Subdivision of the main task — 46
How long for how much? — 46

6 Organising the intellectual content — *page* 50
Elaborating the first outline — 51
Beyond the pilot exhibition — 53
Mapping content on to available space — 55

7 Laying out the exhibition — 56
The starting point — 56
A case study — 57
Estimating the space — 60
Island displays — 61
Expressing a theme — 61

8 The individual exhibits — 64
Some hazards of communication — 65
Function and sequence — 66
Maps and signposts — 71
Numbering exhibits — 72
Housing the exhibits — 74
Travelling exhibitions — 76

9 Choosing media and their modes of use — 78
Selecting the medium — 78
Modes of use — 79
The ends to be attained — 80
The range of choice — 83
Helping the user — 99
Postscript — 100

10 Disabled visitors — 102
Accessibility for the physically disabled — 102
Accessibility for the blind and the partially sighted — 104
Accessibility for the deaf — 104
Accessibility and the mentally disabled — 104
Conclusions — 105

11 Conservation — 106
Light — 106
Humidity and its effects — 107
Air pollution — 107
Microclimates — 108
Security — 109
Maintenance — 110

12 The specification   *page* 111
      The specification document   111

13 Scheduling, monitoring and controlling
      exhibit production   115
      Activities and outputs   115
      Scheduling and monitoring   118
      Three different timescales   120
      The smaller team   121

14 Improving the performance   122
      Publications   122
      Support activities   124
      Learning from experience   125
      Planning and organisation   126

15 Evaluation: its nature, limitations and
      dangers   127
      Evaluation and conflict   128
      Walking the tightrope   130
      A second look   132
      Evaluation in action   133
      Methodological limitations   136
      The psycho-dynamics and politics of
        evaluation   141

16 Designing and carrying out the evaluation
      study   144
      Classification of evaluation
        techniques   144
      Types of investigations in summative
        evaluation   145
      Types of investigations in formative
        evaluation   146
      Sampling visitors for museum
        evaluations: preliminary
        considerations   147

      The arithmetic mean ($\bar{x}$) and standard
        deviation (s) of a sample variable *page* 147
      Standard error of the mean and
        sample size   150
      Randomness and random sampling   153
      Sampling museum visitors: practical
        considerations   155
      Sampling and experimental designs
        for formative evaluation   156
      Methods of data collection   158
      Observation studies   159
      Interviewing   159
      Designing a questionnaire   161
      Further issues of data collection:
        objective tests and rating scales   162
      Validity and reliability   163
      Coding the data   164
      Analysing the data   166
      Tables and graphs   166
      Measures of central tendency and
        variability   166
      Measures of relations or
        correlations   167
      Analysis of differences   168
      Reporting the data: writing the report 168

17 Replacement and renewal   171
      The simple model   171
      Balancing replacement and renewal   174
      Two types of output   178
      Looking forward   180
      The short-term situation   182

      Glossary   185

      Bibliography   189

      Index   194

1 Introduction

This book is concerned with the problems that arise in designing effective **exhibits**, and with ways of overcoming them.

The British Museum (Natural History) has pioneered the development of several new-style **exhibitions** over the last few years. In doing this work, we have discovered numerous pitfalls and obstacles to progress, and with our colleagues have developed systematic procedures to cover all stages, from the initial germ of an idea for an exhibit to its design and eventual construction, evaluation and revision. We believe these procedures apply generally and could be a useful starting point for other people involved in the design of 'educational' exhibitions. As far as possible we have recorded our experience in the form of practical guidelines.

Although the literature on exhibition design, particularly where it concerns museums, gives the impression that those who are responsible for exhibitions are people who know what to do, are content with their knowledge, and who do not cultivate an enquiring frame of mind, it is our contention that things can, and frequently do, go wrong unless systematic procedures are adopted. What is needed is an approach that will help identify the sorts of mistakes that are likely to be made and give assistance in avoiding critical errors.

Background

The word 'educational', as applied to exhibitions, sometimes causes difficulties because it can mean different things to different readers. The context in which we are interested in the word is explored in some depth in Chapter 3 in the section on the psychology of the exhibition visitor. Before embarking on this enquiry, however, it is worth making two observations. First, all exhibitions, by their very nature (i.e. by virtue of their being described as exhibitions), invariably have *some* educational content. Secondly, although exhibitions almost always try to tell visitors things that they are unlikely to have known before, there are many kinds of exhibitions in which the educative component is *not* the most important.

For example, so-called 'trade exhibitions' are primarily designed to boost sales. Personal exhibitions by artists may similarly be designed to promote the reputation (and, hence, the commercial value) of the artists concerned. A police exhibition of torture implements, or weapons of violence used by criminals, might be put on to shock and move the public conscience. An exhibition of military power might be intended to imbue the public with a sense of security, or respect for authority. On the other hand, a display of folk dancing, or an exhibition of roses, might be set up solely to give pleasure. In all such cases, there is an educative component in the sense that visitors and spectators are likely to learn things which are of interest to them, and which they did not know before. But the educative component is only of secondary importance.

Let us also notice that some exhibitions are essentially *self-congratulatory* in purpose. An exhibitor might simply want visitors to know how rich or clever or discerning or dedicated he is. A common example of the self-congratulatory exhibition occurs when schools mount exhibitions of the work and accomplishments of their pupils. In a society that reveres prowess of almost every kind, such 'look-at-what-we-have-done' exhibitions are enjoyable occasions for doting parents, and for the pupils and staff on whom praise gets bestowed. Such exhibitions may also be part of a deeper political game in which 'good publicity' – e.g. a splash across the front page of the local newspaper – can be exploited to request additional resources from, say, the local education authority or the parent-teacher association. Once again, education is by no means the *primary* objective of such exhibitions. It remains true, however, that such exhibitions will fail to achieve their sought-after objectives (of admiration, publicity, additional funds, and the like) unless the appropriate messages – of success, accomplishment, and so on – are got across.

According to the *Oxford English Dictionary*,

an exhibition is a display of some kind. It is something that is submitted or made available for human inspection. If one assumes that all exhibitions have to have a *purpose*, it will seem to follow that exhibitions must always be man-made. But there is a more general sense (metaphorical, perhaps) in which people sometimes speak of exhibitions that occur naturally. Examples of naturally occurring exhibitions would be the dawn chorus, a mating dance, a blanket of wild flowers in spring, a spectacular cloud formation, a display of thunder and lightning, an avalanche, a volcanic eruption, and so on.

If we ask ourselves why we are inclined to describe such naturally occurring events as exhibitions, we find ourselves justifying the description on the grounds that the events in question all have a *spectacular* quality about them and are, partly for that reason, *educative* experiences. This book does not concern itself with exhibitions that are 'put on by nature', but it is worth pausing to note the essential ingredient of *emotional impact*. To describe something as an exhibition is to raise the expectation that it will in some way move or touch us, emotionally. If we fail to find ourselves moved or touched by something that has been described to us as an exhibition, there is a corresponding tendency for us to feel 'let down'.

Exhibitions can have a variety of objectives. Among those already mentioned are the objectives of sales promotion, advancing of personal reputations, arousing of public concern, inducing of sense of security, sheer pleasure, self-display, and so on. Countless other objectives (aesthetic enjoyment, inducing of conformity, propaganda . . .) are also possible, and particular exhibitions may well be designed to achieve several objectives at once. People who are responsible for mounting particular exhibitions are therefore faced with two difficult questions. First of all, they must ask themselves exactly what objectives they are most desirous of achieving. Secondly, they must ask themselves how such objectives, once identified, can best be achieved. In other words, they must first of all *commit* themselves to the pursuit of a justifiable and worthwhile set of objectives. Next, they must place the objectives in a suitable order of priority. Finally, they must discover ways of ensuring that the objectives are accomplished in a competent manner.

Museums and educational exhibits

Museums are readily associated with exhibitions and much of what we have to say will be said in the context of museum displays, although our points are intended to apply to all educational exhibitions regardless of where they are mounted.

In various ways, and with differing emphases, most museums are concerned with the collection, conservation, study and display of objects. An interesting exception to this rule is provided by some modern science and technology museums – or science centres – that are primarily concerned with the concepts of science and whose collections, if they exist at all, are not the primary reason for their existence. But, by and large, the generalisation holds true and the display of objects gives museums their main claim to an educative purpose. The reason for this will be clear from a brief look at the history of museums.

Wittlin's *Museums: in search of a usable future* (1970) and Hudson's *A social history of museums* (1975) and *Museums for the 1980s* (1977) provide the necessary background information. Having their origins in the private collections of rich and leisured men, museums (at least in England) progressed slowly from admitting visitors as a privilege to admitting them as a right. Magnificent collections were built up over many years, and even in quite small museums these may now be without parallel as records of man's natural and cultural heritage. They are often priceless and irreplaceable. These collections have tended to make museums unique centres of reference and research because they attract scholarly activity. For all of these reasons, museums are widely considered to be ideal places for mounting significant educational exhibitions.

Not surprisingly then, large sums of money are spent annually by many museums on activities that are claimed to serve a predominantly educative purpose. Exhibits are designed and installed, books are written, lectures are arranged and specialist staff are employed to assist school groups and casual visitors. These activities occupy the time of many specialists and account for a considerable part of each museum's budget. Almost without exception, these educational activities are carried out in the name of the general public. Museums regularly claim to serve the public at large, rather than just the professional scholar or university student, and it is on these grounds that funds are provided for new exhibitions and related educational activities.

If museums claim funds in this way, it becomes a matter of some importance to enquire how well they are fulfilling their general educative purpose. Do they give value for money? Educationalists and students of museums have recently started to form some definite opinions on this. The consensus is that museums fail in general to provide the lay visitors with a good educational experience. The **displays** may be full of interest for a minority audience of scholars who already know the subject, but their meaning and significance tend to be lost on the uninformed visitor. This person simply wanders round in a comparative state of bemusement, so that at the end of the day very little has been learned. In these circumstances museums have, as Hudson puts it, remarkable powers of making the uneducated feel inferior.

Our own view, in writing this book, is that where this unsatisfactory state of affairs persists year after year, the public is entitled to ask whether the museums that fail in this respect are getting part of their money under false pretences. This is particularly the case because museums could, at almost no extra cost, make significant improvements to their existing educational provision. What is more, at some extra cost, they could offer new educative facilities of a demonstrably superior kind.

The design tradition

Museums are idiosyncratic institutions each of which is unique in some way, but nevertheless, rather than attempting a general history of design in museums, we give below an account of the changes in approach of the one we are most familiar with. This brings out a story which is far from unique.

The doors of the British Museum (Natural History) in South Kensington first opened to the public on 19 April 1881, the general arrangement of the galleries having been decided by Sir Richard Owen in the early 1860s. Setting out to show the Plan of Creation, Owen acknowledged at the lowest level the role of public showman, but generally he wanted exhibitions 'of a wider and higher nature than to gratify the gaze or the love of the marvellous', or 'charm the eye and gratify the sense of beauty and of grace'. His

educational aims were to be met by three separate displays (Fig. 1.1). The first of these was arranged in the front and back galleries of the Museum to give a 'comprehensive, philosophic and connected view of the classes of animals, plants, or minerals' and fulfil 'obligations of a distinct and peculiar, if not superior, kind'. The second display, placed in the central hall, was planned as the Director's personal introduction to the exhibitions, an 'Index Collection' or 'elementary account for those uninformed in natural history'. The third display was a Gallery of British Zoology in the north hall, a 'series of exhibited specimens so complete, and so displayed as to enable him [the local collector] to identify his own specimen with one there ticketed with its proper name and locality'. In these three displays, all the natural objects that could be obtained readily and exhibited permanently were to be put on show.

As this arrangement makes clear, natural history was to the Victorians almost entirely factual. Little attempt was made to go beyond the appearance of the objects on display and explain their significance, and in this respect the British Museum (Natural History) was typical of museums, whether concerned with science, art or history.

Owen regretted the limited educational means available to him in the public galleries, and he proposed that 'the chief Curator of each class or department' should deliver 'an annual course of lectures on the classification, habits, instincts, and economic use of such class or department of Natural History'. However, the lectures were never arranged, and the view that the specimens could be left to speak for themselves became firmly entrenched. This view was supported by the assumption that people could be left to educate themselves, all that a public body need do was provide the opportunity.

The exhibition that arose from the early planning of the Museum must have presented the lay visitor with a puzzling arrangement of objects, each carefully placed beyond his reach, with a label in a language he could barely understand. Rarely would he have found a simple connecting narrative to help him make sense of what he could see. One feels that Brown Goode's (1891) much quoted definition of an 'efficient' educational museum, 'a collection of instructive labels, each illustrated by a well-selected specimen', would have done little to help in such circumstances. And this must have been true as long as the

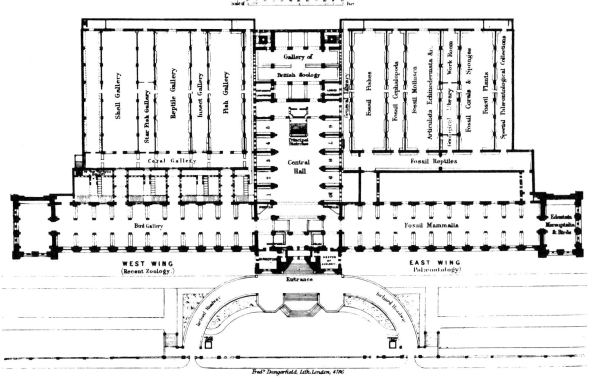

Figure 1.1 The original arrangement of exhibitions on the ground floor of the British Museum (Natural History). From the first guide to the Museum published in 1886.

question, '"Instructive" for whom?' was disregarded.

The educational attitudes behind the exhibition are revealed in the writings of Günther (1880), one of the early Keepers of Zoology:

> The exhibition will probably be found more liberal than may be deemed necessary by some of my fellow-labourers; but if a visitor should, on leaving the galleries, 'take nothing with him but sore feet, a bad headache, and a general idea that the animal kingdom is a mighty maze without plan,' I should be inclined to believe that this state of bodily and mental prostration is the visitor's, and not the curator's fault.

The general tenor of such remarks is clear. There were to be no concessions to the ignorant and the uninformed (Fig. 1.2).

The question of exhibition design hardly arises when we consider the early years of the Museum, and this seems to be generally the case,

particularly as regards show-case museums. The setting up of the exhibits proceeded from the **galleries** to the separate displays, with the floor area fitted out with cases, specimens fitted to cases and, finally, labels fitted between specimens (Fig. 1.3). Thus all the important decisions had to be taken at an early stage by the architect, and the contents of the exhibitions had to be accommodated within his constraints. We can call this system 'designing from the gallery downwards', and contrast it with 'designing from the message upwards', where design starts with an analysis of the ideas to be communicated and the methods used in communicating them.

Although the principle of separating study and display collections had been established in 1858, the style of many of the exhibits in the new British Museum (Natural History) was what we now call 'open storage'. This type of display, in which dozens of objects are crowded together with little or no explanation, has survived in all sorts of museums down to the present day. Design

Figure 1.2 'Among the crocodiles. In one of the galleries at the South Kensington Natural History Museum the bodies of dead and gone crocodiles lie like mummies upon tables, waiting for the student who has been created by Act of Parliament, but who rarely comes to improve his mind by examining these stuffed emigrants. Small wonder is it then if weary of idleness the official gives way to yawns, and even the crocodiles seem to imitate his example, and to lift their lank jaws in sympathetic response.' *The Graphic*, 25 November 1893.

Figure 1.3 Designing from the gallery downwards. A 19th-century show-case museum. The fossil fish gallery of the British Museum (Natural History) in 1923.

only begins to enter the scene when the objects are thinned out and some further explanation is provided (Fig. 1.4). The result is close to the instructive-labels-and-well-selected-specimens style of exhibit recommended by Brown Goode. Even now this is perhaps the commonest type of display, though it is often disguised under a thin veneer of contemporary

Figure 1.4 '... instructive labels, each illustrated by a well-selected specimen.' Brown Goode's formula for an 'efficient' educational museum.

Figure 1.5 A 'modern' Brown Goode type of exhibit.

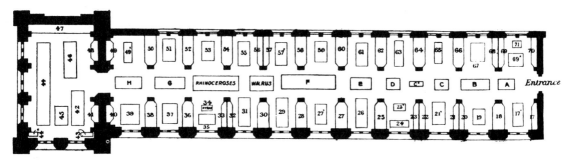

Figure 1.6 Plan of a 19th-century gallery showing an arrangement of cases that provides no simple circulation route.

finish (Fig. 1.5). It tends to be characterised by the length and technical detail of its 'scholarly' texts, and its disregard for the difficulties of the lay visitor.

To understand the next stages in the development of exhibition design, it is necessary to go outside the world of established museums. The problem was that design from the gallery downwards gave a rigid layout that channelled visitors into circulation routes that discouraged full and orderly coverage of the displays (Fig. 1.6). The way in which this type of design was practised – as a continuation of architectural design – also resulted in a lack of variety in the spaces that were to house the exhibits. There was no subdivision into areas that could be taken in easily by the visitor, i.e. perceived as wholes. In short, there was no attempt to meet the physiological and psychological requirements of the visitor.

This problem was solved in a bold and convincing way by Walter Gropius working with a handful of ex-Bauhaus colleagues. The key

Figure 1.7 Exhibition of the Building Workers' Union, Berlin, 1931. From Bayer (1961).

events were the 1930 Deutscher Werkbund Exhibition in Paris and the 1931 Building Workers' Union Exhibition in Berlin. Gropius and his team used the space in these exhibitions in a new and revolutionary way (Fig. 1.7). They divided it up into areas of different character and arranged the displays so that they followed a logical sequence from room to room. They paid special attention to circulation, promoting a smooth flow of visitors by, among other things, the introduction of curved walls. Drama was achieved by the use of a bridge or raised viewing gallery which overlooked the space; by the imaginative presentation of objects no longer confined to glass cases; by the use of bold lettering, photography, charts and the latest graphic techniques; and by the introduction of displays that moved or lit up at the touch of a button.

These Bauhaus innovations influenced exhibit design all over the world, and can still be strongly felt at the present day. They may even have been responsible, ultimately, for the introduction of full-time professional designers in the museum world. In the United Kingdom the first real wave came in the 1960s, stimulated possibly by such happenings as the 1951 Festival of Britain, and the British Museum (Natural History) appointed its first professionally trained three-dimensional designer in 1965. In museums as a whole, the introduction of this new breed of workers met

with some resistance, and it would be idle to pretend that the designer's lot has been an easy one. It has been difficult for him to find a niche and a way of working in these long-settled institutions; his relations with curators have often been fraught with woe; and designers themselves have been divided as to their exact role – whether it be to take over the entire process of mounting exhibitions, or package for popular consumption the goods provided by the curators. On this last point, in neither case does the system work to the obvious advantage of the general public when it comes to designing educational exhibitions. But designers can take some comfort from the knowledge that they are now an integral part of the exhibition team in any large museum. For educationalists this is still far from the case.

For all its importance in the history of exhibition design, the work of Gropius and his team was still concerned essentially with working down from the space to be filled to the message to be communicated. For a different approach, centred on the act of communication and the difficulties likely to be faced by the receiver in understanding the message, we must turn to the Social and Economic Museum in Vienna. Otto Neurath was the moving spirit behind this museum, founded in 1924 out of the Museum of Housing and Town Planning which opened the year before. Neurath's main innovations were in

Figure 1.8 The Social and Economic Museum, Vienna, c. 1927. Reproduced from the Otto and Marie Neurath Isotype Collection, The Library, University of Reading.

the field of graphic design. He was concerned with helping the man in the street to understand social change, and he sought a method of representing statistics in a way that was both correct and interesting. Another of his concerns was the humanisation of knowledge; that is to say, he wished to make technical matters accessible to lay people through the quality and structure of his communication. He saw humanisation as the antithesis of popularisation, which aims only at a semblance of understanding through the translation of technical terms into popular language.

The Social and Economic Museum was housed in the Gothic New Town Hall of Vienna (Fig. 1.8). It included some three-dimensional material, models of buildings and so on, but its main claim to fame rests on its statistical charts. These were mounted on frames of natural wood, specially designed so that they did not detract from the charts themselves. Each display unit was lit separately so that attention was further fixed on the charts, and a crimson carpet helped to draw attention away from the building. The basis of the charts was a sign language in which a greater number of things was represented by a greater number of signs (Fig. 9.14). Originally known as the Vienna Method, this later developed into Isotype (International System of Typographic Picture Education), and is usefully reviewed by Marie Neurath (1974).

Neurath is important because he approached exhibit design with the clear purpose of communicating with the visitor. Artistic fulfilment played no part in his work. He started with an analysis of what he wanted to say, and carefully considered how he might best succeed in saying it. He expected to improve the quality of his presentations by criticism and by trial and error. Although Neurath's innovations in exhibit design have been less influential than those of Gropius, in our view *both* approaches are needed, and we suggest that the successful exhibit designer is the person who can work from the gallery downwards and from the message upwards *at the same time.*

Objects, ideas and exhibits

The new-style exhibitions in the British Museum (Natural History) have called into question some widely held notions of what an exhibition should look like and what it should contain. The argument tends to revolve around the role of objects, or 'real things', in museum displays and is closely linked with the question, 'What is a museum?' There are a number of issues here of general interest to the designer of educational exhibits, and these are worth looking at in advance of the rest of this book.

Throughout we use the word 'museum' in its broadest sense, to include art galleries, science centres and shows of all kinds whether they include 'museum' in the title or not. The important thing for us is that it should be possible for a rational person to use the word 'museum' in describing any one of these institutions. This is not an orthodox view, and books on museums commonly begin by trying to clarify the object of their attentions. This approach is often sound and it might seem no more than common sense to define what one is talking about before launching into a detailed exposition. Yet experience shows that in this case the attempt is doomed to failure; the word 'museum' simply covers too wide a range of institutions with too many different functions to be captured in a useful, formal definition. We suggest that such a definition might be regarded as the culmination of an investigation into museums rather than as a starting point, though this end point is still nowhere in sight.

Another view of the problem is that the question 'What is a museum?' is unanswerable and must always remain so. This is because a term can be explained in a definition only by using some other terms, which are themselves not defined. By way of example, look at the International Council of Museums' 1971 definition – '... an institution which serves the community. It acquires, preserves, makes intelligible and, as an essential part of its function, presents to the public the material evidence concerning man and nature. It does this in such a way as to provide opportunities for study, education and enjoyment' – and ask what the terms 'community', 'makes intelligible' and 'presents' mean in this context. And then ask what 'understood' or 'clear' means in a definition of 'makes intelligible', for example. And so on, and so on. It is easy to see that we are quickly cast into a dispute about the meaning of words. This is why people are still arguing about the meaning of 'museum'.

Many writers have sought the essence of museums in 'real objects', or argued that the study of museums is properly concerned with the study of the non-verbal 'language of real things'. These writers have generally argued that the proper function of a museum is to put its objects on view and leave them to speak for themselves. As we have seen, this was the Victorian attitude, and it still persists with the justification that visitors are left free to derive their own concepts and draw their own conclusions, without risk of bias being introduced by the exhibition team.

There are a number of things to say about this argument and these are important when it comes to the practical business of designing exhibitions. First, it must be said that it goes against all knowledge of perception. In a metaphor suggested by Popper (1972), our minds are not 'buckets' which become filled with sensory data

as we passively acquire knowledge from the outside world, rather they are 'searchlights' actively seeking out meaning in the things we observe and experience. It follows that what we perceive is determined by our previous experience, our knowledge and our expectations; there is probably no such thing as a pure and simple fact. That visitors should derive their own concepts and draw their own conclusions from a brief examination of specimens placed out of reach is firmly denied by the whole history of scholarship. Such concepts are the creation of exceptional minds and often of many years of thought. Similarly, Levin (1976) shows that the American Museum of Natural History curator who labelled some small stone flakes, 'choppers of the African neolithic period', was begging several involved questions about the origin and use of such objects, which could never be answered by the objects themselves.

None of this is intended to deny the oft-asserted importance of objects or 'real things' in museums. But even under ideal circustances, the fact remains that objects, by themselves, can communicate little beyond their own existence. The lesson for the exhibit designer must be that unless he wishes to restrict himself to an elite audience of scholars who already know the background information, he must present his objects in a coherent and informative context.

A second point is that human memory is well served by the exhibit that is built around a strong and easily understood narrative. We think in terms of stories, and while random facts, such as the length of the longest dinosaur, may be remembered, it is generally true that isolated and poorly understood facts are soon forgotten unless they can be related to other facts with the help of some broad unifying ideas.

But should this sort of information be left to books? With dynamic exhibits this is clearly not the case, for there is no way that the printed word could achieve the same results. It is the traditional kind of static display that can most easily be translated into words and pictures. There is a further point. Many people do not regard books as a prime source of information, even when they are profusely illustrated. This is easily forgotten by the highly literate organisers of exhibitions. In an attempt to explore the question further, the Swedish Museum of Natural History displayed a series of popular books on the same subject as a temporary exhibition. Visitors were asked how many of the books they had read. Of the 20 or so books displayed, 80 per cent of the visitors had not read any at all. Although the experiment is far from conclusive, Engström (1973) rightly remarks that the museum appeared to be reaching a wider and rather different public from that reached by the books. There is no reason to assume that visitors to an exhibition are willing or able to acquire background knowledge from some external source.

A second look at objects

In order to mount an effective educational exhibition, it is essential to construct some kind of story-line or theme that is likely to be comprehensible to the intended **target audience**. Such a theme will obviously be constructed with a view to making use of physical objects already available, or easily obtained. However, the theme will almost certainly indicate that some objects are more important than others from an educative point of view. And it might even indicate that certain objects are not required at all either because (a) their presence would be misleading, or (b) their presence would be irrelevant. In this sense it has to be acknowledged that the theme or story-line determines the objects displayed and not the other way round.

2 The general framework

This chapter is concerned with the development of a framework within which successful educational exhibitions can be designed and produced. Several distinct skills are involved in this work (Ch. 5), and normally a team of people is required. This means that well defined procedures must be adopted. These include management and consultation, though here we are only concerned with the stages of the work. Systems of management and consultation will vary strongly from institution to institution.

Stages of the operation

Almost *all* 'team projects' (not just projects to do with the setting up of educational exhibitions) comprise a series of activities. Of these, a given activity can usually be started only after some work has been done on one or more other activities. Sometimes several activities can be carried on at the same time, and sometimes one must be completed before another can be started. Thus we find that educational exhibitions characteristically (and almost inevitably) pass through a series of fairly distinguishable stages. These may be described in different ways, and the detail is liable to a good deal of variation from one account to another. In this chapter we shall characterise them as follows.

(1) Pre-planning and authorisation.
(2) Planning.
(3) Implementation:

    (a) Development;
    (b) Production;
    (c) Installation and dressing.

(4) Presentation and evaluation.
(5) Maintenance.
(6) Updating and revision.

These six stages can obviously be given somewhat different names. There is nothing sacrosanct about the way we have chosen to characterise them; it is just a matter of convenience. For particular purposes, it might be useful to subdivide some of the stages, or run some of them together, but in general all projects progress through stages concerned with 'getting started' (1 & 2 above), 'making it happen' (3), 'trying it out' (4 & 5) and 'doing it even better' (6). And it should be clear that these stages often overlap. For example, some sponsors may require very detailed plans before agreeing to underwrite the costs of mounting an educational exhibition. In this case, a lot of detailed work that is normally deferred until the *planning* or *implementation* stage will have to be done, speculatively, at the *pre-planning and authorisation* stage. This could save time later, but it could also cause difficulties if the project is committed to tight advance plans that turn out at later stages to have unforeseen defects.

Pre-planning and authorisation

Typically, the whole process of exhibition design starts with some individual or group of individuals – or some official body, perhaps – thinking it might be a good idea to mount a particular exhibition. Steps are then taken to try and arouse support and enthusiasm for the idea, e.g. by enquiring whether appropriate experts and helpers can be found, and whether the necessary finance can be made available.

A key step at this stage is to define the mission, e.g. to produce a clear statement of purpose. This will normally include a synopsis of the proposed intellectual content, thereby clarifying what the exhibition is to be about. It must also consider who the exhibition is to be aimed at, what the designers are trying to achieve, and what sort of resources are available. As a rule, this statement will fix the *type* of exhibition the organisers are concerned with. Thus decisions will be taken as to whether the exhibition will need interpretation by a third party, or is to be designed to communicate directly with the viewer; whether it is to be permanent or temporary; and whether it is to be fixed or travelling. At this stage, decisions may also be taken about the location of the exhibition.

Armed with a clear statement of purpose, it is

then possible for the organisers to consider the feasibility of the project and give some preliminary consideration to the procedures likely to be involved. Lobbying for support can begin, preliminary plans can be presented to sponsors, and discussions arranged. Negotiations are pursued until such time as the requisite support is obtained, and the official 'go ahead' signal is given.

Planning

As soon as the 'go ahead' signal is given, the whole operation moves into the *planning* stage, and this brings us to matters dealt with in some detail later in this book. There are essentially three aspects to the work at this stage: the theme of the exhibition, the resources to be used and scheduling.

The initial statement of the intellectual content of the exhibition must now be worked out in more detail. The aim is to produce a skeleton structure that defines the units of content and orders them in some way. It may usefully take the form of a network, a hierarchy or even a simple chain, accompanied by a brief description of each unit. Hand in hand with this work goes the further development of the statement of purpose, with the original aims made more precise and, if appropriate, the formulation of detailed objectives.

Resources are assessed by listing those that are available and quantifying their extent. They consist of money, manpower, machines or materials and all must be considered. For example: What skills are required and which are already available? Can additional staff be recruited? How should the team be organised? How are outside helpers to be contacted? And so on. The aim is to finish up with a resource policy that promotes effectiveness and efficiency in later stages while relating directly to the original statement of purpose.

A scheduling procedure is required to coordinate the various resources and activities, and to promote the harmonious working of the team. The various activities of the next stage, *implementation,* need to be well defined and their relations to each other understood in some detail. But the key activity is the breakdown of the intellectual content of the proposed exhibition into manageable units. These can then be related to the resources policy and the time required for each step in the process.

The end-products of the *planning* stage are a brief for the exhibition and a first schedule for its design and production. Together these cover the aims and objectives of the project and the various constraints under which it will be designed. They provide the basis for all subsequent work on the exhibition, including the production of catalogues and books, and educational programmes for schools, other special groups and casual visitors.

Implementation

At this stage designers and technicians start work in earnest, their ultimate end-product being the finished exhibition ready to be opened to the viewers. Most of the work on the project takes place now, and there are many activities that must be successfully completed, whether carried out by a handful of people or a large team. Development of the displays may involve subject-matter experts, designers, educationalists and editors. The purpose is to transform the (often abstract) ideas of the exhibition brief into specifications for the physical realisation of displays. Production normally involves draughtsmen, graphic designers, artists, and printers, as well as various technicians, and perhaps conservation and security experts. Installation, particularly for a permanent exhibition, usually involves site preparation work, with the cleaning or painting of the fabric of the building, the renewal of electrics and possibly plumbing, and the laying of new floors (Fig. 2.1). Panels, glass cases, audio-visual theatres, and so on must then be made to receive the displays before the final dressing and adjustment of lighting, audio-visuals, and so on can be done. Because of the complexity of all these activities, and the large amount of time required, it is normal for site preparation to run concurrently with other aspects of production, and sometimes with the last phases of development.

Presentation and evaluation

Since the people responsible for mounting the exhibition almost invariably find themselves working on it (putting the finishing touches to it) right up to the last minute, the *implementation* stage continues right up to the time of the opening ceremony. The arrival of the first visitors, however, marks the beginning of the *presentation and*

Figure 2.1 Installation of the 'Hall of human biology', British Museum (Natural History), 1977.

evaluation stage. During this stage, two concurrent activities go on. First, visitors are inspecting the fruits of what is often many months of hard work on the part of the exhibition team. Secondly, attempts are being made to 'evaluate' the success of the final product. With the advent of this stage, the exhibition staff stop worrying how on earth they will manage to get the exhibition ready in time for the opening. They start worrying, instead, about what the visitor reaction will be to their endeavours.

If the exhibition is a short, 'one-off' affair, the evaluation activity undertaken at this stage will typically be used partly to satisfy the curiosity of the exhibition staff and their sponsors (since it is natural for people to want to know how well they have done), and partly to form the basis for some kind of official end-of-product report, e.g. to the sponsors of the exhibition, and possibly to the mass media as well. But if the exhibition is designed to stand for (say) a year or two, there is usually financial provision for it to be revised and updated from time to time, in addition to routine maintenance. This brings us to the last two stages of the operation. They run side by side, but whereas maintenance activity is obligatory, and in fact usually practised, the updating and revision of exhibitions far more rarely takes place.

Maintenance

A regular maintenance check is essential to ensure that an exhibition is functioning as intended. The check covers audio-visuals and other dynamic displays as well as cleaning and lighting. Where conservation is important, it may also be necessary to check temperature, humidity and light levels, as well as looking for the harmful effects of vibration and dust. All of the problems are, of course, greatly eased if likely maintenance problems are kept in mind throughout the *implementation* stage.

Updating and revision

The evaluation activity carried out at the *presentation and evaluation* stage assumes much greater significance if there is the possibility of updating and revising the exhibition from time to time, because it can be used actively to inform and guide the revision process.

It would be a big mistake, however, to assume that evaluation does not need to go on *prior* to the *presentation and evaluation* stage. There is a general (but no less important) sense in which evaluation needs to go on all the time, and from the very start. The business of mounting effective educational exhibitions can be plagued with unforeseen obstacles and pitfalls. If we want to increase our chances of avoiding such obstacles and pitfalls, it makes good sense to adopt a *careful evaluative stance* towards almost everything we do.

Consider, for example, the activities that need to be undertaken during the *pre-planning and authorisation* stage. If we just focus on the matter of trying to arouse the support and enthusiasm of relevant experts and possible sponsors, it is clear that these people, when approached, will themselves evaluate the proposals that are being put before them. If the proposals strike them as being inadequately thought through, they will tend to be unsympathetic. Thus, before putting the proposals to potential sponsors, the proposers should say to themselves, 'Let us evaluate these proposals ourselves in an attempt to forestall the kinds of objections that our potential sponsors might make when *they* come to evaluate our proposals.'

Similar comments can be made in respect of virtually every other activity that might go on in the following stages. However trivial or 'obvious looking' a particular activity might seem to be, it is always worth pausing to wonder whether there might be a better way of doing it. The prescription is entirely general, in fact. In all walks of life, whatever we are doing, it always pays us to keep a weather-eye open for possible mistakes that we might be making. To learn from experience is to be able to identify and (hence) rectify mistakes that we had not previously noticed. To see this deeply, so that it sinks right into our bones, is to make evaluation – in the Buddhist sense of 'constant mindfulness' – a permanent way of life. In the context of designing educational exhibitions, the cultivation of a continuing evaluative stance is especially desirable, if the ultimate objective is to mount a whole series of educational exhibitions, all of which need to be authorised and paid for. By carefully evaluating *over all six stages* the difficulties that obstructed the smooth setting up of the first exhibition, we significantly enhance our chances of doing better the next time round.

Learning from experience

The need to pause, reflect on what one is doing, and consider whether there might be a better way of doing it, may not be widely perceived among those responsible for mounting educational exhibitions. A glance at almost any issue of the relevant journals will reveal a satisfaction with the way things are and a distrust of innovation and change. These attitudes are often coupled with a fondness for conclusions reached without any reference to evidence or supporting arguments. In these circumstances, it is not surprising that exhibitions continue to fail in a number of fairly straightforward and well documented ways, e.g. in the use of captions which – with their coded information and esoteric language – are to a greater or lesser extent meaningless to the lay visitor (Fig. 2.2). Such failings are repeatedly exposed, but rarely acted upon. They are passed on from generation to generation of exhibitions, despite the apparent ease with which they are remedied. One piece of work after another is

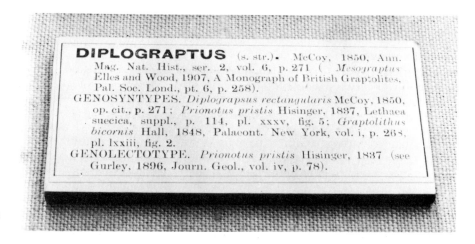

Figure 2.2 An esoteric label.

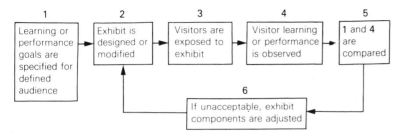

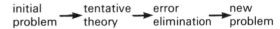

Figure 2.3 The basic developmental cycle for educational exhibits. From Screven (1976).

completed, opened to the public, and then (its shortcomings ignored) forgotten about until the time comes for it to be replaced, usually for reasons that have nothing to do with its qualities as an exhibition. In short, there is a failure to reflect on what is happening and to learn from experience.

In recent years, however, there have been signs of a growing disenchantment with the accepted way of doing things, and a climate of opinion has been forming in which it is recognised that some traditional procedures are ripe for change. Thus several workers in the United States have set up a system of exhibition design in which events are contrived so that the participants are 'forced' to consider what is going on. This is done in the hope that lessons are learned from the experience of designing that will improve the quality of the final work. A practical guide to this system has been provided by Screven (1976) under the heading *Exhibit evaluation – a goal referenced approach*. However, as will become apparent later, the main concern is with avoiding errors – i.e. moving *away* from undesirable situations – rather than with moving *towards* goals, and therefore this title should not be taken to imply a foolproof set of rules for designing effective exhibits.

The basic developmental cycle is summarised in Figure 2.3. An important link in the depicted chain of activities is the feedback of information so that the design of exhibits is informed by knowledge of exhibit performance. In fact, in all 'experimental' methods where experiences are contrived in this way, the outcome of the action must be ascertained or else the method is worthless. Thus Waddington (1977) criticises the failure to obtain corrective feedback in the building of Britain's new towns since the Second World War. Policy has undergone several changes over the years based on vague hunches and personal opinions rather than carefully collected facts.

The system of trial and error, or 'suck it and see', that Screven proposes is basically a three-

stage iterative process which can be represented in generalised form as follows:

initial problem → tentative theory → error elimination → new problem

For the exhibition designer, the *initial problem* may take many forms. It may concern the layout of an exhibit on the floor of a **gallery**, the attraction and holding of the visitor's attention, the best way of guiding visitors around the displays, or the intelligibility of a piece of text. In practice, these problems are often translated into the language of goals or objectives, as in Screven's diagram.

The designer's equivalent of a *tentative theory* is a design in the form of drawings and specifications for the whole or some part of an exhibition. This is the proposed solution for the initial problem. However, it is not a general solution believed to hold true over a wide range of circumstances. Exhibit designs are normally special-purpose solutions. They deal with particular problems in particular circumstances.

Error elimination involves the criticism of the proposed solution by building or making a **mock-up** of an exhibit, exposing it to visitors and judging how well it measures up to expectations. In this way the tentative theory is put to the test to reveal its limitations. The outcome is a comparison between 'what is' and 'what ought to be'. (This evaluation work can usefully be conducted at Development in stage (3), as well as at stage (4), as we discuss in Chapter 15.)

The elimination of errors leads *ideally* to a more refined solution of the initial problem. During this process the data surrounding the problem are explored and tentative solutions tried out, so frequently the problem comes to be seen in a new light. A new solution can then be pitted against a deeper interpretation of the original problem. In theory at least, there is no reason why this process should not go on indefinitely, because we have no way of knowing when we have arrived at a perfect answer. However, in practice, exhibition designers are not concerned with ultimate truths or perfect solutions, but with the more mundane questions of what to do next and what to do so that the chance of making errors is minimised. Further, the number of possibilities that can be explored is limited, and so the trial and error process is broken off when solutions are judged to be acceptable in the existing circumstances.

Evidence of success

The process of trial and error outlined above has been used in the design of a number of educational exhibitions, and valuable case studies have been published. These will repay study, both for the methods used and the results obtained. They include projects at the Children's Museum, Boston (Nicol 1969), the Lawrence Hall of Science, University of California, Berkeley (Eason and Linn 1976, Friedman, Eason and Sneider 1979) and the British Museum (Natural History) (Griggs 1981, Griggs and Manning 1983). Work in progress is shown in Figs 2.4 and 2.5. In every case, a sensitivity towards the sorts of things that can go wrong and a desire to avoid mistakes are as important as the routing out of errors during evaluation.

As already indicated, feedback can be collected on a range of timescales, in the short term at each step in the design of a single exhibit, and in the

long run as work progresses from exhibition to exhibition. To get some idea of the results that have been obtained, we may look at the development of an astronomy exhibition at the Lawrence Hall of Science. The following questions were answered.

(a)   Do the displays work as planned?
(b)   Are the directions at an appropriate reading level?
(c)   Can visitors follow the directions provided?
(d)   Are the diagrams clear to visitors?
(e)   How long do visitors generally spend at each display?
(f)   What part of the visitor population is interested in optics?

The organisers concluded that the exhibition would have been an expensive failure had it not been tested out during development.

At the British Museum (Natural History), the experience of working on a *series* of exhibitions has shown the need, among other things, to:

(a) produce an exhibition brief that gives considered attention to the aims of the exercise and the constraints under which it will be carried out, and does not set out the subject-matter in such detail that new constraints are introduced which stifle creative development;

Figure 2.4 Formative evaluation of new instructions for a display illustrating the carbon cycle, British Museum (Natural History), 1980.

Figure 2.5 Mock-up of part of a new display introducing cells, for the 'Hall of human biology', British Museum (Natural History), 1980.

(b) ensure that the same team carries out both the construction and maintenance of mechanical and electronic devices, otherwise design errors will be propagated from one new exhibit to the next.

At a different level of work practice, we have learned the need to:

(c) design **orientation** systems – maps, signposts and so on – at the same time as the exhibits, so that they are not superimposed on the gallery as an afterthought;

(d) link evaluation policies to flexible design so that changes can be made to exhibits with reasonable ease and at a reasonable cost;

(e) control the leakage of sound from individual exhibits, e.g. by showing audio-visual programmes in enclosed auditoria;

(f) inform visitors of the length of audio-visual programmes and how often they are shown;

(g) use electronic rather than mechanical devices because of their greater reliability;

(h) avoid printing text on transparent surfaces, e.g. on the glass fronts of show-cases.

But whether we look at our own work, or at the short-term, corrective feedback of the Lawrence Hall of Science, it does seem that there are limits to the sorts of problems that can be handled by this approach. These concern work practice (how to organise the design and production process), ergonomics and mechanical efficiency, and the intelligibility of the message. However, so far it has not been able to provide strong help with more subtle problems concerning exhibit effectiveness, such as selecting the best medium, or motivating the visitor to attend to the message. In other words, it enables the designer to respond to problems and perhaps make adjustments, but there is no evidence that it helps him transcend the constraints of the original design. It is, therefore, worth looking at the trial and error approach in more detail, to see exactly what the limitations may be.

Problems of trial and error

The trial and error approach is subject to a variety of constraints. First, there is the need for an informed starting point and the difficulty of achieving this position. Trial and error is not a matter of plucking a guess out of the air to serve as a tentative theory, trying it out, rejecting it, and making another guess. This would waste resources and lead nowhere fast. Rather, trial and error requires as a starting point a conjecture that has a reasonable chance of paying off and is worthy of serious attention. This means that the designer who wishes to proceed in this way must have some knowledge of the alternative courses of action that are open to him, and there must be some underlying theory that enables sensible choices to be made among them. In fact, lack of an adequate theoretical base for educational exhibits seems to have been a major stumbling block in the past. Secondly, there is the need for adequate procedures for trying out proposed solutions and for generating better alternatives. It is common knowledge that different people evaluate a particular exhibit (or film, painting, football match, and so on) in different ways, depending on their background and expectations. Shettel (1968) has investigated the matter further by looking at the criteria habitually employed by specialists developing, producing and teaching from exhibits, and asking them whether these criteria provide a sound basis for judging the worth of exhibits. He selected 55 criteria from the literature and listed them in 15 basic types (Table 2.1).

Table 2.1   Shettel's basic exhibit categories.

(1) attractiveness of exhibit	(13) design of exhibit size
(2) ease of comprehension	physical layout
(3) unity within the exhibit	use of colour
(4) ability to attract attention	use of light
(5) ability to hold attention	use of contrast
(6) appropriateness of presentation	(14) exhibit items quantity
(7) accuracy of information	attractiveness
(8) location and crowd flow	size
(9) visitor characteristics	(15) communication techniques
(10) focus of attention	sound
(11) textual material	motion
(12) relation of exhibit to surrounding and other exhibits	demonstrations
	charts
	films
	models
	auxiliary teaching
	visitor participation

He then developed a six-point scale, later reduced on trial to four points, which could be applied to these criteria and against which exhibits could be rated. The revised scale read:

excellent   good   fair   poor

We shall ignore some of the subtleties in the design of the draft list of criteria (such as to check the internal reliability of the ratings), and consider only the results of the first trial. Although this was only a pilot experiment, it seems safe to conclude that the results give no comfort to those who believe they can produce generally valid judgements out of their own feelings. To cite an example, six specialists rated one display for its overall design. Using the earlier six-point scale, one said it was excellent; one, very good; one, high average; one, low average; and two, fair. Shettel concluded, 'Whatever *overall* design means to the authors of the exhibit literature, it certainly means different things to the six raters.' A further conclusion of particular interest relates to the trial and error approach itself. It is this. While each rater knew what he would do to improve a particular display, the raters disagreed among themselves as to what sort of action was

needed. Therefore, there was no certainty that a given action would result in an improvement according to some independent criterion such as educational effectiveness. Under these circumstances, rather than removing errors, designers might find themselves replacing one set of errors by a different set. Shettel's solution to this problem was for exhibition designers to use **behavioural objectives.** These are considered in the next chapter.

In general terms, then, the problem with trial and error is not simply that of recognising and removing erroneous ideas (or actions), but also of knowing what to put in their places. The crucial point is that there is no objective procedure for replacing the tentative theory of the trial and error cycle with a new theory that is guaranteed to give better results.

A third constraint also arises from the question of knowing what needs to be done to improve things. It is largely a practical matter and arises because, in the usual run of events, the design team will have limited scope for its investigations, and a limited range of alternatives for further action. The team is therefore forced to look at a fairly restricted number of consequences in evaluating its trial solutions, and the decision as to what to test and what not to test is likely to be somewhat arbitrary. In this way interesting and important consequences of designs are liable to be overlooked, with the attendant danger that good features are thrown out with the bad. So, unless there is some strong underlying theory to guide matters, not only to indicate the sorts of mistake that are likely to be made but also to show what needs to be done, there is the distinct probability that the whole system will simply lurch from one set of errors to the next without any real improvement in its performance.

The last constraint we shall consider concerns the exercise of power. So far we have looked at difficulties that are intrinsic to the trial and error system or are internal to the workings of the design team. However, some of the most important problems arise externally. They depend upon sociological and psychological factors and play an important role in almost all projects.

Going back to the *pre-planning and authorisation* stage of mounting an exhibition, it should be noted that *only rarely* is support given, and means allocated, according to a master plan or overall policy. Normally, as Etzioni (1968) has shown in the broader field of planning, the interests and relative power of the applicants and members of the authorising and funding body interact in a complicated way. Thus decisions are rarely taken on the basis of knowledge alone; more often they stem from the interplay of knowledge, values and power, in varying proportions.

Value judgements enter at all stages of the work, not just at the beginning. Thus trial and error may indicate that a particular course of action is desirable. But if it goes against the prevailing view of how things should be done, it may be rejected despite the strength of the arguments in favour. In the same way, a design that succeeds in educational terms may be objected to if it is felt to be inappropriate on some other, broader grounds such as style of treatment; while a design that is seen to be 'right' may be accepted regardless of evidence that show it fails in its educative purpose.

In making decisions and reaching conclusions such as these, the decision-makers, as Etzioni shows, are also influenced by the play of power. Basically, this is a question of how much pressure the various interested parties are able to exert. Hence the design team's results from trial and error will count for little or nothing if an outside party can wield sufficient political power to realise *its* preference. A decision-taker can always choose to ignore facts, but he cannot ignore power. Thus for those carefully developing an exhibition by trial and error, there is no necessary connection between knowledge (of what needs to be done, for example) and power, and no immunity from outside pressures.

Recommendations

Where does this leave us in seeking a new approach to exhibit design that will assist in the avoidance of critical errors? As we have just seen, trial and error as a process of developing exhibits is able to give some help, but it is subject to a number of constraints. It is also clear that it can never be a substitute for a real understanding of the problems that are being tackled; and it is always necessary, whatever the circumstances, to keep a watchful eye open for the consequences of any particular course of action. Nevertheless, it is very difficult to pinpoint an alternative approach that has had the same success in producing effective educational exhibits. Therefore, until very much stronger design procedures become available, we recommend the rough and ready experimental method of trial and error as the best way of ensuring that exhibitions are produced which work broadly as intended. Several of the themes introduced here are taken up in more detail in Chapters 15 and 16.

3 Psychological and educational aspects of exhibition design

The primary aim of this chapter is to consider the psychological and educational aspects of exhibition design, with special reference to museum exhibitions that have a predominantly *educational* intent. More precisely, we shall be considering what the disciplines of psychology and education have to offer, by way of helpful advice and guidance, to the designers of such exhibitions.

To some readers, it may come as something of a surprise to be told that psychologists and educators do have worthwhile insights to offer the aspiring exhibition designer. For many years, exhibitions have, after all, been mounted by people who have manifestly had little formal training in either psychology or education. Some of these exhibitions have achieved considerable public acclaim. And, even in cases where an exhibition has been subjected to heavy criticism, it has seldom been suggested that the advice of the professional psychologist and educator would necessarily have made it significantly better. This being so, it might be legitimately wondered whether such advice is really necessary. What can such 'experts' possibly offer that the experienced exhibition designer does not already know, albeit in an intuitive way?

There are two kinds of response to this question. First of all, it is obvious that, in order to achieve the kind of success that its sponsors and designers are hoping for, an exhibition *must* take account of the needs, interests and abilities of the intended audience. And this amounts to saying (whether we realise it or not) that an exhibition is unlikely to be successful, in the eyes of the visiting public and its critics, unless it satisfies certain psychological and educational criteria. There is consequently a clear *prima-facie* case for supposing that professional psychologists and educators *might* have worthwhile things to say about the design of educational exhibitions. The second response is somewhat different. In addition to

claiming the *prima-facie* case, we can offer evidence that, in the absence of professional guidance from appropriately qualified psychologists and educators, exhibition designers are likely to do things wrong – or, at the very least, do things less well than might otherwise be the case. For convenience, we shall describe this second kind of response as the empirical and theoretical case. Let us now examine these two cases more closely.

The prima-facie case

The strength of the *prima-facie* case derives from the fact that educational exhibitions are designed to teach, and the disciplines of psychology and education are centrally and vitally concerned with the conditions under which learning can successfully occur. Really, this is all that needs to be said. However, it is still possible to find cynics who, knowing almost nothing about psychology or education, have nevertheless convinced themselves that these disciplines are a monumental waste of human effort and are, in consequence, best ignored. There is little point in trying to convert people who do think this way. The best that can be done, perhaps, is to call attention to the kinds of issues discussed later in this chapter. Apart from that, the only challenge to the professional psychologist and educator is that of trying to be more charitable about the cynics than they are about him.

By way of additional comment, we remark that a search of the psychological and educational literature reveals large amounts of material and research findings on such matters as learning and motivation, cognitive and emotional obstacles to learning, fatigue effects, the psychology of perception, the use of audio-visual aids in education, and so on. A walk through almost any educational exhibition also reveals numerous examples of ineptitudes (e.g. the failure to place key exhibits at a comfortable viewing distance), which an appropriately experienced psychologist or educator would never have missed.

The empirical and theoretical case

The strength of the empirical and theoretical case derives partly from commonsense considerations, and partly from a large mass of theoretical, conceptual and experimental research on subjects to do with the phenomenon of human learning. It needs to be said at once that researchers in the fields of psychology and education are still quite a long way from having all the answers that they would like to have (concerning, for example, the conditions under which humans do and do not learn). As indicated in the Preface, it is also the case that much useful information is still buried deep in the professional literature. But it is quite untenable to suggest that this massive body of knowledge has nothing to offer the experienced exhibition designer at all.

At a commonsense level, for instance, everybody knows that exhibitions should not 'go over the heads' of the majority of visitors. Everybody knows that visitors will not in general welcome the kind of exhibition that makes them unduly foot-sore. Everybody also knows that people dislike being talked down to. And so on. However, these essentially informal and commonsensical insights into human nature are by no means *reliable* guides to success. For example, it is one thing to say that an exhibition should be neither too simple nor too complicated, but it is quite another thing to know *how* to strike an acceptable balance between simplicity and complexity. Again, it is quite easy to say that an exhibition should avoid features that are likely to irritate members of the visiting public, but it is quite another thing to know *how* this might be best achieved. What the professional psychologist and educator can contribute is information regarding *how* certain desiderata can be achieved. When exhibition designers express scepticism about the need for advice from professional psychologists and educators, they are usually assuming either (a) that they are already sensitised to the salient psychological and educational issues, or (b) that the benefits accruing from such advice would not be worth the additional time and effort involved in getting it. The claim being made in this chapter is that neither (a) nor (b) is correct.

By way of substantiation, we offer a short and largely *ad-hoc* list of 'things that tend to go wrong' with educational exhibitions and other materials that have not had the benefit of advice from professionally qualified psychologists and educators.

(a) Introduction of new concepts too often in obscure, clumsy or vague ways.

(b) Tendency to explain the unfamiliar in terms of the even less familiar (i.e. starting beyond the learner's familiar knowledge, explaining things by reference to other things with which the learner is not sufficiently conversant).

(c) Presence of confusing clouds of detail. Talking points and teaching points appearing to 'jump all over the place'.

(d) Use of unexplained procedures of inference.

(e) Presence of actual mistakes in texts or legends. (It takes a greenhorn a long time to realise that this might have happened.)

(f) Assertion given before justificatory reason for it. (It is possible to worry for hours about the grounds for an assertion – in a mathematical textbook, for example – if one does not realise that the reason for the assertion has yet to be given . . .)

(g) Visitor is able to follow step by step, but not to grasp the overall conceptual structure. (Ability to follow, but not to understand. Inability to see underlying basis for argument. Inability to generate argument unaided, etc.)

(h) Visitor is unable to see why something is suddenly introduced.

(i) Fixed 'personal' associations of meaning that interfere, either because the text author is unclear of *his* assignation of meaning, or because his and learner's meanings collide – to the confusion of the latter.

(j) Bad composition of sentences, long qualifying phrases.

(k) Notation is often poor, and poorly explained, and (hence) hard to remember.

(l) Introduction of off-putting warnings to the effect that something is 'likely to be found difficult'. (The challenge is to reassure and make things easy . . .)

Improvability and its limitations

Humans may not be perfectible, but they are surely improvable. Almost everything that we set out to do can, given the requisite inclination and resources and know-how, be done a little better. Many of the things that we humans do are in fact capable of being done *very much* better. There would seem to be no exceptions to this general rule. It applies to entirely commonplace activities such as washing up dishes and making beds. It applies throughout the entire realm of work and sport and leisure. It applies to the running of businesses and the governing of whole nations. Without any doubt at all, it applies to the mounting of educational exhibitions.

Of course, not all improvements are *worth* striving for. An ambitious athlete might well be willing to train twice as hard to obtain a 1 per cent increase in his running time. But few exhibition designers are likely to want to work twice as hard to secure only a 1 per cent increase in the educational effectiveness of their exhibition. When people reach a certain level of proficiency, the Law of Diminishing Returns begins to make further improvements not worth the additional effort involved. In prowess-type activities such as athletics, it will presumably *always* be worthwhile for the very best athletes to go on fighting this particular law. The rewards for gaining even a miniscule improvement can more than justify the expenditure of quite gruelling additional effort. In saner activities, such as exhibition design, this is not the case. It is therefore not enough to claim that present-day educational exhibitions are generally capable of significant improvement. We must also show that the effort needed to bring about such improvement is not 'out of proportion' to the benefits obtained. In other words, we must show that the design of educational exhibitions has not yet reached the sort of proficiency level at which the Law of Diminishing Returns is seriously starting to bite.

Another point that needs to be noticed is that the Law of Diminishing Returns can sometimes give rise to seriously misleading conclusions. The law is convincing enough in the field of athletics, because our best athletes do seem to be approaching a natural limit to what is achievable. But this is not necessarily the case in other areas. In the 1940s, for example, many people thought that the speed of airplanes was approaching an absolute upper limit. With the recognition that planes could be propelled by jets, rather than propellers, this view underwent an order of magnitude transformation. The fact that intelligent people cannot *see* how things can be improved does not by any means imply that no improvement is possible. It may imply, instead, that they are operating with assumptions that are partly in error and, for that reason, unduly limiting.

One further point needs to be made, and it concerns the interpretation that is being given, in this chapter, to the concept of *improvement*. Unfortunately, the notion of improvement has been corrupted, in recent years, by the introduction of notions of 'cost-effectiveness'. In the eyes of some people, improving is nowadays roughly synonymous with 'doing things more cheaply'. The aim of the cost-effectiveness expert is to cut corners – to try to find ways of doing things that superficially look the same as before (or will 'do the job' just as well), but that actually save time and money. In the context of exhibition design, this kind of improvement would consist of finding ways of mounting exhibitions with fewer staff, cheaper materials, smaller overheads, etc. It may well be the case that cost savings of this kind *can* be found. But this is not what the present chapter is primarily about. Although financial considerations must be taken into account to some extent, our overriding concern in this chapter is not with the business of saving money, but with the business of helping to ensure that educational exhibitions really do provide their target audience (e.g. the ordinary man in the street) with 'a good educational experience'.

The psychology of the exhibition visitor

The well known distinction between work and leisure tends to obscure a rather more important *psychological* distinction – namely, the distinction between activities that are performed under conditions of stress, and activities that are performed under conditions of *no* stress. As we all know, many activities that are commonly described as leisure activities are intensely serious and stressful to those who take part in them. For example, the amount of stress involved in playing games like chess or football, or the amount of stress involved in keeping a treasured garden in good condition, can far exceed the amount of stress involved in doing one's day-to-day job. Conversely, there are some people (master craftsmen, for instance) for whom 'work' – in the sense of doing things for a living – is an almost continuous pleasure. Such people are completely on top of their job, and their working environment may be almost completely free of stress, harassment and other pressures.

The crucial distinction, then, is between doing things under conditions of stress, and doing things under conditions that are largely (or, better still, totally) free of stress. Stress can, of course, arise in a variety of different ways. A person can feel stressed if he considers himself to be under time pressure, or if he feels that other people will criticise him unless his actions come up to certain standards. Even if there are no external threats at all, a person will still feel stressed if he *imagines* that external threats exist, or if he is the kind of perfectionist who imposes unrealistically high standards upon himself.

Roughly speaking, a stressful situation is any situation that people consider (not necessarily correctly) to be threatening. Perhaps they feel they do not have enough time to do things properly, or to acquit themselves well. Perhaps they feel that they are vulnerable to criticism or punishment, or even attack, if they make a wrong move. Perhaps they feel wrong-footed, in the sense of being obliged to choose among the lesser of several evils. These feelings do not have to be objectively 'correct'. In order to create feelings of stress and urgency, it is sufficient that these people should *imagine* such feelings to be correct. What characterises the stressful situation is the feeling that there could be some kind of disappointment or trouble if certain problems are not handled in the right way.

There are some people for whom almost every situation in life contains elements of actual or incipient stress. But there is another way of living. And, for want of a better name, we can describe it here as 'the pure play mode'. What characterises stress-free play is the total absence of such things as worry, feelings of time pressure and overload, and (above all) any kind of *recriminatory evaluation*. In the pure play mode, problems, paradoxes and challenges are essentially non-threatening because we can either ignore them or else 'have a go' at them without feeling that anyone (including ourselves) is going to stand in judgement over us. If we fail to solve a particular problem when we are in the pure play mode, it does not matter, because we can either drop it, or go back to it later, or just laugh at ourselves for getting caught.

The pure play mode differs from the much commoner 'feeling stressed' mode in several important ways. If we are feeling stressed, our approach to problems tends to be one of how to get rid of the trouble that the problem is causing (or is likely to cause) us. In the pure play mode, problems are not seen as things that need to be got rid of. Rather, they are seen as *invitations to understand.* In the pure play mode, we are able to indulge ourselves in the luxury of intellectual honesty. Instead of trying to guess or bluff our way out of a problem situation (which is what stressed and busy people tend to do when they are put in some unexpected quandary) we can, if we are in the pure play mode, afford to take a relaxed look at the problem with a view to trying genuinely to understand what it is all about, and what response it really (as opposed to apparently) calls for. In the pure play mode we are able, in fact, to 'learn for the love of it'. Much more could be said about the difference between acting under conditions of felt stress and urgency, and acting under conditions in which such feelings are absent. But most readers are likely to be already aware of the salient differences from their own experience. They are likely to recall, for example, the difference between the learning that they were compelled to do at school, under threat of criticism, ridicule, punishment, ostracism, and the like, and the 'learning for the love of it' that they did *on their own account* (e.g. outside of school) in pursuit of knowledge and skills that really interested them. Just consider, for example, the learning that teenagers do for the sheer enjoyment of it – learning about pop stars, motor bikes, football, computer programming, chess, or whatever.

The point being made here is that there is a significant *qualitative* difference between the kind of learning that takes place under conditions of stress, and the kind of learning that can take place under conditions of *conviviality.* In the latter case, problems and paradoxes – things that we do not immediately understand – can take the form of thoroughly enjoyable challenges. In the former case, they are much more likely to take the form of potentially worrying threats. The designers of educational exhibitions would be well advised to take this difference seriously. The first rule of successful exhibition design is to ensure that, to as great an extent as is possible, the exhibition is a generally convivial occasion for the people who visit it. If certain visitors find the exhibition intimidating, or 'all too much for them' – if, in other words, it is the sort of exhibition that makes them feel inadequate and foolish because they cannot understand it – then the whole atmosphere will be soured, and the exhibition will be a failure so far as these particular visitors are concerned. If, on the other hand, visitors can sense the friendliness and conviviality of the exhibition as soon as they walk into the main exhibition hall, and if they are offered experiences, information and challenges that they can genuinely appreciate and comprehend, and if there is no stage at which they ever have cause to feel anxious or foolish or 'informationally lost', the exhibition will almost inevitably be both instructive and warmly remembered.

The lure of novelty

Modern man is an inquisitive creature. He speculates endlessly, he shops around for ideas, he studies newspapers and television and other mass media to find out what is going on, he gossips for much the same reasons, and so on. It is almost as if the need for novel experiences is as pressing and as natural to him as the need for food. Actually, animals often seem to behave in rather similar ways. Some animal psychologists have noted this fact by postulating the existence, in all living creatures, of an instinctive tendency to *explore*. Animals do not, however, seem to be quite as demoniacally inquisitive as man. If a rat is placed in a strange environment, it will cautiously explore. But, after establishing that there is nothing to be scared about, it is likely to go to sleep. Humans do not relax so easily. Experiments have been conducted in which humans have been placed in bleak and impoverished environments (e.g. small bare cells) in which there is almost no novel stimulation to occupy their minds. Under such conditions, many people break down. The impression one gets is that the average human mind continually *searches* for novelty – for novel events and happenings to think about and adapt to. If such events cease to occur, the most common result is a feeling of severe stress and boredom.

It is debatable whether humans *have* to be so dependent upon novel stimulation from the outside world. But the fact that so many people are dependent in this way is good news for the designer of educational exhibitions. Among other things, it guarantees that, when people enter an exhibition, they are at least likely to be looking at what is going on around them! They will be predisposed, also, to *attend* to the novelty that is being presented to them. There are, however, some snags.

First of all, it has to be noticed that although most people like to have a certain amount of variety to attend to, and although they often get bored if such novelty is lacking, they do not in general like 'too much' novelty. Too little novelty can be boring, but too much novelty tends to be bemusing or even frightening. Since people also *differ* in respect of how much novelty they can tolerate, educational exhibitions should be arranged so that visitors have some personal control over the amount of novelty that they need to absorb. This can be done by running the exhibition at several different levels, and by distinguishing between (a) novel ideas that the visitor really ought to try to take in, and (b) novel ideas that are of lesser (subsidiary) importance. It helps, also, to incorporate a certain amount of repetition or 'redundancy' in the exhibition, so that visitors can pick up at a later stage any particularly vital pieces of novel information that they might have missed at earlier stages.

Secondly, we must recognise that although visitors are likely to be looking at what is going on around them, they will *not* necessarily be looking too hard at the exhibition itself. In many cases, they are just as likely to be looking at one another and, to a large extent, ignoring the exhibition. The obvious reason for this is that other people can be just as attractive a source of novelty as the exhibits themselves. Let us therefore consider more carefully the conditions under which the *exhibits*, rather than other people (or, for that matter, the architecture of the building, or the wooden cabinets, or the restaurant facilities, or whatever), get attended to.

The problem of attention

If we ask why people behave in the ways that they do, one kind of response that professional psychologists often give is to cite a variety of different (but interrelated) 'factors' that collectively tend to determine our everyday behaviour. The most general thing that can be said is that our behaviour is determined partly by the situation that presents itself to us, and partly by the past experience that we bring to bear on the situation. Of course, our past experience is itself likely to influence, quite heavily, the way in which we *perceive* the situation confronting us. If we want to go into this matter in a little more detail, it can also be said that our behaviour, at any given time, is largely influenced by our needs and interests at that time, and also by our abilities and our perception of what the situation demands.

These are very general statements. By themselves, they do not get us very far. At the very least we need to know how such factors as needs, interests and abilities are interrelated, and how they relate to other relevant factors such as our perception of what the situation demands. Indeed, we even need to ask whether there are better ways of talking and theorising about the origin and causation of human behaviour. It is obviously beyond the scope of this chapter to pursue these matters in detail. There is, however, one 'factor' that *is* worth singling out for special consideration, because it has an all-pervasive effect on the way in which *humans* behave, and on the things that humans choose to *attend* to. The factor in question is what psychologists sometimes describe as the self-image factor. And the key idea is that most humans, most of the time, tend to act *in accordance with the image that they have of themselves.*

Roughly speaking, a person's self-image is whatever *matters* to the person in question. If it matters to a person to look smartly dressed, then we can say that 'looking smart' is part of the image that the person has of himself. Similarly, if a person moves in circles in which it is considered fashionable or 'the right thing to do' to attend a particular happening (an exhibition, gathering, theatre, or whatever), and if it matters to him to maintain the approval of such people, he may well attend for the sole purpose of being able to say, after the event, that he was also there. Again, if a person has an image of himself as being someone who ought to be better informed, or who ought not to miss out on a once-in-a-lifetime opportunity to see something, he may well go for one of these reasons. More generally, if a person has an image of himself as being the kind of person who is capable of benefiting from a visit to, say, an exhibition, this will be a strong incentive for him to look around. In all such cases, the person will be attending the exhibition with the aim of attending to the exhibits, in an aspiringly intelligent manner.

There is nothing especially recondite about the notion of people behaving in accordance with the image that they have of themselves. Most people live and act in accordance with standards and precepts that they have come, over the years, to value. And this is one reason why it comes as a surprise when someone seems to act 'out of character'. The point being made here is that one's character is hardly likely to change the moment one walks into an exhibition hall. If a visitor has an image of himself as being (say) a dutiful or long-suffering father, he may well attend an educational exhibition for the sole purpose of making sure that his children have a good look around. It might not even occur to him that he also might profit from having a good look around.

The inescapable conclusion that has to be drawn is that people will visit exhibitions for a wide variety of different reasons – to instruct or entertain themselves (or their families), to show off their knowledge to whoever they go with, to have something to talk about to their friends, to while away an odd half hour, to use the restaurant facilities, to get out of the rain, and so on. Some visitors will enter exhibitions with a genuine desire to learn, and others will enter either (a) with hardly any such desires at all, or (b) with strong doubts as to whether they will be capable of learning, even if they want to.

As already indicated, the exact state of mind of a visitor, on first entering an exhibition, will depend upon a whole cluster of predominantly psychological factors, e.g. his level of relevant knowledge, the time at his disposal, his eagerness to learn, his experience of other exhibitions that he has visited in the past, and the kinds of expectations that have been induced in him by hearsay and media publicity. Because of the multiplicity of reasons that can exist for visiting or not visiting a particular exhibition, or for attending or not attending to particular exhibits, it is largely a waste of time to speculate about why particular visitors behave in particular ways. The most that can be said is that a whole range of underlying needs, motives and aspirations and the like *will* be operative during any given visit. And one way of making sense of visitor behaviour is to examine the image that visitors have of themselves. If we know how a person sees himself – if we know, for example, the extent to which learning about a particular topic really matters to him, and if we know whether or not he sees himself as being generally 'good at learning' – we can make reasonably strong predictions (a) about that person's initial eagerness and motivation to learn, and (b) about the rapidity with which he is likely to get discouraged in the face of difficulty. In the absence of information of this kind, relevant predictions are difficult to make. Certainly, it would be unwise to assume that people who visit exhibitions – even avowedly educational exhibitions – do so with learning as their primary aim. A high proportion of visitors may be attending for reasons that have little to do with the possibility of learning. It is therefore no easy matter to *induce* such visitors to try to learn, once they have crossed the threshold into the exhibition.

Balancing reward and effort

However much we may deplore the fact, increasing numbers of people nowadays tend to adopt a 'what's in it for me?' attitude to most of the things that they are invited, or called upon, to do. When confronted with the possibility of doing something, they ask themselves whether the rewards are likely to be worthwhile. For example, people will not usually buy a book unless they perceive the benefits of having it as being commensurate with the purchase price. Likewise, they will not spend too much time and effort reading it unless they think that the expenditure of such effort will produce an appropriate pay-off. There is, in fact, a continuous mental balancing of 'likely effort for likely reward'. The main factors that are mentally weighed up, and balanced against one another, are:

(a) the amount of effort (in terms of time, money and energy) that the proposed course of action is likely to call for;
(b) the magnitude and value of the consequences ('pay-off'), in terms of rewards obtained or punishments avoided or both, if the proposed course of action is successful;
(c) the likelihood, or otherwise, that the proposed course of action will indeed be successful.

The operation of this mental balancing act can be seen in all walks of life. For example, people will do the football pools because the amount of effort involved (in filling up the coupon) is very small, whereas the pay-off (if successful) can be

enormous – notwithstanding the fact that the likelihood of success is only miniscule. Similarly, our athlete might spend huge amounts of effort to win an important race, if he believes that he has a genuine chance of winning.

It is easy to see that each of the above three factors directly influences the others. For example, many people would stop doing the pools if the financial outlay were to be significantly increased, or if they got too disillusioned about their chances of winning. And some people would expend very much more effort on the pools if, by studying form intensively, they believed that there would be a significant increase in the chances of their winning substantial sums. In the context of educational exhibitions, the operation of the above factors has salutary implications. Among other things, there is a clear implication that visitors are unlikely to spend very much effort studying the exhibits unless they feel that the rewards for doing so *will* be worthwhile. They must also have confidence in their own ability to learn. There must, in fact, be *hope*. And the exhibition must do its best to ensure that hope is justified. The effect of the three factors listed above is to induce people to expend effort if and only if there is a hope of getting some worthwhile reward. It is hope that keeps the 'what's in it for me?' personality going. In recognition of this fact, educational exhibitions must incorporate features that have the motivational effect of cheering the visitor on. Although a person may not visit an educational exhibition with any serious intention to learn, it remains true that, once he is in the main hallway, he may well prefer to try to learn, rather than just wander around in a state of bemusement. The lesson to be learned from the three factors just considered is that he must be convinced, from the very outset, that his efforts to learn are likely to be well repaid. The question that arises, therefore, is how can appropriate motivational and informational conditions be contrived. Let us pause to consider some of the difficulties that stand in the way.

Some difficulties of empathy

Every good teacher knows that teaching is difficult. Conversely, any teacher who claims that teaching is easy is, in all probability, *not* a good teacher. In recent years, researchers have started to give increasing attention to the problem of *why* teaching is difficult. Several distinct sources of difficulty have been identified.

First of all, it has now become increasingly clear that many teachers (even teachers of comparatively long standing) are not at all good at empathising with the aspiring learner. Among other things, they simply cannot understand how ignorant or misinformed the comparative beginner might be. They cannot put themselves in the beginner's shoes and 'see' that ideas that are transparently clear to themselves might be wellnigh unintelligible to the novice. This difficulty is essentially a failure of imagination on the part of the would-be teacher. However conscientious and well meaning such a teacher may be, he is simply unable to come down to the beginner's level.

The inability to empathise is particularly likely to afflict *specialists* who tangle with the problems of how to educate the general public. The high powered expert of (say) microprocessors and computer programming may well be quite unable to see that things that he takes for granted are by no means obvious to the beginner. He may also be quite unable to see that statements that admit, in his eyes, of only one interpretation, are actually capable of numerous kinds of misinterpretation by the uninformed.

It is, of course, easy to see how this state of affairs comes about. The trouble is that, as people get more and more conversant with a particular subject, ideas that were initially opaque and difficult start to look more and more obvious. Eventually, as increasing familiarity breeds more and more confidence, the ideas in question become so 'obvious' that it is hard to see how anybody could possibly have difficulty in grasping them. When this point is reached, teaching tends to be seen (by the confident expert) *not* as a matter of carefully introducing and explaining basic ideas, but as a matter of saying things that any intelligent layman ought to be able to comprehend almost at once. If the intelligent layman fails to comprehend, the next step is to suggest that he has not really tried.

Unfortunately, we humans too easily lose our innocence. When we first try to come to grips with some complex subject-matter, it seldom occurs to us that we ourselves might one day want (or be called upon) to teach it to others. In consequence, we do not bother to note down the numerous difficulties, confusions and inadvertances of teaching method that we ourselves encounter on

our pathway to mastery. By the time we *have* mastered the subject-matter, such difficulties have already faded from our memory. However much we try, we cannot recapture the state of mind that we ourselves were in, during our earliest faltering attempts to discover what the subject was all about.

The validity of these comments is demonstrated in almost every household in the land – whenever, for example, some loving father tries to tell his son about decimal multiplication or the addition of fractions or Euclidean geometry. A pad and pencil are produced and, with a few flourishes, father tries to explain to his son things that took him (when *he* was a boy) weeks or even months to understand. Consider, also, the teacher who cheerily talks about the need to pre-check the 'entry knowledge' of some new group of students. Knowledge? What such students need is not a test of knowledge, but a test of their ignorance. The priority need is not to discover what they know but to discover what they do not know. Contrary to much popular opinion, a check on the former does not necessarily yield satisfactory information about the latter. The point is not a trivial one. Before we can even begin to teach some people, it may be necessary to spend time and effort releasing them from the grip of erroneous and obstructive presuppositions.

Techniques of effective teaching

Not so long ago, people were known to travel hundreds of miles, often under difficult and dangerous conditions, to sit at the feet of a Great Teacher. What is more, the purpose of the journey was not to be able to answer a hundred multiple-choice questions at the end of the day. The goal was to achieve significant understanding, and such journeys were undertaken in the belief that Great Teachers are born, rather than made. The essence of a Great Teacher is that he has both (a) a profound understanding of what he is teaching, and (b) the empathic ability to impart such understanding to the ardent seeker.

Today's teachers, through no fault of their own, are often seriously lacking in both these qualities. In recognition of this fact, effort tends to be directed towards building in safeguards that will 'automatically' give sufficiently satisfactory results.

Among the safeguards that have been developed over the past 20 to 30 years, the following deserve special mention.

(a) Techniques for helping teachers to determine the content and conceptual structure of subject-matters that they wish to teach.

(b) Techniques for determining the suitability of some proposed set of teaching materials, having regard to the needs, interests and abilities of the students involved.

(c) Techniques for determining the *order* in which particular teaching points can best be presented. Ancillary techniques for determining the most promising-looking media of communication and their modes of use (e.g. conventional textbook, programmed text, audio-visual displays . . .).

(d) Techniques for enabling teachers to determine, with minimum equivocation, how 'successful' their teaching has been.

(e) Techniques for enabling the students *also* to determine (preferably at each stage of the learning process) how well they are doing. Ancillary techniques for enabling students to 'back-track' in cases of difficulty, and to detect and correct any errors in their understanding.

(f) 'Overarching' techniques for integrating (a) to (e) within a unified teaching system that both arouses and maintains the motivation and good will of different kinds of students.

It would take a full-length book to cover these techniques in carefully worked out detail, so we will restrict ourselves to discussing each in comparatively brief outline form.

Subject-matter, content and structure

One way of teaching is to present the learner with one fact or principle after another. If the facts are sufficiently interesting in themselves, the learner may well be entirely satisfied with this procedure. In an exhibition on wild animals, for example, a visitor might consider his visit to have been worthwhile if he emerges with odd snippets of information that he did not know before – if he learns, for instance, that elephants cannot jump, and that they are the only creatures that have four knees. There is, however, a snag. It stems from the fact that, having absorbed such delectable morsels of information, there is little that the visitor can do except memorise them and repeat them.

There is more to significant teaching than this. Significant teaching is teaching that, at the very least, tries to induce in the learner some insights into the ways in which relevant facts and principles are *related*. If such relationships are not pointed out, knowledge is of necessity fragmentary. The situation is analogous to that of a person who wants to become a taxi driver and who knows the names of some of the main streets *without* at the same time knowing how they are geographically related to one another. Let us explore this analogy more closely.

If a man wants to become a taxi driver, he must build up a detailed relational image of the terrain he is proposing to cover. The build-up can proceed in several different ways. For example, he might choose to obtain a gross bird's-eye view of how the main roadways are related, so that he can then work on filling in the finer detail to do with lesser interconnecting roads and backwaters. Alternatively, he might tackle one locality at a time –the business area, the market area, the new housing estate, the recreational district, the area where Charlie lives, and so on – and eventually piece the localities together into one integrated whole. However, these two approaches are essentially similar in so far as they both call for the establishing of appropriate 'whole-to-part' relationships.

The analogy and its implications are worth taking seriously. In solving almost any problem whatever, and in getting a *familiarity* with almost any subject-matter whatever, the overall aim is always to establish appropriate whole-to-part relationships. Until the parts are conceptually 'available' to the learner, they cannot be meaningfully composed into wholes. The taxi driver thus learns his way around a district in piecemeal fashion – first by learning local relationships of adjacency (knowing what roads are most closely connected to what other roads), and later expanding his knowledge to connect one cluster of roads to another. Only when a sufficient number of local clusters are available can the bigger compositions be conceived. And even this calls for the help of certain linguistic (e.g. terminological) tricks. For example, the taxi driver will find himself giving *names* to particular groupings of streets – names such as 'the market area', and 'the area around the main theatre'. Each such name will stand for a constellation of roads that he can describe in detail. So, in relating one named area to another, he is effectively relating one constellation of streets to another constellation of streets. The process of building up the requisite relational structure is inevitably slow. And, although the final result may look complex, the complexity is actually compounded out of a lot of simplicity.

The analogy of the taxi driver is quite a useful one because, in trying to teach people intellectual subject-matters, we do (metaphorically speaking) take them on a set of tours, so that they can learn certain paths, and see the patterns that these paths make, and see also the regions that they cover – so that the 'areal' geography can *then* (and only then) be grasped. In effect, the students are initially obliged to follow, step by step, without really understanding why they are passing the things that they are passing. They know that they can 'go left' here, but not *why* they do not go right, or go in some other direction. If left to themselves, they might of course wander indefinitely. With the help of a good teacher, the learning process is greatly facilitated. Small component abilities are established first, and these are later given names and compounded with other component abilities.

Let us also note, in passing, a fundamental difference between (a) understanding a subject-matter, and (b) being able to *follow* what some expert has to say about a subject-matter. There is all the difference in the world between being able to follow the steps that some teacher lays out in a path (from 'problem' to 'solution'), and being able to generate *for oneself* the steps in question. To revert to our taxi driver analogy, it is a bit like the difference between being able to follow a map, and being able to give someone precise directions on how to get somewhere. The trainee taxi driver can do the former, but not the latter. And the difference is in the kind of familiarity that enables the experienced taxi driver to think without looking, and to consider possible routes and possible obstructions to them. 'Understanding' a subject is having *that* sort of familiarity with it.

When the man in the street looks upwards into the heavens on a cloudless summer day, what he sees is a bright yellow sun in a bright blue sky. When Goethe looked upwards in the same circumstances, he was perceptive enough to 'see'

that the blueness of the sky *had something to do with* the yellowness of the sun. In other words, he perceived the two phenomena – of blueness and yellowness – as belonging together. For Goethe, the phenomena were related. This is relational thinking, *par excellence.* What marks out the subtle thinker from the crude and fragmentary thinker is this ability to perceive relationships (and, better still, relationships between relationships) that are not immediately obvious. To have this ability is, among other things, to be able (a) to perceive significance in what lesser mortals regard as trivial, and (b) to perceive triviality in what lesser mortals regard as significant.

Educators who appreciate the importance of inducing high-level relational thinking are nowadays tending to give this matter absolute priority (over all other considerations) in their curriculum planning. Their starting point, therefore, is a delineation of the 'to-be-taught' subject-matter in the form of a relational network that explicitly shows how key concepts in the subject-matter are to be related. Shortage of space prevents us from developing this matter in greater detail, but we append one example of such a network (Fig. 3.1). It is taken from Rowntree's *Educational technology in curriculum development* (1974), and it deals with the matter of how to teach one comparatively straightforward subject-matter – namely, the formation of tree rings.

To a large extent, Figure 3.1 speaks for itself. For example, it is clearly a 'quasi-causal' diagram showing what things affect what other things. The arrows in the diagram can be read as meaning 'gives rise to'. Thus, if we start in the top left-hand corner of the diagram, we learn that low precipitation gives rise to less cloud cover which in turn gives rise to more solar radiation. And so on. No doubt it is obvious that teaching arranged in accordance with diagrams of this kind is *fundamentally* different from the kind of teaching that simply conveys isolated facts . . .

Much more could be said about the advantages of teaching in the relational manner advocated in this section. We might notice, for example, that – contrary to much popular opinion – effective teaching is *not* primarily concerned with the careful presentation of one fact or principle after another. The effective teacher is not in the business of telling or showing students 'what is the case'. Instead, he is in the business of teaching the student *what to do next*. This is a subtle and far-from-recognised point that we will come back to.

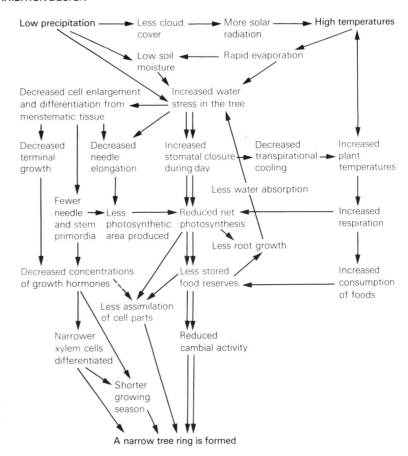

Figure 3.1 A relational network to show how the key concepts in studying the formation of tree rings are to be related. From Rowntree (1974).

Assessing suitability

A diagram of the kind in Figure 3.1 is something of a source document. First of all, it can be expanded and annotated in a variety of different ways. Among other things, the technical terms in the diagram can be extracted, and subjected to scrutiny, to see what needs to be done to convey their meanings effectively. In all probability, the teaching of any one technical term – e.g. 'photosynthesis', might itself call for a further relational diagram. By carefully unpacking the implications of the diagram given in the last section, it may become obvious that there is actually a very large amount of careful teaching that needs to be done. The question that then arises is whether the intended population of students is likely to have the time or the inclination or the ability to put in the minimum necessary effort. If the answer is No, it will be necessary to revise one's ideas as to what is teachable, and what is not.

Again, it is beyond the scope of this chapter to pursue these matters in depth. It must therefore suffice to assure the reader that the relevant techniques *have* been largely worked out. For example, techniques exist for assessing how long a given learning task is likely to take, having regard to the needs and interests and abilities of the target student population. Techniques also exist for guiding certain difficult decisions about what to include, in a proposed teaching programme, and what to leave out. And techniques exist for 'sampling' the proposed student population, to test out their views and likely reactions to particular kinds of teaching material.

In standard educational settings, it is always helpful to have volunteer students on whom to 'try out' some proposed set of teaching materials. Likewise, it is always helpful to have volunteers to try out some proposed sequence of exhibits for an exhibition. The reason why it is helpful is that even the most experienced and imaginative exhibition designers cannot be relied upon to foresee all the ways in which their materials might be misunderstood. It is therefore a good idea to get a few volunteers, in the form of 'typical members of the visiting public', on site for a few hours, to see what sort of sense or nonsense they make of the materials in question.

On the other hand, it would be dangerous to *over*estimate the usefulness of volunteers. Volunteers will generally pick up things that are crassly wrong (e.g. from exhibits that go right over the heads of everyone), but different volunteers may offer different opinions and, in all probability, *none* of the volunteers will have any vision of how the sequence of exhibits might be significantly improved. If exhibits are modified in the light of comments from volunteers, it is entirely possible that the modified sequence of exhibits will introduce new defects. To safeguard against this possibility, more volunteers will have to be obtained. And so on. This can obviously be an expensive and time-consuming business – subject, in fact, to the Law of Diminishing Returns. For reasons such as this, effort is nowadays being directed towards the challenge of assessing the suitability of teaching materials, educational exhibits, and the like, with only *minimal* reference to the proposed target audience.

Order and format

Having decided what to teach, problems arise about the best *sequence* in which the relevant teaching points should be made. Again, there are assorted techniques for helping to answer this question. The matter is quite complicated, however, because different factors tend to compete with one another for consideration. For example, it is generally desirable to teach in a way that minimises the need for repeated 'recapitulations'. If we want to build up the student's confidence (without at the same time building up any false confidence), we *must* maintain his expectation and hope that he will 'be able to advance'. Too much chopping and changing – picking up one topic, and then dropping it to deal with another – creates feelings of discontinuity, and a sense of not being sure what is going on. A priority goal, then, is to discover a teaching sequence that builds up smoothly. This is especially important in the context of educational exhibitions, because visitors cannot easily sort out errors by 'back-tracking' to previous exhibits. With conventional textbooks, back-tracking is comparatively

simple. The reader just flips back a few pages to re-read something that he thinks he might have misunderstood. But the exhibition visitor is unlikely to go wandering back (in opposition, perhaps, to the onward flow of other visitors) to recheck what he saw at the other end of the hall.

In addition to minimising discontinuities and recapitulations, we must also try to avoid the need for initially *distortive* simplification. If we introduce some topic in an *over*simplified manner, and if we then have to confess to the learner, at some later date, that we have done this, two unfortunate consequences can ensue. First of all, confidence can diminish, because he will wonder what other half-truths and oversimplifications he has been subjected to. Worse, we are effectively asking him to change his conceptual framework 'in mid-stream'. In effect, we are telling him to discount or forget what he was told earlier, and to start looking at the subject-matter in some 'new and better' way. This is what psychologists sometimes describe as 'negative transfer' of knowledge. It occurs whenever knowledge is of a kind that is *disruptive* of the acquisition of additional knowledge. Ideally, teachers always want to achieve the exact opposite – namely, 'positive transfer'. To teach in a way that facilitates positive transfer is to teach in a way that tries to ensure that each new bit of knowledge *assists* the acquisition of further knowledge.

Next, we need to notice that it is always a good idea, at the beginning of a teaching programme, to try to return high psychological satisfaction to the student on the basis of *simple* conceptual material. To do this, we need to find intricate and delighting 'achievements' (of insight or of doing) that, from the standpoint of the conceptual material just presented, are transparently obvious. For example, we might search for some engineering attainment that looks both surprising and highly impressive, until it is realised that it follows entirely naturally from an understanding of the simple extra concept that the student has just been given. To teach in this way is to teach with impact. It induces the student to think (and to think correctly) that what he is learning is *worth* learning, because the content is usefully applicable in the real world.

There is much more that could be said about the problem of sequencing. Psychologists have, for example, distinguished between logical sequencing, psychological sequencing, and epistemological sequencing. Logical sequencing is perhaps the most compelling (see Ch. 6). If concept A cannot be understood until concept B has been understood, then, from a logical point of view, concept B *must* be taught before concept A. However, even if no strict logical ordering can be found, it might still be the case that, *psychologically*, it turns out to be easier for most students to learn concept B before concept A. And, occasionally, there are additional epistemological considerations to do with the whole way in which a particular subject-matter is conceptualised within a given society. Such considerations can *also* suggest that concept B should be taught before concept A.

On the matter of format, there is again a lot to be said. Most readers will be aware that, in recent years, a whole new range of 'instructional formats' has appeared on the educational scene. These include such things as programmed textbooks, computer-aided learning, audio-visual teaching techniques, teaching by radio, cassette, or television, and so on. There are, in fact, several other significant additions that are less well known, such as the so-called **algorithmic** approach (Lewis & Horabin 1977), the so-called **mathetics** approach (Gilbert 1969), and the so-called **information mapping** approach (Horn 1976–80). These different instructional formats all have characteristic features of their own, and an understanding of what each has to offer can be quite helpful to any aspiring teacher. Most of these formats are in themselves not particularly relevant to the design of educational exhibitions, but the thinking that lay behind the development of these formats most certainly *is* relevant, and worth knowing about.

With regard to educational exhibitions in particular, it is no doubt obvious that learning must take place (if it takes place at all) primarily through looking – supplemented, perhaps, by a certain amount of relevant listening, touching, smelling, and even tasting. What is more, the looking that is involved is mainly directed towards visual displays, and the text and captions that accompany them. It is not the kind of looking that is involved in working one's way through a conventional textbook. As it happens, learning-by-looking is quite a fundamental human skill. In all probability, it is more 'basic' than 'learning-by-reading'. Learning by looking can also be made very much more effective if there are opportunities for the learner to *do* things, and to

check out the consequences or results of his doings. Recognition of this fact accounts for the sharp increase, in educational exhibitions, in the number of 'interactive devices' that visitors are invited to play with. There are good psychological reasons for expecting such devices to be powerful aids to learning, in a museum environment, provided they are constructed in a suitably motivating and non-frustrating way.

The problem of success

Since the designers and sponsors of educational exhibitions are invariably anxious that their efforts should be considered a success, it is worth *planning* for success from the very outset. One way of doing this is to adopt what is nowadays widely known as the **'behavioural objectives approach'** to education. Briefly, the method consists in stating what it is that the student ought to be able to say and/or do, as a result of undergoing a given educational experience, that he could not say and/or do *before.* In other words, the method consists in drawing up a specification of the consequences of going through a particular educational experience – the consequences taking the form of well defined *questions* that the student should be able to answer, and well defined *tasks* that he ought to be able to perform.

It is both a strength and a weakness of the behavioural objectives approach that it can be used with almost any kind of educational programme – indoctrinal or otherwise, relational or otherwise, and so on. For example, an exhibition on wild animals could have, as one of its objectives, the objective that visitors should be able to answer the question, 'Can elephants jump?'. If, on the other hand, the teaching is of a putatively higher order than this, the objectives will be of a kind that can be derived from Figure 3.1. Our personal recommendation, of course, is that significant objectives are of this latter kind. Thus, if we were training taxi drivers, we would not wish to specify the objective of 'being able to follow a local road map'. Instead, we would specify some such objective as 'The proficient taxi driver should be able to give the quickest route from any road to any other, without reference to a local map.'

The point about the behavioural objectives approach is that it 'comes clean' on what the teachers (or exhibition designers) are trying to achieve. If a group of designers assert that the visitor, after passing through the exhibition at a reasonable pace, should be able to answer such-and-such questions, and be able to perform such-and-such tasks, there is a clear basis for evaluating the success of the exhibition. First of all, the professional evaluator can examine the kinds of questions that the visitor is expected to be able to answer, and the kinds of tasks that he is expected to be able to perform, with a view to seeing just how searching and exacting they are. Next, he can take steps to see whether the visitors have, in the main, actually acquired these abilities.

It is worth bearing in mind, however, that there may be more to the notion of success than this. Other indices of success might be favourable reviews in the press, large queues to get into the exhibition, demonstrated tendencies for visitors to return, and to recommend the exhibition to their friends, more funds made available by the local authority to continue or revise the exhibition, or to mount another like it. And so on. If such indices of success are considered to be important, it is worthwhile for the design team to think, from the very outset, how they might improve their chances of meeting such criteria.

Student success and difficulty

One of the best ways of teaching is to teach in a manner that enables the learner to tell (a) whether he is doing something wrong, and (b) how to rectify his mistake if he *is* doing something wrong. The goal, here, is to provide a teaching experience that makes the student optimally 'error-sensitive'. If a student can spot the errors that he has made (or is making) and can also put them right, virtually nothing can go wrong' with the learning process.

It is important to see that the behavioural objectives approach does not automatically ensure that the student will have a smooth passage. A behavioural objective is, in fact, an objective for the teacher. It is a device by which the teacher can satisfy himself that the student has learned what he ought to have learned. It is *not* a device by which the *student* can be satisfied that he has learned to the teacher's satisfaction. The two cases are different. What is important is that the student should know how well he is doing. In

the absence of the requisite error-sensitivity, this cannot be guaranteed to happen. All too often, the student will be left wondering whether he really has done what is expected and, if so, whether it is now in order to move on to the next teaching point.

If the student does run into difficulties, what can he do? In the context of educational exhibitions, there is not much that can be done. As already indicated, there is no ready facility whereby the visitor can back-track to an earlier display, even if he happens to know which display to go to. Extra care must therefore be taken to minimise the likelihood of visitors misunderstanding, in any serious fashion, what they *do* study.

Overarching principles

The last five sections have all dealt with techniques that are richly and deeply interrelated. Taken as a whole, they imply the need to take heed of the following considerations.

Knowing what is going on

Ideally, the aspiring learner should at all times know what is going on. There is nothing more 'demotivating' than finding oneself in a situation in which one does not know what is supposed to be happening – a situation, in other words, in which one feels 'informationally lost'. In the context of educational exhibitions, this means that the visitor must be given the right sort of orientation, almost as soon as he enters the exhibition hall. There must be some clear and simple 'scene setting' – a conspicuous notice, for example, that tells him what the exhibition is about and what the designers are hoping to get across to him as he works his way round. In view of the fact that many visitors may lack confidence in their ability to understand what they are about to see, an effort should also be made to offer a number of reassurances. Among other things, the visitor should be made to feel that, with a little care, the main teaching points are indeed within his grasp, and that they are also worth grasping. In other words, an attempt should be made to put the visitor at his ease. At an early stage, he should have a good idea of what is going on, and also be fairly relaxed in his own mind about it.

Knowing what to do

In addition to knowing what is going on (e.g. knowing what the exhibition is supposed to be about), the visitor must also know what part he personally is supposed to play in the proceedings. What, exactly, is he expected to do? Is he supposed just to gawp at the exhibits? Is he supposed to take them really seriously? Is he supposed to study each display for two minutes, or half an hour? Somehow, the exhibition must signal its expectations of the visitor. And it may well be the case that different visitors are expected or invited to play different roles. It would be entirely possible, for example, for an exhibition to have special little pamphlets to hand out to 'mums and dads', or teachers accompanied by pupils of various ages – inviting these people to do different or extra things.

Wanting to do it

A visitor cannot know what to do, unless he first knows what is going on. And whatever it is that he is supposed to do, he cannot know whether he wants to do it, unless he first knows whether 'it' fits in with what is going on. Naturally, there is no way of making visitors want to do certain things. But we can try to encourage them to do so. And we can try to ensure that they are not frustrated in their first (possibly grudging) attempts to do what is asked.

Opportunity to do it

If we are wanting visitors to do certain things, we really must give them the opportunity to try. We also remark that a visitor cannot even know whether the opportunity will persist long enough to try, unless he first of all knows what is going on.

The provision of appropriate opportunities completes the set of very general conditions that need to be satisfied. In summary, we can tell the visitor *what* we are offering him the opportunity to do, and *why* this is what we are offering him. We can let him know what will be going on *if* he wants to take the opportunity. And we can try to ensure that, if he does want to take the opportunities offered, his attempts are not frustrated.

Ways of knowing

As already indicated, there now exists an enormous amount of literature on the subject of teaching and learning. Much of it is highly technical in nature, because professional educators and psychologists have found it necessary to invent large numbers of technical terms and expressions to assist the various theorisings that they engage in. Throughout this chapter, we have tried quite hard to avoid going into these technicalities. In this respect, the content of this chapter exemplifies one of the main precepts of this book – namely, that one should try to avoid going over the head of the learner, even if this means that one fails to do full justice to the subject-matter in question. To emphasise the fact that there is very much more to be said about the pedagogical issues that have been touched upon over the last few pages, we now briefly mention one of many alternative (and partly complementary) approaches. This is to do with the matter of how people come to know about things.

One good way of coming to grips with almost any teaching problem whatever is to ask oneself, 'How could a motivated person *come to know* about this particular subject-matter?' When the question is posed in this way, we find ourselves embarking upon an intriguing exercise aimed at elucidating the different ways in which aspiring human learners can come to know about things with which they were previously unfamiliar (Figs 3.2–6).

For example, there is what some writers call the *method of definition.* Thus, we can come to know that an equilateral triangle is a triangle that has all three sides equal, by being given a definition to that effect. Next, there is the *method of demonstration.* For example, we can come to know that the internal angles of a triangle add up to 180°, by following a demonstration to that effect. However, these are both essentially passive ways of coming to know about things. They are ways that require us to do nothing more than sit in a chair and read a book. Are there *more active* ways of coming to know about things?

The answer is *Yes.* One of the most active ways of coming to know about things is via the *method of interaction.* We come to know what a lemon is like by breaking it open and sucking it. We come to know (at first hand) what a horse is like by rearing a foal, feeding it, patting it, nursing it through sickness, riding it, and so on. We come to know what cooking is like by interacting with food and cooking utensils. And so on.

Figure 3.2 Ways of knowing: the method of definition. From 'Introducing ecology', British Museum (Natural History), 1978.

Figure 3.3 Ways of knowing: the method of demonstration. From 'Man's place in evolution', British. Museum (Natural History), 1980.

Figure 3.4 Ways of knowing: the method of interaction. From the 'Hall of human biology', British Museum (Natural History), 1977.

Figure 3.5 Ways of knowing: the method of enactment. The visitor investigates a genuine problem in a computer-based display. From 'Introducing ecology', British Museum (Natural History), 1978.

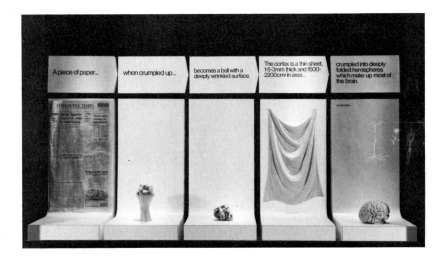

Figure 3.6 Ways of knowing: the method of analogy. From the 'Hall of human biology', British Museum (Natural History), 1977.

The point about the method of interaction is that we induce events in the real world (not just on paper) that make the real things real to us. By the method of interaction, we generate experiences that we can think about and talk about. Although the matter cannot be pursued in detail here, it can be said that the method of interaction provides a learning experience that is qualitatively different from the kind of learning that can be acquired by passively reading a book. Consider, for example, the difference between learning about horses in the manner just discussed, and learning about horses by reading books, watching films, and the like. Or consider the difference between watching a cookery demonstration on television, and actually trying to cook the same dish oneself.

Are there yet other ways of coming to know about things? Again, the answer is *Yes*. Another slightly different, but nevertheless active, method is the *method of enactment*. Roughly speaking, the method of enactment asserts that people understand best the things that they can *do* (and, as a corollary, they *think* that they understand the things that they *think* they can do ...). Yet another method – perhaps the most fundamentally important of all – is the *method of analogy*. This method acknowledges the fact that we make sense of current events, problems, etc. by referring such events and problems to similar-looking events and problems that we have encountered in the past. In brief, we look for promising analogies.

The method of analogy probably underpins all the other methods. For example, when we give a definition we are actually saying that X is a sort of Y (i.e. an analogy). If we go so far as to assert that X is Y, we have asserted an identity – which is actually only the limiting case of an analogy. Again, if we give a demonstration, the demonstration will be understood only in so far as there are relevant analogical concepts in the student's mind. And when we break open a lemon and suck it for the first time (i.e. using what we have called the method of interaction), we say something such as, 'Oh! This is *like* an orange, only more sour'. So, here again, analogising plays an essential role in our conceptual understanding.

Some physical convincers

About seven years ago, one of the national television networks in Britain put out a 40-minute programme on the subject of homeopathic medicine. The programme was widely acclaimed as a highly interesting and (partly for that reason) highly successful introduction to the subject. In the space of little more than half an hour, it managed to give a very fair overview of what homeopathic medicine is all about. Among the many (related) topics covered were:

(a) the climate of dissatisfaction (with conventional medicine) out of which homeopathic techniques grew;
(b) the key personalities (and main concepts) involved;
(c) the ways in which homeopathic medicine can convincingly claim to be different from, and even superior to, more conventional modes of allopathic medicine;
(d) the historical development of the homeo-

pathic techniques now in current use;
(e) the range of applicability of homeopathic techniques, e.g. to animals, and even to creatures that are asleep or unconscious at the time of treatment;
(f) the pros and cons of various disputes that have arisen (e.g. the accusation that homeopathic techniques have only a placebo effect), and the attempts that have been made to resolve such disputes;
(g) the relationship of homeopathic medicine to other recent innovations in 'alternative medicine', e.g. the emphasis of homeopathic practitioners on trying to treat the whole person, rather than a particular symptom or disease.

The programme was visually attractive, the language was comparatively simple and, when the occasional technical term had to be introduced, this was done with care and effectiveness. It can be said, with some conviction, that the programme would have (a) held the attention of a wide range of viewers of not more than average intelligence, and (b) *moved* such viewers from a state of crass ignorance about homeopathic medicine to a state of having a useful overall view of what the subject was all about.

Actually, there is nothing unduly surprising about this. There are many other 'general feature' programmes, on television, in glossy magazines, and elsewhere, that are just as effective in their own way. What is more, there are numerous 'short workshops' and 'short seminars' that are run by management consultants and that *also* manage to move people rapidly from a state of ignorance to a state of 'knowing something worthwhile' about a particular topic. In every case, the designers of these 'happenings' have succeeded in solving the problem of *rapid information transfer*. There is not the slightest doubt that the trick can be done. And it is important to bear in mind the fact that it *is* possible, because there is a common tendency to believe that there are almost impossible obstacles to success. Whenever we see a successful piece of rapid instructional communication, it pays us to remember that these are the physical convincers that testify to the possibility of teaching a heterogeneous audience both quickly and well.

Finally, let us note that the kinds of successes just mentioned were in all probability achieved *without* very much help from the professional educator or psychologist. It is still very common to find instructional films and workshops and seminars designed by people on an almost completely intuitive basis. In cases where the designers have intuitions of the right (i.e. near-optimal) kind, no harm is done. But the existence of a massively larger number of *non*-successful instructional films and workshops, etc. suggests that there is a very real need to enhance private intuitions with an understanding of the pedagogical conditions of success.

General comment

Learning is essentially a creative process, and the burden of it is always upon the learner. The teacher cannot make it happen, but the would-be learner *can* stop it happening. The teacher can also stop it happening by omitting to arrange conditions that are necessary for it to happen, or by introducing elements that prevent it from happening. Contrary to popular opinion, learning (as opposed to conditioning) involves no guesswork. It grows out of the learner's understanding.

In summary form it can be said that learning consists in distinguishing the relevant from the irrelevant.

It can *only* occur for its own sake. Learning that is engaged in for the sake of other people, or under duress, is more accurately described as conditioning. The chief characteristics of conditioning are emphasis on escaping from problem situations (rather than understanding them), plus a chain of adverse consequences that the psychological literature describes as cognitive fixity, mental blindness, guessing, self-limitation, and the like.

Not every reader will understand the preceding three paragraphs. And, among those who understand what is being said, not everyone will agree with the view of learning that has just been offered. It would take a full-sized book to elaborate and justify the foregoing statement in fine detail, but it needs to be stressed that the content and recommendations of this book are all broadly compatible with the viewpoint just presented. The significance of the viewpoint is that, duly elaborated, it provides an outline pedagogical basis for the design of *convivial* learning environments of any kind.

4 Planning the work

Mounting an exhibition is a considerable under-taking, the magnitude of which depends, of course, on how big the exhibition is. Whatever the size of the project, it is a salutary exercise to consider the capacity of the exhibition team in relation to the total floor area to be fitted out. When the time it takes to renew or replace the whole of the exhibition has been worked out, unless the team has more money and other resources than most are blessed with, it will become obvious that some thought should be given to the policy to be followed, especially to the balance between minor projects involving the titivation or replacement of individual exhibits and major ones involving renewal of whole sections of the exhibition, be they large or small. We consider this balance in Chapter 17.

Critical path analysis

Many modern projects are conceived on such a large scale that the organisation of the necessary resources of manpower and materials presents a formidable task. To ease this task there came into being a series of scheduling techniques known collectively as critical path analysis. In addition, the more general name of network analysis is widely used, though this is also given to a set of quite different techniques used in the electricity supply industry. In these scheduling techniques, the project is represented as a network of activities, and attention is focused on one particular path through the network that determines the minimum time in which the project may be completed – the so-called critical path.

The classic example of the benefits of critical path analysis is provided by the Polaris Fleet Ballistic Missile project of the US Navy, for which the Programme Evaluation and Review Technique (PERT) was devised. A network comprises a set of points (in formal terms, **nodes**) connected by lines (arcs). The nodes of a PERT network correspond to events and the arcs to activities from which the events result (Fig. 4.1). Typical activities include the production of sub-assemblies for manufactured articles such as cars, and the usual event is the completion of some activity or other. (Readers who would like more detailed examples are recommended to dip into two eminently readable books by Battersby 1975, 1967.)

Because later activities can sometimes be started before earlier ones have been finished, it is often necessary in PERT networks to split an activity into two or more and to link otherwise disconnected events by introducing artificial or

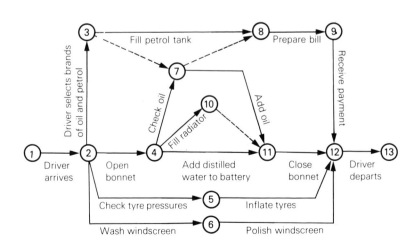

Figure 4.1 A simple PERT network linking activities involved in visiting a petrol station. From Battersby (1975).

'dummy' activities which are really non-existent because they do not take up any time or bring about any change. All this enlarges the network and adds to the work of calculating the critical path.

The alternative network is exemplified by the Metra Potential Method (MPM), in which the nodes represent the activities and the arcs correspond to restrictions on how soon the particular activity at the right-hand end may follow the one at the left (Fig. 4.2). The lag between the two activities may be less than the time it takes to complete the earlier one: since all the constituent activities must be completed for the project to have finished, there is no need either for dummy activities or dummy nodes. This minimises the size of the network and hence simplifies the work of developing it and of calculating the critical path. There are other advantages too with the MPM type of network, such as the facility to pick out subcritical paths in order of criticality. But the biggest gain is in simplification, since the benefit of critical path analysis stems largely from the discipline imposed by the need to specify component activities in precise terms and to think about the sequential constraints to which they are subject.

Organising an exhibition is not, on the whole, a project of the sort or size for which critical path analysis was designed. It is less like building a new factory and more like organising production in the factory once it has been built, because an exhibition team is a sort of production line for exhibits. Each exhibit is the end-product of a fairly short chain of activities, all of which enter into the production of every exhibit, and the order in which the exhibits are produced is generally less important than that they should all be completed and in place by the date announced for the opening of the exhibition. It is easy to picture quite small projects involving the production of a single exhibit in network terms, and this may be a useful exercise for a student on a systems and procedures course (Howell 1971). However, a network that splits 59 man-hours of work between 60 events is hardly an appropriate management tool, even when planning one year's work for one person.

The usefulness of critical path analysis in organising the work of an exhibition team is a conceptual one. It is helpful to picture exhibition production as an operation that involves a bunch of otherwise independent chains of activities that diverge from the starting point and join up again at the finishing point. The order in which the individual activities in the various chains are undertaken is not constrained to anything like the same extent as in the exemplary critical path analysis. Many of them could go on concurrently if only sufficient resources were available – which they never are! The critical path in these circumstances is not so much a constraint on management decisions as an outcome of them, whereas in the classic case the reverse is true. However, a basis for effective management control is available if a standard chain of activities can be defined and each activity given a standard time allowance. We return to this point later.

There is, of course, more to mounting an exhibition than just producing the exhibits. The hall or gallery where the exhibition is to be staged has to be prepared, which usually involves redecoration and perhaps structural alterations, or even starting from scratch with a new building. Literature such as catalogues, explanatory or other material to supplement the exhibition,

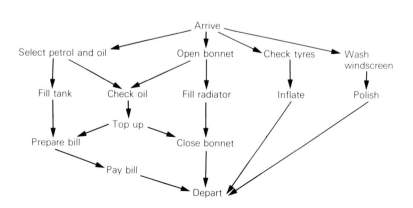

Figure 4.2 An MPM network for the same activities as in Figure 4.1. Note that the numbering of the activities is not critical.

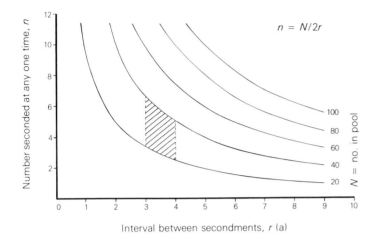

Figure 4.3 Secondment graph.

teaching aids, and souvenirs such as badges and pictures, have to be designed and produced. Publicity has to be arranged well in advance of the opening date, but not so far in advance that it loses its impact. It is useful, therefore, to analyse the overall situation to the extent of drawing up a coarse network in which all the constituent activities are fairly substantial, and to use this to coordinate the efforts of the various groups involved. The amount of detail that it is worth incorporating, and hence the complexity of the network, must of necessity depend on the way in which the organisation functions, and more particularly on how much it does for itself and how much it depends on others. Perhaps the best reason for drawing up such a network is that it allows the opening date to be set on an informed basis, instead of by a purely arbitrary decision which may subsequently give rise to unforeseen difficulties.

The secondment problem

Though much of the work of mounting exhibitions may be the responsibility of people for whom this is a full-time occupation, some of the load invariably falls on the shoulders of those who are primarily concerned with other things. This is often the case in a museum that is associated with, or part of, a research institution. One of the major problems in organising an exhibition department in these circumstances is therefore likely to be that of choosing between the provision of expertise from within the permanent staff of the

exhibition department or by secondment from other departments, e.g. those concerned with research and curation.

Where the latter course is followed, it is important that the implications of secondment are examined at the outset because it is quite possible for secondment stints to come round at unacceptably short intervals for the staff concerned. Furthermore, it is only right that staff who are taken on to do work from which they are liable to be seconded from time to time for other duties should be aware from the very beginning of the extent of this liability. This is especially so when the people concerned are highly motivated specialists and by nature academics rather than popular communicators. It is important to minimise the number of occasions on which staff get seconded against their will, although it is also worth noting that staff who are initially reluctant to be seconded often find that they enjoy the experience once they get into it.

As is so often the case, it is much easier to come to grips with the problem if it is summarised graphically. Figure 4.3 relates the number of people seconded at any one time to both the size of the pool from which they are seconded and the time between successive secondments of the same individual. The size of the pool is usually constant, but the other two figures should be treated as averages – if only because it is impossible to foresee the future with certainty. A further factor that enters into the diagram is the length of the secondment stint. In Figure 4.3 this is taken as six months.

People joining the staff of a large museum may

expect to devote a proportion of their time to planning exhibits for the public galleries. In the more junior grades the contribution will generally be given as a temporary member of the exhibition team, but senior members of the staff are excluded from this pool because a lot of their time is already taken up by administrative duties. They may nevertheless contribute in other ways, e.g. by advising on the briefs from which the exhibits are developed (see below).

Accurate prediction of what will happen to a particular person in the secondment pool is impossible, because the whole system for producing the exhibits has to respond to circumstances that change from time to time, so the best that can be done is to deal with what will happen on average.

The situation is determined by the values of four variables:

N the number of people in the pool;
n the number of people on secondment at any one time;
r the average interval between successive secondments for the same individual;
m the average duration of the secondment.

These are linked by the constraint that the proportion of the people in the pool who are on secondment must be the same as the proportion of his time that the average member of the pool spends in this way – having 10 per cent of the people in the pool on secondment all the time is equivalent to having all of them on secondment for 10 per cent of the time. Since it is convenient to measure r in years but m in months, we may then write

$$\frac{m}{12r} = \frac{n}{N}$$

It is also convenient to regard the secondment period as a parameter, a variable whose value is fixed by other circumstances. Secondment must be full-time for the work to proceed at an acceptable pace and for full use to be made of the designers' time. It must not be too long or the seconded person's curatorial work or research will suffer and promotion prospects will be adversely affected. On the other hand, it must not be too short or it will be impossible for the seconded person to function as an efficient member of the exhibition team, so m is set at six months in Figure 4.3.

The size of the pool is another parameter, one which it is difficult to fix with any precision. Wider considerations, outside the scope of the exhibition team, may have to be taken into account at this stage.

The diagram (Fig. 4.3) focuses attention on what the secondment policies involve by making it easy to predict n in relation to r (or vice versa) for any likely value of N, the last being regarded as a parameter of lower order than m because its value is uncertain, whereas that of m is set by separate considerations. The diagram thus consists of a series of curves relating n and r, each for a different value of the parameter N – which illustrates the definition of a parameter as a fixed variable, the value of N being fixed for any particular line but variable from line to line.*

The shaded area in the diagram is based on the supposition that logistic difficulties will result if secondment comes round more often than once every three or four years (r is measured from the beginning of one secondment to that of the next, i.e. it includes the secondment period, six months in the case under discussion). With a pool estimated to consist of between 20 and 40 people, this suggests that at any one time four or five will be available for planning exhibitions. Thus if more than this number are needed to maintain an acceptable pace of exhibition work, the balance must be provided in some other way, e.g. by increasing the number of permanent members of the exhibition team. The diagram makes two other important points. First, a little simple algebra and a few lines on graph paper will often enable the implications of a decision on policy to be explored before the decision is taken. Secondly, though only three variables can be represented with ease on a flat graph and many situations involve more than this number, it is still possible to proceed. A little thought about the set of variables will often bring to light relationships between them (constraints) that reduce the number that can be treated as independent, in the sense that if there are four variables linked together by one constraint, fixing the values of any three of them will enable the fourth to be calculated from the constraint. It is much better to handle the situation in this way than to attempt to simplify it by assigning arbitrary values to one or

---

* It is useful to have a clear idea of what a parameter is because confusion can arise if 'parameter' is used when what is really meant is 'variable'.

more of the variables at the outset, which almost inevitably produces a distorted view of things.

The exhibition brief

In the past, many exhibitions have been set up in the way described in Chapter 1. Subject-matter experts listed the objects to be displayed and wrote labels for them, then responsibility passed to other people who arranged the specimens in standard cases. More recently these other people have included trained designers, but the process of preparing the exhibits has remained very much the same – the starting point has been a decision to display this, that or the other rather than a critical examination of what the exhibition was intended to accomplish in broader terms. The approach we have adopted draws on a wider variety of specialised skills, as will be apparent from the next chapter. When this situation obtains it is important that everyone in the small group responsible for a particular section of the exhibition should have a clear idea of its place in the general scheme of things, and of the purpose its section of the exhibition is intended to fulfil. Doing the job properly takes a lot of money and effort, resources which are always scarce, and these should not be wasted by avoidable overlap between sections or unnecessary repetition of what has been done before. For these reasons, the team, as a whole, needs to be properly briefed at the outset.

The brief provides the basis of control in the whole operation, especially in the initial design (or development, Ch. 5) of the exhibits. It translates the generalities of the policy of the organisation or sponsor, and within this policy that of the exhibition team, into the specifications appropriate to the work in hand. It also provides the means for putting into action the lessons learned from previous work. In short, it sets out the constraints under which the exhibits must be developed, but must nevertheless leave proper scope for creative work during the developmental stage.

The larger the scale of the operation, the greater the number of people involved, therefore the greater the opportunity for misunderstanding and the more obvious the need for a proper brief. In a large team a brief quite obviously serves a useful purpose, but what of the small team? The answer is that however many or few people are involved,

the effective pursuit of a recognised long-term goal and the efficient use of scarce resources requires conscious attention to the same points. And it is these points that provide the structure of the brief. They make the brief important irrespective of the scale of the operation.

Like many aspects of our work in the British Museum (Natural History), the briefs have evolved as requirements have become more sharply defined in response to experience. The broad aims, however, have been the same throughout, namely to:

(a) set out the specific aims of a particular phase of the work;
(b) outline the ideas with which the phase is concerned and the way in which they are related to one another;
(c) explain the way in which the subject-matter is to be approached so that it accords with the basic principles of the exhibition programme as a whole;
(d) feed into current work changes in policy and findings from evaluation;
(e) provide a basis for planning and scheduling, particularly for the development stage, but also for the subsequent stages which are greatly affected by the rate of progress in development;
(f) set out any constraints additional to those implied by the preceding five aims.

With these aims it is all too easy to be repetitive. Furthermore, there exists a natural tendency to pay too much attention to the details of the subject-matter and too little to practical considerations (which are much more difficult to handle!). It has been said that to specify a piece of educational material all that is needed is a statement of objectives, a specification of the target audience, and a list of the operative constraints. This is at heart nothing but a self-evident truth – you need to know what you are trying to do, who you hope will benefit from it, and under what conditions you have to work in doing it. It is the overall purpose of the brief to meet these three requirements, which are quite distinct from one another, whereas the six aims listed above merge into one another. From the two together there emerges a standard list of contents of a brief.

(1) *Introduction.* This comprises a list of aims, a synoptic story-line, and any general comments.

(2) *Concept hierarchy.* This sets out the intellectual structure of the exhibition, which is also the starting point for scheduling (Chs 6 & 13).

(3) *Notes on the concept hierarchy.* Many concepts will be represented on the diagram in shorthand by technical terms that need definition or amplification. References to the literature (see below) help to prevent the brief from taking the form of a learned monograph.

(4) *Visitor considerations.* More is called for than the mere statement that the exhibition is aimed at such and such a target audience. The aim should be to say something about the assumed expectations and prior know-ledge of the visitor, the level of treatment, any special facilities that are needed, and any other educational considerations.

(5) *Constraints.* These include spatial, structural, temporal and financial constraints.

(6) *References.* These should be limited to key works that provide a way into the literature.

Regarding the brief as the arch on which the exhibition is supported, the keystone is without doubt the concept hierarchy, which specifies the constraints on the sequence in which the ideas are to be presented (Ch. 6). Experience has shown that it needs to be depicted at high resolution and in considerable detail, so that the concepts are

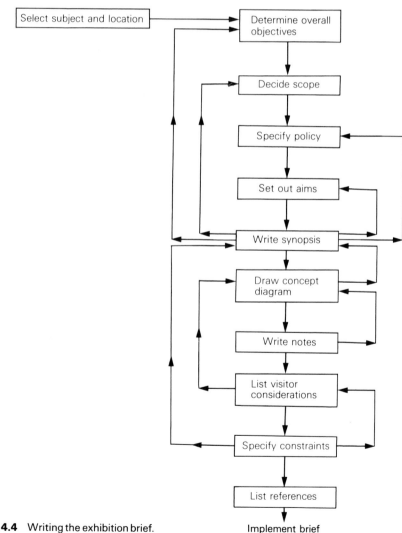

Figure 4.4 Writing the exhibition brief.

sharply defined. At the same time, development must not be stifled by overspecification at the outset. This throws a considerable burden on the people managing the exhibition team, who are responsible for producing the brief and then for seeing that it is properly implemented. They need to think it through very carefully indeed if they are to forestall disruptive changes to it later. Thus it is not possible just to sit down and write a good brief at the first attempt. The writing is above all an iterative process because of the complicated way in which the parts of the brief affect one another. This is summarised in Figure 4.4, which shows that one has to keep going back and forth, revising what has already been done in what appeared at the time to be a perfectly satisfactory manner.

It is the response of the management team to the challenge of writing a clear and effective brief that determines the speed and efficiency with which the exhibition policy is implemented and, to a large extent, the effectiveness of the exhibits.

Cost control

Exhibition planners never have an infinite amount of money at their disposal. On the contrary, it is almost inevitable that initial ideas will sooner or later prove to have been too grandiose for available resources. When this time comes, economies have to be made; and the further in time this point is from the instant of conception, and the nearer to opening day, the more difficult it is to reduce costs. If the development work has been carried out carefully and thoroughly, there will be nothing redundant to discard; something that is really essential will have to go. The whole project is then marred.

It is not sufficient just to include a contingency sum in the budget, even from the outset. As the plan becomes more and more detailed, it becomes less and less flexible. The situation is thus very much as portrayed in Figure 4.5.

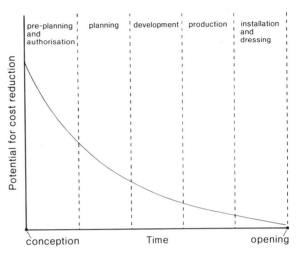

Figure 4.5 Potential for cost reduction.

From the instant of conception to the day of opening, the potential for reducing expenditure falls asymptotically from the total cost to zero. The period between these two events is divided between the activities of stages (1) to (3c) as described in Chapter 2. In Figure 4.5 we have quite arbitrarily shown these stages as of equal length because it is not possible to make a more precise generalisation. The sole purpose of making the subdivision is to emphasise the point that initial enthusiasm must not be allowed to swamp prudence. It is not just when production contracts are being placed that costs need to be taken into consideration. By then, the ability to make substantial savings is severely limited without going back to an earlier stage, perhaps even to the beginning, and starting again from there.

We deal with other aspects of front-end analysis in Chapter 15; for the moment our concern is with costs alone. From the outset, no decision should be taken without as precise an evaluation as possible of the way it will affect the overall cost of the exhibition.

5 The exhibition team

When an exhibition is being planned, there are more things to be considered than the subject-matter. Above all, careful thought needs to be given to the organisation of the team that is going to have the task of developing, producing, installing, dressing, maintaining and perhaps evaluating the exhibition. Success or failure in achieving what was intended at the outset hinges on a very fundamental question – how long does it take how many people to cope with how big an exhibition?

If the reader can answer this question precisely off the top of his head, he can probably skip the rest of this chapter, the main purpose of which is to describe one way of arriving at a satisfactory conclusion. A more likely state of affairs is that he will start to wonder what sort of people should be considered, how the overall responsibility for achieving the overall target should be shared out between them, how to measure the size of an exhibition, how to assess progress as time passes, and similar things. The content of this chapter is likely to be alien to people who are not used to thinking in this way. Nevertheless, we make no apology for presenting the material as we have found it to be a great help in our work.

Subdivision of the main task

The easiest way to cope with this multitude of questions is to start at the beginning and work steadily and systematically forward. The first step is to think of an **exhibition** as a series of **exhibits**, and to subdivide the work of preparing an exhibit and putting it before the public into a series of consecutive stages. We have, in fact, already carried out such a subdivision, when we spoke in the first paragraph of parts of the overall task – developing, producing, installing, dressing and maintaining. For the sake of clarity let us say a few words about our mental picture of these constituent tasks. An exhibit is something physical, something which somebody has to make or put together in some way. It has to be produced. But the person who produces it need not necessarily be the same as the person who thought it up in the first place, though on the

other hand he might be – or then again there might be more than two people involved. The important thing for present purposes is that we have distinguished two tasks that require rather different skills and abilities, in much the same way as a builder distinguishes between the different skills of his workmen. He may have a bricklayer who can turn his hand to plastering, or an electrician who is a dab hand at carpentry, but walls have to be built before they can be plastered and quite a lot of carpentry has to be done before the wiring can be installed. In the same way, some thought needs to be given to an exhibit before it is constructed if it is going to be at all useful.

We use 'development' as a convenient name for the process of thinking up exhibits, as an alternative to the more obvious word 'design', because we see development as a team effort and it is convenient and conventional to reserve the word 'designer' for certain people in the development team who possess particular skills. More of this later. The important thing for the moment is to see the developers as the people who get the exhibition under way, just as the bricklayers are the first tradesmen involved in building houses.

How long for how much?

The output of the bricklaying process is an obvious one, walls. And the rate at which the walls go up determines the rate at which houses are built. It also determines the rate at which the other trades must work, because if there is a mismatch there will either be people standing idle or a growing number of unfinished houses. Similarly, if we can identify an end-product for the process of development and devise a measure corresponding to the number of bricks an average bricklayer can lay per hour, we can then make a start on balancing our team so that in the long term the outputs for each of the post-development processes are the same as that for development.

The end-product of development is the information needed for the next stage, that of production, to go smoothly ahead. In physical terms this is a set of **working drawings** supplemented by a written specification (Ch. 12), but it would be rather silly to measure the productivity of the development team by the area of the drawings or the volume of the specifications. We can, however, take a leaf out of the builder's book and relate output to floor area. Cost per square foot (or in these days metre) is, in fact, a commonplace measure for comparing different buildings. We can then base our planning on a development team that produces each year the working drawings and specifications that allow us to produce so many square feet or square metres of exhibition.

Obviously exhibits differ from one another, and some call for more work in development than others, but what is lost on the swings is gained on the roundabouts. All we need is a reasonably accurate average figure. When starting out it may seem difficult to decide what figure to use, but in this sort of situation there is usually some experience somewhere that can be drawn upon, and the initial figure can and should always be modified in the light of experience.

We have conjured up a picture of a team of bricklayers, but who are the corresponding people in the development team? The skills of a bricklayer are fairly obvious ones, but what are those of a developer? We came to the conclusion quite early on in our own work that there are two quite distinct skills involved in developing exhibits. One is the skill of rationalisation; the other that of imagination. The former is characteristic of science, and relies upon the imagination to the extent that hypotheses must be thought up, but thereafter is self-consciously rational. The other skill gives much freer rein to the subconscious, centring on hunch rather than on rationalisation, and it predominates in the arts (including the art of management) in the way that rationalisation predominates in the sciences (including management science). In setting up the team at the British Museum (Natural History), it was felt that both approaches had a great deal to contribute to the development of effective exhibits, but that the sort of training that would develop the one would inhibit the other. This is not to say that people with design qualifications are irrational or that those with a science background are unimaginative, it is just that the two types of training attract different types of people and are intended to give different results. This made it unlikely that one would be able to find

people well endowed with both the skills, which is how the elements of the development team came to be partnerships, each comprising a scientist and a designer.

Each partnership develops on average 160 m² of exhibition a year. It specifies each exhibit in writing and with drawings, but it does not produce a full set of working drawings such as could be used by a contractor to build an exhibit. Producing these calls for the exercise of a further skill, that of the engineering draughtsman. Thus the output of the development team passes to the drawing office where the draughtsmen produce a full set of working drawings. The average exhibit occupies 33 m² of floor space, and it takes four weeks of draughtsman's time to prepare the working drawings for it, including costings.

It is thus a simple matter of arithmetic to work out the number of draughtsmen needed to cope with the output of a given number of development partnerships, or how many partnerships are needed for a drawing office of a given size. For instance, if there are five partnerships, each developing exhibitions at the rate of 160 m² per year, and the average exhibit occupies 20 m², the number of exhibits developed per year will be 160 multiplied by 5 and divided by 20, i.e. 40: if a draughtsman can produce the working drawings at the rate of 10 exhibits per year it will require four draughtsmen to cope with the output of the five partnerships. However, as has already been implied, there are no exact figures on which to base the arithmetic. In such circumstances it is useful to see how sensitive the results of the calculation are to variations in the figures used. The easiest way of doing this is to draw a simple diagram that links together the important variables in the situation under consideration. It is, in fact, a useful principle whenever a course of action has to be decided upon and there are several factors that have to be taken into account – a point we made in Chapter 4 and one to which we attach so much importance that we have no hesitation in making it again. The actual calculation, as in the present instance, may be simple, but the starting point is usually somewhat arbitrary – for instance, does one start with a development team of a given size, or a drawing office team? This is an example of a more general principle, which is never to select a particular value for variable factors at the beginning of a calculation if this can be avoided. For instance, if we are concerned about the running costs of a thermostatic electric heater, it is best to refrain from assuming at the outset that it will be on for a particular number of hours per day, and to work out instead the cost per hour, day or (most probably) year, were it to be on all the time. This leaves the arbitrary factor to the end of the calculation instead of putting it at the beginning, which makes it easier to see the effect that changing the assumption about the value of the factor has on the outcome, in this case the running cost.

Having got this far by identifying a quantity that is outside our control (the cost per hour when the heater is on) and another the value of which is unknown (the percentage of the total time that the heater is using electricity), as well as the one that we have been seeking to establish (the running cost), we have no need to restrict ourselves to a particular view of the situation as presented by the calculation. We can take a general view by drawing a diagram like Figure 5.1. This shows the relation between the thing we are seeking to establish (the dependent variable – call it y) and the unknown factor (the independent variable – call it x) for the given value of the thing which is fixed for the particular situation (the cost per hour when the heater is on, which is a 'fixed variable' or parameter – fixed in the situation with which we are immediately concerned but none the less variable for a different situation, e.g. different for a different heater).

When we return to the matter of development and drawing office teams, we are faced with a

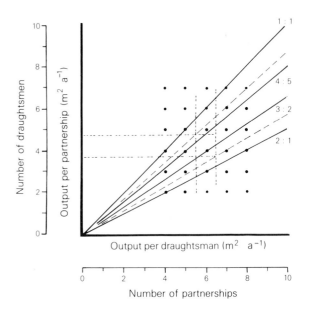

Figure 5.2 Graph to show the relationship between the size of the exhibition development team and the number of draughtsmen.

more complex situation. The basic problem is to balance the sizes of the two teams when we are uncertain about how much work a development partnership, or for that matter a draughtsman, can do in whatever period of time we choose to work with. This means that we have four variables to contend with, two numbers and two output rates. Furthermore, the numbers must be whole ones – people cannot be split in two!*

We can reduce the number of variables to three by deriving a new variable that is the ratio of two of the primary variables, as we did in defining the parameter in the case of the electric heater. In the present instance there is a fairly obvious way of choosing the variables to be combined, because the need for the output of the drawing office to match that of the development team means that the ratio of the two numbers must be the inverse of that of the two rates of output. It is convenient to take this ratio, expressed in terms of whole numbers, as our parameter and then draw the

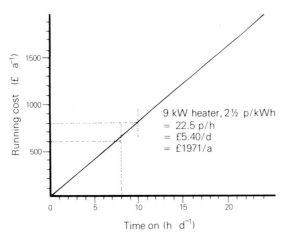

Figure 5.1 Graph to show the running costs of a thermostatic electric heater.

---

* This is not to deny that it is a convenient statistical artefact to state propositions that assume they can, e.g. by regarding the average family as composed of one overworked female, one underpaid male, and 2.6 underfed children! Also, of course, a person's time may be subdivided, and half a person working full-time could be assumed for the purposes of calculation to turn out as much work as a whole person working half-time.

dual-purpose diagram shown in Figure 5.2. The diagram thus provides a simple yet complete picture of the situation under consideration, and may be used to explore the various possibilities that come to mind. The inner two axes, one horizontal and one vertical, allow the plausible range of the ratio to be selected; the outer two allow the sizes of the two teams to be determined. For instance, suppose that our best estimates of the two rates are such that they lie between the respective pairs of dotted lines. We can see straight away that unless we have more than one draughtsman per partnership we shall be in trouble, but if the ratio is 2:1 there will not be enough work to keep all the draughtsmen occupied. If we start off with four partnerships, we need three draughtsmen – two would be too few and four too many. We can probably add an extra partnership without overloading the draughtsmen, but if we add two of the one we should add one of the other. And so on. Whatever we do, we should aim to keep within the band defined by the two inclined dotted lines that are drawn from the origin and through the outer corners of the rectangle defined by the output estimates.

Although there is no direct link from the development partnerships to the teams beyond the drawing office, it is the output from development that is the determining factor in every case, and so we can draw a whole series of diagrams like that in Figure 5.2. In planning the composition of the entire group, it is useful to look at the diagrams side by side; there is always some constraint on the total number of people that can be engaged, and with the set of diagrams in front of us it is easier to identify the best places in which to economise.

In the smaller museum the exhibition team will, of course, be smaller too, but the same principles can be applied even if the approach is different because the tasks that have to be undertaken differ only in scale, not in their fundamental nature. The starting point is the same, defining the tasks and the time each takes per unit of output. It may be that people are less specialised, one person having to undertake several different tasks. Figure 5.2 can be modified to suit this situation by replacing output per partnership by output per hour for development work, and so on. It can then be used to decide how time should be allocated between the various tasks.

The biggest danger is epitomised in the old adage, 'Don't bite off more than you can chew'. It is a waste of time and energy to devote so much of the available effort to designing splendid new exhibits that there are not enough resources left for the subsequent stages in the operation – preparing the working drawings, getting the main structure made and erected, preparing and installing the objects, drafting and laying out the textual matter, including labels. And a certain amount of maintenance is always required; an exhibit starts to deteriorate from the moment it is finished, and no exhibit lasts for ever. Furthermore, no exhibit is perfect, and very few are completely suited to the purpose for which they were designed. Maintenance, evaluation, renewal and replacement are all essential activities, and we shall consider them in some detail elsewhere in this book.

6 Organising the intellectual content

What we have to say in this chapter deals with exhibitions that are intended to communicate knowledge and understanding, and that are designed to provide a convivial and unconstrained learning experience as described in Chapter 3. Learning is closely related to knowledge and understanding, and the three terms are to some extent interchangeable in everyday conversation. To clear the air a little before describing a practical way of organising the intellectual content of an exhibition, and laying the foundations for the management of the work of the exhibition team, let us draw a few distinctions. In so doing we shall find that it helps to concentrate on verbs, or activities, rather than things and objects of thought.

A person – like any animal – has a repertoire of behaviours, and *learns* by adding a new behaviour to this repertoire. The evidence that he *knows* a particular thing is that the behavioural repertoire includes a particular item related to that thing. Sometimes what is learned is a skill, when the item added to the behavioural repertoire is' that self-same skill. However, we are not at the moment concerned with skills, only with knowledge and understanding.*

The point that we wish to make is that a behaviour that indicates that a person *knows* some particular thing may or may not indicate that he understands it, but a behaviour that indicates that he *understands* it also indicates that he *knows* it.

One big difference between knowing and understanding is that it is possible to know something as a result of rote learning but understanding requires something more than this. Another difference is that a given item is either known or not known, whereas there are different degrees to which it may be understood; some people will know it, others will not, and of those who know it some will understand it better than others.

To take an example, Newton's Second Law of Motion is represented by the equation

$$s = ut + \tfrac{1}{2} f t^2$$

in which s is the distance travelled by a body in time t when its initial velocity u is increased by an acceleration f. The test of whether or not a person *knows* this particular thing (the law) is the ability to quote the formula when asked, but he can quote it without understanding what it means or how it may be usefully employed. He does not, for instance, need to know any algebra, or even that $t^2 = t \times t$, but he does need this extra knowledge to give the value of s when given values for u, f and t. The ability to give the correct answer in this case (guessing apart) is an indication that, to some extent at least, he understands the law. Furthermore, to square t he must be able to multiply, and to multiply he must be able to add (multiplication being repeated addition), and to add it is necessary to be able to count. To answer the question 'How does a body move under the influence of an applied force?' requires a deeper understanding which takes in the ideas of distance, time, velocity and acceleration and the use of a letter to represent any element of a particular set of numbers (i.e. elementary algebra).

The ideas that together constitute knowledge can be given the more specific name 'concepts', and they are all linked together. To depict the structure of any particular body of knowledge requires a diagram that has no particular beginning or end; it is just a complicated network. Whatever else knowledge is, it is certainly not hierarchical – but understanding is, in the sense that some things cannot be understood until others have been, such as squaring, multiplying, adding and counting in the example above.

The point is that though learning does not necessarily involve an hierarchical sequence of events, understanding does. When the aim is to produce understanding, there are sequential constraints on the learning objectives and hence

---

* Whether or not an exhibition can, in the normal run of things, provide environments appropriate to the learning of manual or intellectual skills is an interesting point, but not one of immediate relevance.

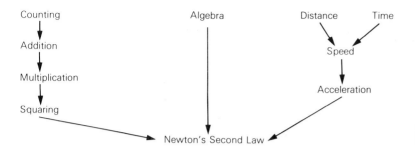

Figure 6.1 Concept hierarchy for Newton's Second Law of Motion.

on the order in which concepts are presented in an exhibition. Some concepts can be taken for granted, sometimes either one of a pair may be presented before the other, but for many pairs of concepts it will be obvious that any understanding of the one presupposes some grasp of the other. Diagrammatic representations of knowledge structures tend to be very complex, and there is little to be gained by trying to draw one for an exhibition, but a concept hierarchy provides a very useful way of organising its intellectual content. One for the movement of a body under the influence of an applied force is illustrated in Figure 6.1. Here the concepts form the **nodes** of the diagram and they are linked by arcs.

The drawing up of a concept hierarchy is an important aspect of elaborating the first synopsis of an exhibition, as described in our comments on *planning* in Chapter 2.

Elaborating the first outline

The uniqueness of an exhibition as an environment for learning mainly resides in its informality and the complete freedom of the learner to do as he pleases, at least in the context of learning (Ch. 3). In the wider context, the visitor must of course conform to opening hours, not wander around chewing sandwiches, and so on. The exhibition needs to be structured to facilitate learning (Gagné 1970), but the structure is not conceived as something to be imposed upon the visitor. Its purpose is solely to unify the presentation of the intellectual material and make it easier for the visitor to find his way around the exhibition, following his own inclinations, delving deeper here, skating over something there, going back to something already seen when he feels the need to.

The depth of the understanding that results from a visit is entirely the visitor's own affair, all the exhibition organisers can do is present the knowledge at what seems to be the appropriate level.

What we are suggesting is treatment at not less than two, possibly three or even more levels of resolution, suitably identified for the visitor's benefit, the components being organised around a spine that corresponds to treatment at minimum resolution (Fig. 6.2). The multi-level structure not only accommodates the wide range of the visitors' interests and attainments but also provides a way of handling the wealth of material available for inclusion in an exhibition. To distinguish between the three levels, the main chain or spine (level 1) includes the *absolute minimum* of the concepts and detail consistent with the coherence of the theme. Level 3 takes the visitor up to the frontiers of knowledge, but at selected

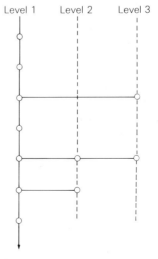

Figure 6.2 A three-level exhibition structure.

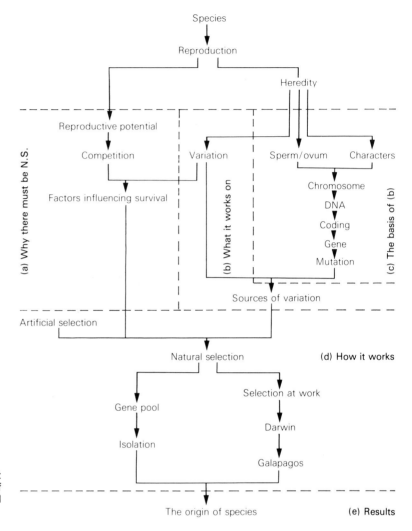

Figure 6.3 First draft of a concept hierarchy for an exhibition on 'Origin of species', British Museum (Natural History).

points rather than over the whole region. Level 2 is introduced (a) where necessary to bridge the gap between levels 1 and 3 and (b) where the level 1 treatment can be amplified but there is no frontier in the immediate offing.

For each concept in the structure there needs to be:

(a) a concise statement;
(b) a specification of the means of attaining the necessary preconditions of learning;
(c) a specification of means for demonstrating that learning has occurred.

The third requirement, and to some extent the second also, can be left to the development stage, but drawing up the concept hierarchy is an essential part of the operation of producing the brief to which the development team works. This is not to say that it does not get revised afterwards. Like so many things, brief writing is an iterative process (Ch. 4). For learning purposes the content of the exhibition-to-be must be analysed in terms of capabilities, not subject-matter. A brief that results from an analysis that is essentially content-orientated and illustrated with topic maps is a less than satisfactory planning and design tool. Analysis of a topic best begins with a statement of the terminal objective and proceeds by the identification of subordinate topics and learning acts, each of which is a prerequisite for those that come after. The analysis continues until the known or assumed current performance of the learner is reached.

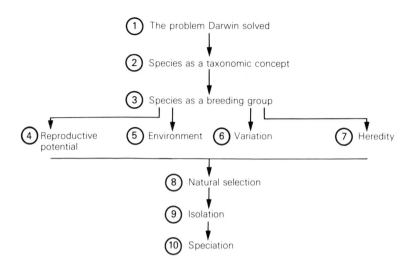

① The problem Darwin solved

② Species as a taxonomic concept

③ Species as a breeding group

④ Reproductive potential   ⑤ Environment   ⑥ Variation   ⑦ Heredity

⑧ Natural selection

⑨ Isolation

⑩ Speciation

Figure 6.4 Final concept hierarchy for an exhibition on 'Origin of species', British Museum (Natural History), 1981.

To illustrate the process of drafting the concept hierarchy, we show in Figure 6.3 the hierarchy from the first draft of the brief for an exhibition in the British Museum (Natural History) on 'Origin of species', and in Figure 6.4 the final version produced some eight weeks later, which is appreciably simpler.

Beyond the pilot exhibition

When our new programme of work was initiated at the British Museum (Natural History), the scope and content of the new exhibitions were studied by a series of working parties dealing with the four themes of Man, Ecology, Life Processes and Behaviour, and Evolution and Diversity. It was then decided to mount a pilot exhibition on the subject of Human Biology, and an area of approximately 1100 m² was earmarked for this exhibition, to be based on the report of the working party on 'Man'. After devoting considerable time and effort to the formulation of **behavioural objectives**, the realisation dawned that the exhibition could contain only a fraction of what was in the report, and that each theme would require a whole series of exhibitions.

A series of exhibitions that sets out to show the whole of biological knowledge must of necessity cover a great deal of intellectual ground. By no means are all museum exhibitions conceived on such a grand scale, but the organisational problems that have to be overcome are much less unusual. The specification of the necessary tasks and activities, and the constraints that affect the order in which they may be undertaken, are important steps towards producing the plan upon which control of the project can be based. The arrangement of the underlying knowledge in a way that facilitates the unambiguous definition of the tasks and activities in any exhibition project plays an important part in this process, because it is the key to the elimination of overlap in the specification of the different exhibitions.

It would be a very unusual museum that set up the whole of its exhibitions in one fell swoop. The work has to be undertaken in stages. There are several reasons why this is so, of which the most telling is the limited availability of the more important resources – manpower, money and space. If the exhibitions are to form a coherent whole, there must be a structure into which they fit like the pieces of a jigsaw puzzle. If the project is to be free from resource-wasting repetition, there must be no ambiguity about what goes where and the sections must be defined in a way that makes them mutually exclusive. Naturally enough there was a great deal of overlap and duplication amongst the reports of the working parties, who had started from scratch with no experience to go on because they were completely rethinking the whole business. Once the brief had been prepared for the pilot stage, it became a matter of some urgency to reconsider the structure of the whole series of exhibitions from the standpoint of avoiding all unnecessary overlap and repetition. Once again the approach adopted would be equally apposite to other exhibitions, even if they were smaller.

The approach was based on the system concept which plays such a central part in cybernetics and general systems theory (Beer 1959, von Bertalanffy 1973, Pask 1975). The theme of the exhibitions as a whole is a system that comprises all living things, i.e. the biological system. In any system there are four main things to consider, though the emphasis may vary from one occasion to the next. These are:

(a) components;
(b) structure;
(c) environment;
(d) behaviour.

It is sometimes useful to consider the abstract concept of a closed system (Klir & Valach 1967), though in real life it is usually impossible to describe the behaviour of a system without taking its environment into account. The environment of the biological system is wholly physical and non-living. The behaviour comprises some phenomena that arise from interaction between the components of the system, and some that result from interaction between the system and its environment.

Difficulty often arises in separating system and environment. There is no unequivocal rule to say where the boundary should go, which is usually a matter of mere expediency. In the present instance it is much easier than is often the case. All of the components of the system, but none of those of the environment, are living things. Once this distinction is made, and the four topics listed above are taken into account, it is comparatively easy to ensure the necessary exclusivity.

To relate the subjects studied by the working parties to these four topics, in broad terms 'Diversity' corresponds to the components of the system and 'Evolution' to its structure. More specifically, evolution is a process with two outcomes that lie in different dimensions, one being the structure of the living world and the other the diversity of its components. 'Life Processes and Behaviour', like the process of evolution, are aspects of the behaviour of the system, and so in the broad sense is 'Ecology', conveniently defined as being concerned with the interactions of living things with one another and with their non-living environment. The subject of the 'Man' theme is merely one species amongst many thousands from the standpoint of 'Diversity', but one in which the visitor to the museum may safely be assumed to have a special interest. Man is also extremely important from the ecological standpoint.

Thus there emerge four major subdivisions of the series of exhibitions: (1) evolution, (2) forms of life (diversity), (3) how life works (life processes) and (4) ecology. While meeting the criteria of mutual exclusivity and no overlap, they nevertheless fail to solve the problem of subdivision into units of suitable size for planning and organising the stage by stage work on the exhibitions. None of them is small enough to be dealt with as a manageable project without further subdivision, especially that dealing with the forms of life. Fortunately, they do lend themselves to further subdivision, so they are at least a step in the right direction.

At the other extreme, there is the single concept (a 'node' in a concept hierarchy), which represents too fine a subdivision for many purposes but is, in fact, eminently suitable as the basis for the organisation of management at the 'grass roots' level (Ch. 13). In between these extremes, there is a need for an intermediate unit that meets certain practical requirements. The traditional unit for this purpose is the **gallery** or exhibition hall, the usefulness of which is in no way diminished because of the wide variation in size from gallery to gallery. Sometimes a particular stint of exhibition work may involve only part of a gallery, but there is a much more important reason for setting this particular tradition aside. It belongs to the era in which, as we have seen in Chapter 1, galleries and show-cases were set up with scant regard to the exhibits they were to house. A central tenet of this book is that the housing should be designed to fit the exhibit, the design of the exhibit being determined by educational considerations. Furthermore, the unit that is most appropriate from the standpoint of content is not necessarily the most practical one. For these reasons, the best thing to do is to divide the work into *phases* of suitable size, a phase being of around 12 months duration. This allows new exhibitions to be opened regularly and provides something new for the visitor at reasonably short intervals. Phases are thus individually defined by operational considerations. The intermediate unit as far as content is concerned corresponds roughly to a phase but is determined by different factors – those which stem from the nature of the information to be communicated. Each phase may cover more than one content unit, or conversely more than one phase may be devoted to a single unit (unless the context specifically indicates the contrary, we use this word in the narrow sense of a content unit). The order in which the units are arranged stems from the nature of the content, the order of the phases depends on practical considerations.

Mapping content on to available space

Mapping the intellectual content on to the space available is one of the most difficult parts in planning any exhibition. It cannot be stressed too strongly that, for satisfactory long-term results, the starting point must be a detailed analysis of the information to be conveyed, preferably in diagrammatic form so that the whole scene may be surveyed as one. The amount of space allocated to each unit should be in proportion to the information it contains. There exist objective methods for measuring information content which are much used in the telecommunications and computer fields (Pask 1975), but to resort to them in planning most exhibitions would be to use a sledgehammer to crack a nut. In any case, in the comparatively lengthy time it takes to cope with all the exhibitions in a substantial museum of science or technology, the subject is bound to develop and change. Therefore, the appropriate time to detail the content is at the time of writing the brief, not at the outset when drawing up the exhibition strategy.

To give a hypothetical example, suppose the plan for the exhibitions in a natural history museum divides the content into 60 units. About half of these are likely to be accounted for by 'Forms of life', each covering one or more biological groups arranged to represent the gradual diversification brought about by the process of evolution, 10 by 'How life works', nine by various aspects of ecology, and seven by topics in the 'Evolution' division. The remainder are needed to introduce the entire series of exhibitions and explain how the various sections fit together. 'Forms of life' could reasonably have four sub-divisions: two small ones dealing with viruses, other primitive organisms, fungi and lichens; one dealing with plant diversity; and a large one (of around 25 units) dealing with animal diversity. With a total space of, say, 24 000 m², this allows an average of 400 m² per unit. The tentative allocations are likely to vary over a wide range, e.g. from 50 m² for one of the small units, such as that dealing with viruses, to 2 500 m² for one dealing with mammals.

What principles can be drawn from this hypothetical example to help others responsible for exhibitions, particularly when working on a smaller scale? Obviously anyone concerned with the life sciences could exploit the general structure without much ado, adapting it to his own particular circumstances and requirements. Others would have to break newer ground. The first step is to look for a system and define what the project is all about. The second is to examine that system in terms of its environment and its components or elements, then look at its behaviour and structure, e.g. what links one element to another, and how the elements inter-act with one another and with the environment. The emphasis throughout should be on processes rather than on entities, because the former are better when it comes to defining mutually exclusive sets – the key to the whole business of structuring the intellectual content of an exhibition.

7 Laying out the exhibition

Earlier sections of this book have described a theoretical framework for the design of educational exhibits and the organisation of the design team and its work. We now move on in Chapters 7, 8 and 9 to consider practical aspects of exhibition design. These involve a discussion of **media** (the vehicles of communication) and **modes** (the ways in which media are used) in Chapter 9, but we note here that decisions about media and modes determine the sort of stimuli that are presented to visitors.

The decisions preceding the choice of a medium, its arrangement and setting in relationship to (a) other media, (b) the space and (c) the visitors, all comprise the process commonly called design. Design is often thought of as a single linear process from conception to specification, and descriptions tend of necessity to be written in this way to avoid confusion. In reality, design is a transactional process involving reason and intuition, in which the message to be communicated, the mode and the medium are played off against one another according to the individual values placed upon them.

The design process is concerned with solutions to practical problems. There is, however, never just one answer, and design can be seen as an attempt to find at least one good way of meeting temporal, spatial and economic constraints in a particular situation. These constraints do not have an independent existence but are created by cultural values and human purposes, and the designer, or the institution for which he works, can change them at will. At the British Museum (Natural History) the constraints imposed are in the main educational rather than aesthetic or economic, but whatever they are it is likely that only some will be answered and that some will receive more attention than others.

Design should begin with a sense of purpose and all those involved in designing educational exhibits should define the purpose of an exhibit by formulating clear and agreed objectives. Having said this, the various constraints influence design in three ways, through *importance, function* and *sequence*. Importance is concerned with the values we place on things, whether it be the amount of space devoted to a particular topic; the emphasis of one part of a display in relation to another; what is thought to be an appropriate style; or the amount of time we spend developing an idea. Function is concerned with the way things work, e.g. the amount of space needed to ensure an uninterrupted flow of visitors through a gallery; the provision of flexible structures to accommodate any change in an exhibit; or the placement of a label so that it can easily be read at the same time as the object to which it refers is studied. Sequence refers to the order in which objects are seen or activities take place. It is about the way the exhibit content is mapped onto the space available; the order in which instructions are written; and the positioning of displays so that they can be seen in a logical succession.

The starting point

One of the fundamental tasks is to take the conceptual plan of the brief and transform it into an overall plan for the gallery. This overall plan must permit an uninterrupted flow of visitors and enable them to visit the displays in a full and orderly way. The designer must, therefore, familiarise himself with the subject-matter at the outset, and identify the kinds of problems that are likely to arise, e.g. is there a demand for a high concentration of specimens? And if so, what sizes are they? Are there concepts that are more difficult to communicate than others and that will require more space? Does the story have a single theme or several subthemes? Are all subthemes to be treated in the same detail? By identifying problems such as these the designer can begin to map the conceptual structure onto the physical space.

The site of an exhibition is nearly always predetermined and its shape, position in relation to other spaces, exits and entrances and internal structure all influence the way in which the ground plan is developed. In 19th-century buildings like the British Museum (Natural

History), lighting was originally from natural sources. This decreed either sidelighting, where more than one floor was involved, or toplighting. In the former case this necessitated narrow spaces so that light could penetrate the volume, or lofty spaces with high windows that would permit light to reach a greater floor area. Such spaces tended to be long and narrow, presenting both designer and visitor with few options for anything but linear circulation. In more recent buildings, the shape of the space is less restricted. It is not determined by the requirements of natural lighting and gives greater opportunities for answering the aims set out in the brief and providing for the physical and psychological needs of visitors. Such flexibility is particularly relevant in the case of educational exhibitions, for they often require updating and improving and this can involve a change in the form of the ground plan. Narrow spaces limit modifications of this kind.

The position of a space within a building also influences the exhibits inside it. Visitors usually begin by exploring the ground floor before ascending to higher floors. Inevitably, fewer visitors reach these higher floors and in consequence the number of visitors at lower levels is likely to be higher than elsewhere. In addition, the attraction of adjacent exhibitions might reduce the time visitors spend in a particular space before moving on. If the space provides a route to other exhibits, this too will affect the way it can be used.

The position of entrances and exits is also important when organising an exhibition. Melton (1935) has shown that visitors pay less attention to displays the closer they get to the exit – the so-called exit gradient effect. Some evidence shows that, all things being equal, there is a pronounced tendency to turn right on entering a gallery and this too might affect the location of displays.

The actual form of the space will influence the plan of an exhibition and may make it difficult to make good use of our knowledge about planning. At the same time the coherence of the space may affect parts of an exhibition. For example, the intrusion of some other accommodation into one side of a square space may produce dead areas, possibly even culs-de-sac, that can lead to parts of an exhibition being underused, congested or confusingly circuitous.

The architectural treatment of a space may also influence the planning of exhibitions. For example, the British Museum (Natural History) is a very attractive, highly decorative, 19th-century building with columns covered in sculptured reliefs of animals and plants. In recognising the merit of the architecture, it must of course be left exposed to view and exhibit structures stood free of the fabric of the building. This is understandable, but less excusable in modern buildings where decorative and heavily textured finishes achieve the same status, in effect becoming works of art in their own right.

A case study

Various problems are encountered in designing an exhibition, but the solutions tend to have certain features in common, making them applicable in modified form in a wide range of circumstances. These considerations can be illustrated by an example from our own work on an exhibition dealing with 'Origin of species'. The exhibition brief specified a hierarchy of 10 concepts (Fig. 6.4) to be explained and illustrated in a first-floor, 19th-century gallery, about 850 m² in area, 57 m long by 15 m wide, with an entrance *cum* exit at either end. The long sides of the gallery were lined with high windows extending almost to the ceiling, and two parallel rows of columns ran the full length of the centre on an approximate spacing of 5 m in each direction. We had previously designed another exhibition in this space (Fig. 7.1) and were able to draw on this experience when we came to deal with 'Origin of species'.

An early decision concerned the entrances and exits (Fig. 7.2). Entry to the gallery was most likely from the central hall of the museum and, being on the first floor, a steadier flow of visitors was expected than at street level. The other entrance *cum* exit at the opposite end of the gallery was closed because the staircase led down to the end of a ground floor gallery which visitors were likely to have explored already. There seemed little advantage in directing them back to it by ending 'Origin of species' at the furthest point from the central hall, which might also have created an orientation problem. As the central hall is a focal point for all visitors, from which all galleries and services can be reached, it seemed sensible to take people up the gallery and down again, returning them to a familiar and convenient part of the museum.

Figure 7.1 The 'Introducing ecology' exhibition on the first floor of the British Museum (Natural History), 1978.

In the previous exhibition, the displays were sequentially ordered around the outside of the gallery leaving the central space clear. This was done to achieve a clear layout of the exhibits and to allow for the fact that visitors are less willing to spend time viewing displays in the centre of a large, open space. It was, however, discovered that this space created more problems than it solved, the most obvious being the reluctance of visitors to commit time to what they could see was a rather large exhibition (Lakota 1975). Visitors were either not entering the gallery at all, or leaving without seeing the displays at the far end. Obviously the space should be partitioned in some way to make it seem less daunting. It was also felt that a 'directional orientation' – a reluctance to go out on a limb, so to speak – may work to discourage visitors from moving away from what they presume to be the remainder of the museum. Hence, previously seen displays should be screened and ways found of encouraging visitors to continue through the story of the exhibition.

In our earlier exhibition, visitors were very easily distracted by the displays they could see across the central space, although the correct sequence was clearly indicated. Some further way of reducing these arbitrary movements was needed so that the visitors were encouraged to

follow the correct route. All of these problems could have been answered by creating a regimented, corridor-like exhibition which restricted the visitor to a single route, but we believe an essential part of the visitor's experience of a museum is the freedom to see what he wants, in his own time, skipping the parts he does not wish to see. Clearly, our earlier exhibition achieved this freedom but it did not provide the right kind of guidance. Visitors did not seem particularly keen on using the orientation cues within the exhibits, especially when they were physically separated from the displays to which they referred. Some other form of direction was required. At a crude level this might have

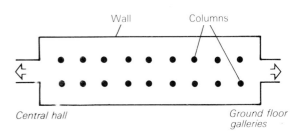

Figure 7.2   Plan of the gallery shown in Figure 7.1.

involved directional arrows and, less overtly, 'movement' created by angled displays and the provision of curved screens. This does not mean that maps and signposts should not have been included, indeed many visitors would probably have found them useful if they were in the right position, i.e. closely linked to the displays.

To try and answer such problems required a radical solution. In this instance the exhibition space was divided down the centre of the gallery (Fig. 7.3). With windows along the side walls and

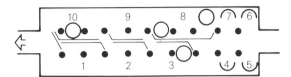

Figure 7.5 Using the areas to reflect the ideas in the 'Origin of species' exhibition, British Museum (Natural History), 1981.

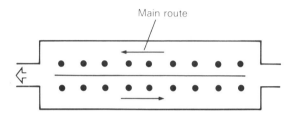

Figure 7.3 Partitioning the space to create an orderly flow of visitors.

the need to leave the architecture open to view, we felt that the best disposition of exhibits was achieved by standing them around this central division. This also gave greater flexibility in the allocation of space for displays within the gallery and freed the display structures from the danger of being determined by architectural features such as columns. Given that most visitors view exhibits from left to right and move naturally from left to right in going from exhibit to exhibit, visitors would begin their tour of the exhibition by turning right into the first displays.

The next decision was to break up the central feature, as yet physically undefined, into chunks that reflected each concept. Freer circulation was allowed at one end where a tight sequence was not needed (Fig. 7.4). Smaller units with gaps in between not only made the structure clear but also allowed the visitor freedom of movement at

appropriate points. Nevertheless, there was still the possibility of arbitrary movement and therefore for visitors to wander about the space without thinking of the choices available to them. To meet this problem a dog-leg was introduced at the end of each concept to conceal the gaps and exit until visitors reached them, thus visitors passing across the space would be aware of short-circuiting the exhibition.

As these design ideas were developed, so was the central feature. It eventually took the form of a fragmented screen wall for graphic displays, plinths for show-cases and machines, and several circular enclosed areas for audio-visuals (Fig. 7.5).

Although no detailed structural features were developed at this stage, these kinds of planning decisions did in general provide the groundwork on which the various media could be mapped. They also ensured cohesion within the exhibition even though some sections were being produced while others were still being developed.

This approach to exhibition design allowed the intellectual content to be communicated in an orderly sequence, so that the visitor was not always asking, 'Where do I go next?' In contrast,

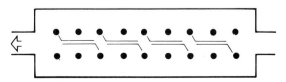

Figure 7.4 Dividing the space into perceptually manageable areas.

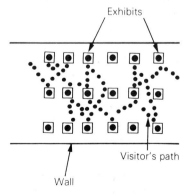

Figure 7.6 Plan of a gallery with regimented show-cases and 'random' circulation.

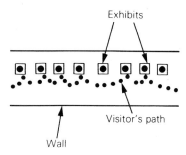

Figure 7.7   Plan of a gallery with regimented show-cases and regimented circulation.

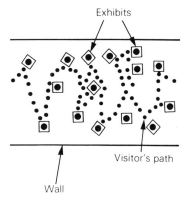

Figure 7.8   Plan of a gallery with a 'random' arrangement of show-cases and 'random' circulation.

the regimented show-cases of the 19th-century (Fig. 7.6) gave no such guidance. Certain modern exhibitions restrict the visitors to a single path (Fig. 7.7) and others give no clear guidance at all (Fig. 7.8).

Estimating the space

The example described above raises several important questions about the space available for an exhibition, e.g. how do you determine the use of space within the gallery and how much space do you allow for each display? Unfortunately, there are no easy answers because the problem requires consideration both of the space needed to accommodate the exhibits and of the space needed for the visitors. Generally, it is extremely difficult to predict visitors' requirements.

The way to proceed is to take account of the factors we do know about and try to decide what kind of problem we are trying to solve. To begin with, it helps to know how many visitors come into the museum each day and at what times most of them arrive and depart. It would be foolish to assume they are evenly distributed throughout the day, when in fact most arrive during a four-hour period around mid-day, half the total number of hours the museum is open. One also needs to know whether visitors come singly, in families or in larger groups; for large groups descending on a single exhibit can cause significant congestion even if the daily attendance figures are insufficient to give cause for concern. If most visitors come in large parties of 10 or more, does one design the layout to accommodate them or does one attempt to encourage them to split up into smaller groups? All such decisions will affect the layout of the exhibition.

If the number of visitors is known, one can get an idea of the numbers likely to visit a particular exhibition. If, for example, we assume that for a peak four-hour period we are visited by 5000 visitors, we might, on the basis of our observations, find that their distribution was sufficiently even to be able to say that 1250 visitors entered the museum during each of these hours. If the subject of the exhibition is a reasonably popular one and our publicity has been reasonably effective, then we could estimate that 25 per cent of our visitors might wish to see it, i.e. some 300 visitors an hour. From similar exhibitions, we estimate that visitors spend about 45 minutes in a gallery and this represents a maximum number of about 220 or about one for every 5 m².

A second way to estimate space is to base one's planning on analogous situations, such as obtain in department stores, where planning figures already exist for counter space and circulation (Table 7.1). Standards also exist to determine the width of gangways as a means of escape in the case of fire, and these too help to define the kinds of space one should provide.

By looking at the exhibits in a general way and then specifically according to the visitor's needs, we have established that each concept in our own work (Ch. 6) needs on average about five displays, and that the average display is about 900 mm wide. Where an exhibit does not need to be seen as a whole, about a metre of space is needed in front to view it, with a further half metre to allow someone to pass behind the viewer. However, it is

Table 7.1 Standards for estimating space.

Type of space	Area (m²/person)
(a) For occupation	
(i) retail shops and show-rooms (including upper floors of department stores)	4.6–7.0
(ii) department stores (ground floor) and special sales areas:	
including counters;	1.0
passages only	0.5
(b) Circulation	
average space for general design purposes	0.8
for people moving at 1.3 m/s (brisk walk)	3.7
for people moving at 0.4–0.9 m/s (shuffle)	0.27–0.37
	Width (m/person)
(c) Exit	
for a building of comparable design to a museum:	
(i) 200–600 people spread evenly on more than one floor	1.0–1.5
(ii) 200–600 people only on one floor	1.1–2.2

likely that more than one visitor will be looking at any one display at a given time, so one must start thinking in terms of, 'How much space do two or three people need so that they do not interfere with the viewing of other displays?' Thus, in a very general way, guesses can be made about the situation, and as the design proceeds these can be reassessed in the light of more specific needs. For example, if a theatre is used every time an audio-visual is specified, the number of visitors wishing to see it must be estimated on the basis of programme length and the numbers likely to arrive at the theatre whilst the programme is running. Ergonomic data can be used in a similar way to define the viewing spaces for displays (Fig. 7.9), e.g. if the whole width of a 900 mm panel has to be seen at once, it will require about 1700 mm of space in front of it. Other considerations then begin to bear on the problem, because at that sort of distance the likelihood of someone passing in front of a visitor viewing the exhibit is high. In

such circumstances, it is possible to set the display back from the general line of displays or to use some other method of keeping the viewing space clear, such as raking the floor or changing the texture in front of the exhibit to discourage visitors from walking there.

By the time these elements are put together along with the objects to be included in the exhibition, one can estimate roughly that about 80 per cent of the space will be given over to circulation.

Island displays

The position of displays in relation to the circulation routes is yet another factor that must be considered. It has been established that the capacity of a gallery to handle large numbers of people is dependent on the width of its major paths (Lakota & Kantner 1975), and so island displays, which by their very nature reduce path width, are best avoided. As there is a tendency for such displays to be situated in the middle of the main pathways through an exhibition, visitors standing in front of them will impede circulation, cause congestion and increase crowd pressure.

Another point is that exhibits with free-standing displays can be confusing, because visitors are not always aware which side of the display they should go to first, and therefore may go to the wrong side before orientating themselves to the message. Having been along one side, they are often reluctant to return along the other side as they will in effect be going back on themselves.

Expressing a theme

The designer may wish to express the theme of an exhibition in its overall form. At its best, this involves immersing the visitor in something real (e.g. a nature trail in a real woodland) or, alternatively, creating an exhibition within the gallery that is as close to reality as possible (e.g. a walk-through diorama of an African village). The purpose is to enable the visitor to experience some of the complexity and sensory richness of the real world. To achieve this in an exhibition requires careful attention to visual and spatial detail, and the integration of sound, smell and tactile experience to reinforce the message.

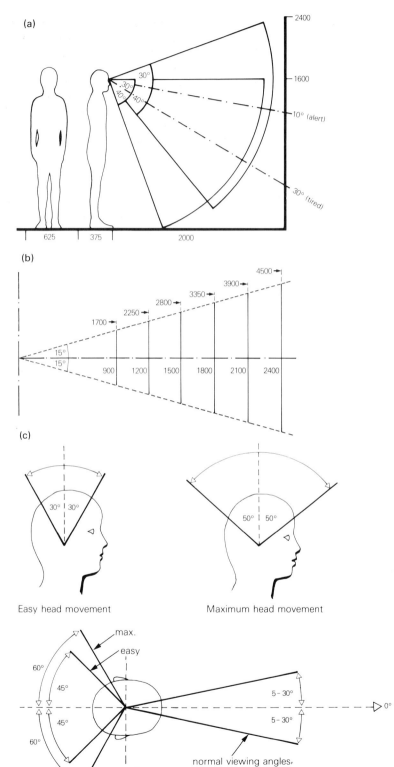

Figure 7.9 Ergonomic data on natural viewing angles. (a) The upper segment requires a viewing distance of 2 m to scan a wall of general information. Most displays are more conveniently viewed in the lower segment. (b) Plan showing the distance required to view conveniently a display of the given widths. (c) Head movements. (Measurements in millimetres.)

Where it is too costly or otherwise impracticable to use the real world, or create a replica of it, the designer can attempt to reinforce the theme of the exhibition by the way he handles the experience the visitor will undergo (e.g. a dark, brown-carpeted interior to create a cave-like environment in which to display minerals and gemstones). Problems arise if the means used are so abstract, and sensory cues so few, that it becomes impossible for the visitor to recognise the designer's intentions without additional explanation. Here one might question the value of attempting to express the theme in this way.

This does not mean that it is essential to create exact or near-exact representations of nature to evoke a theme. If the didactic presentation is both clear and familiar, the judicious use of colour may be quite sufficient. The designer's task is to decide how far it is necessary to go in evoking a theme, and this should be added to the list of overall objectives that the exhibit developer works to. Inevitably, no matter how rigorous the application of practical principles in finding at least one good way to meet temporal, spatial and economic constraints, a great deal rests on the designer's vision, intuition, experience and common sense. These are what ultimately determine the final form of the exhibition.

8 The individual exhibits

One problem in designing an educational exhibition is that the details of the physical structure are not easy to decide at the outset in comparison with a traditional, object-based exhibition, because the concepts to be communicated may call for novel forms of presentation. A further difficulty is that the physical structure should, besides housing the various media, give tangible form to the intellectual argument being presented. Thus, if the visitor is to know what is going on, it helps if he can see relatively easily how the major ideas of the exhibition come together into groups and how the groups relate to each other, as in the analogous case of a text-book organised into chapters. A third consideration is the overall floor plan, which largely determines the order in which the exhibits are seen. And, because considerable physical effort may be involved in visiting an exhibition, the floor plan determines the circulation to a much greater extent than the chapters determine the order in which a text-book is read. And, finally, there is the question of **pacing**, the attempt to strike a balance between consistency (and therefore coherence) and novelty. In deciding on which media to deploy, and on details of physical form, it is important to avoid overwhelming the visitor with variety, and at the same time avoid boring him with the sameness of presentation.

We suggested at the beginning of the previous chapter that *importance, function* and *sequence* are significant factors in planning exhibits and thus in the planning of whole exhibitions. They interact, and begin to build up a pattern for the whole exhibition, as they become expressed in recurring solutions. This pattern reinforces the communication, gives the exhibition its character, and helps the visitor to orientate himself within it. The pattern forms a kind of language which goes beyond the text used in the displays. But these are things that have to develop with the exhibition. The rigid application of some approach or convention can lead to exhibits that, from a design point of view, are inherently dull (Fig. 8.1), or so constraining that they begin to determine the contents of the display to an undesirable extent (Fig. 8.2).

In Figures 8.1 and 8.2 we can see how this rigid approach has affected the exhibits. The message that comes over most clearly in both is one of methodical presentation rather than communication. Clearly this is what mattered to the exhibit

Figure 8.1 The bird gallery of the British Museum (Natural History) in 1980.

Figure 8.2 A rigid arrangement of objects on an under-lying grid.

Figure 8.3 British Lepidoptera in the British Museum (Natural History) in 1980.

developers. In developing educational exhibits one must be continually asking the question, 'Why is it necessary to do it this way?' This is the point at which our own values affect the work. We have to ask whether the things that are important to us are as important to our visitors, and whether we have got the emphasis right.

Some hazards of communication

Wittlin (1971) has analysed the failure to ask such questions when designing exhibits and the resulting **underinterpretive** and **misinterpretive** displays.

Underinterpretive exhibits are those in which, broadly speaking, the objects are supposed to speak for themselves. Such exhibits are, therefore, only likely to mean something to a specialist with considerable previous knowledge and a conceptual framework already in his head. For example, a case full of objects as in Figure 8.3 might be full of significance for the specialist who can bring his own knowledge to bear in interpreting the exhibit, but is likely to mean very little to the average visitor. He may be able to identify individual features in the objects, or different kinds of objects, but if no attempt is made to explain the significance or cause of this variety, the visitor is stuck at this point. Even when explanatory labels are included in an attempt to solve the problems of underinterpretive exhibits, they are pitched at graduate textbook level. Such

exhibits exist because the experts are interested in the things on display and do not need any explanation. Displays are therefore crowded with objects and, while the specialist may delight in this abundance, the layman will probably be bored by it. Unable to appreciate the often subtle differences among a mass of fairly similar objects, he will find the exhibit perplexing and visually monotonous. Wittlin describes such exhibits as combining 'intellectual overload with sensory understimulation'.

In stepping forward to look at an individual object in a crowded display, the visitor is no longer able to see it in the context of the other objects, and cannot judge whether it is a typical or an exceptional example. By stepping back to see the whole, the visitor is confronted with an almost undifferentiated mass, and by labels that are impossible to read. Even if the exhibit is not underinterpretive, there is a definite limit to the human capacity for immediate assimilation of separate items of information. Miller (1970) has pointed out that people can only recall about seven independent items at one time, though much more information can be handled if it is 'chunked' into larger units. It is imperative, therefore, not to overload the visitor with disconnected facts. An underinterpreted exhibit is likely to leave the visitor dismayed, given the limited time he wishes to spend on each exhibit. Should the visitor give time to trying to understand such displays, it is more than likely that he will try to give significance to what is there by making up his own story on the basis of what, rightly or wrongly, the display is thought to be about.

Misinterpretive exhibits are those which combine sensory overstimulation with an intellectual deficit. Here the visitor's attention is concentrated on the arrangement of the display rather than on the message (Fig. 8.4). Object and idea are treated together as a purely visual experience. Everything becomes subordinated to a visual pattern that is little more than incidental decoration. Models are made to a spectacular size or abstracted to the point where they can no longer be recognised; text is printed out on television screens for no other reason than to provide a new experience for the visitor; and so on. No thought is given to the message to be communicated and the visitor is left fascinated but uninformed.

Included in this category are what can only be described as 'book on the wall' exhibits. They are common features of many exhibitions, due, one supposes, to the lack of specimens or unsuitability of the subject for exhibition treatment, or

Figure 8.4 The Evolution Gallery of the Royal Scottish Museum, 1976.

alternatively, to the separation of interpretive text from the objects on display. In the former case, the exhibit combines interpretation (if the text is well written) with sensory understimulation and it must be asked whether a book would have been a more appropriate medium.

If the underinterpretive display is characteristic of the curator fascinated by his collections, and the misinterpretive display that of the designer fascinated by his aesthetic skills, there is a third class of 'failed' displays – the compromise between the two. **A compromise exhibit** attempts to combine a popular display for the layman with a scholar's library of specimens. The problem here is not that the two approaches appear in the same exhibition, but that neither *supports* the other. An obvious example of late, in science museums, is the placing of a computer for use by visitors in amongst displays of computer hardware. Instead of the computer being used to explain what the hardware means, its programs are akin to noughts and crosses games. In contrast, Wittlin recommends *associating* rather than combining the two kinds of exhibit. She envisages an interpretive exhibit leading into another of limited interpretation. The layman, primed by guidance received in the first, could move on to the second if he wishes.

Function and sequence

If we put an object on a plinth or behind glass, we suggest some degree of value and, if we place another object beside it, we have to consider whether its plinth should be of the same height or colour, behind it, or in front of it, and so on. Whatever we do will communicate something to our visitors and we should endeavour to understand what it is we are actually saying as well as what we think we are saying.

If *importance* is concerned as much with what we do not mean to say as it is with what we intend to say, then *function* is concerned solely with the latter. It is about making the displays work effectively, assuming our assessment of the visitors' knowledge and interests is more or less correct. At its simplest level, it concerns making things visible or ensuring that interactive displays are placed within reach. We shall return to this subject in the next chapter, but before moving on to 'Sequence' it is worth considering one or two basic aspects of design from a functional point of view.

Labelling and layout

The first concerns the way that objects are labelled. Labelling can be a messy business, especially where the objects are smaller than the labels. A common way of overcoming this problem is to separate the labels from the objects to which they refer. If the distance becomes too great, key numbers are introduced which enable visitors to locate the objects on the labels. This practice has been extended to the point where labels often appear outside display cases containing the objects in question, sometimes with an intermediate key diagram so that the visitor has to search twice, first to locate the object and then to find the caption. This can be a frustrating business, prone to error, and while displays should be freed from clutter, they should not be purged to the extent of affecting the way they function. The visitor should be able to see both the object and its label within the same perceptual frame. It is very irritating to have to search through a label to find the relevant information or to have to search through a display to find the relevant object. It is all the more frustrating to find that key numbers are too small to be seen easily, or are placed on backgrounds that match those of the display so that they begin to disappear. It is even worse if, as is too often the case, some numbers have been omitted altogether.

If an identification system *has* to be used, it should take the form of a key line-drawing which can be labelled to correspond to the contents of the exhibit. It should not, however, be integrated with other graphics, as it is likely to be the last things to be produced, which will delay the production of other graphic materials and any integral structures. Key drawings should be neither an afterthought nor purely a problem of graphics; their location and form must be considered as the design develops.

The second aspect to consider here concerns the layout of a display. In an attempt to rationalise the design, it is quite common for a grid to be used, similar to those used in designing books. A grid provides some sense of order and relationship, but if used too rigidly it can make perceptual connections that were never intended, so that the display gives entirely the wrong impression.

The photographs and text in the example in Figure 8.5 have been placed in three distinct, vertical columns. These columns create a structure within the panel that extends beyond the immediate limits of photographs and text, so that anything below them appears to conform to the same arrangement. This is critical because the material below appears to give an answer to the question forming the heading, when in fact this is far from the designer's intention.

Lighting

Chapter 7 introduced some ergonomic data that help us to design exhibits which can be viewed without undue physical effort (Fig. 7.9). These data define the perceptual frame, and therefore what the visitor can comfortably see, in particular circumstances. They thus help to determine how exhibits should be put together, one with another, so that the visitor's attention is not persistently distracted by other exhibits. These ergonomic data can now be extended (Fig. 8.6) to embrace the problems of reflection and **glare**, both of which, in their different ways, can make exhibits unviewable.

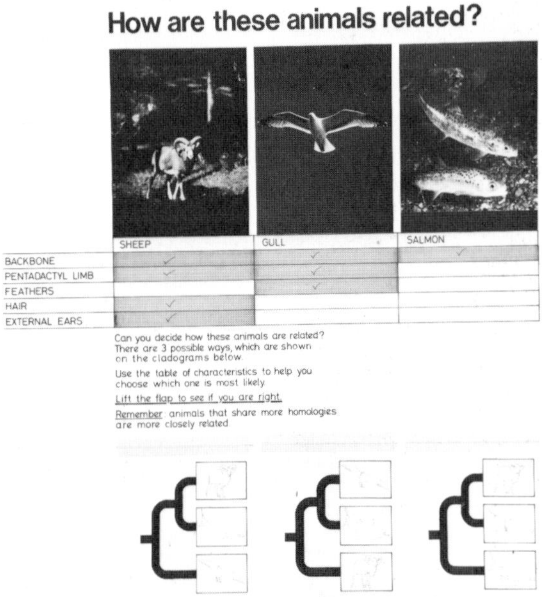

Figure 8.5 Mock-up made during formative evaluation of a new exhibit in the British Museum (Natural History), 1980.

(a)

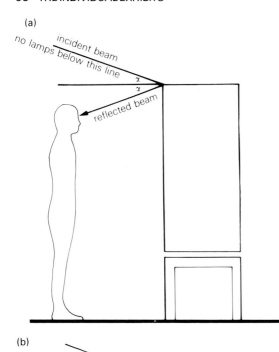

Lighting is a special part of the design of any exhibition and has a significant effect on the visitors. Its purpose is to enable things to be seen by creating contrasts within the object and between the object and its background. Ways in which such contrasts can be achieved are well covered in the Chartered Institution of Building Services' (1980) *CIBS lighting guide – museums and art galleries in London* and in earlier publications (e.g. Gardner & Heller 1960). Visitors should not be aware of lighting beyond an appreciation of the ambience it creates. If they are, it is probably because the designers have got it wrong. Lighting can be internal (in a light-box above a show-case) or external (spotlights, fluorescent tubes, etc.); and general (more or less even illumination over the whole area) or accented (beams of light directed at specific points).

(b)

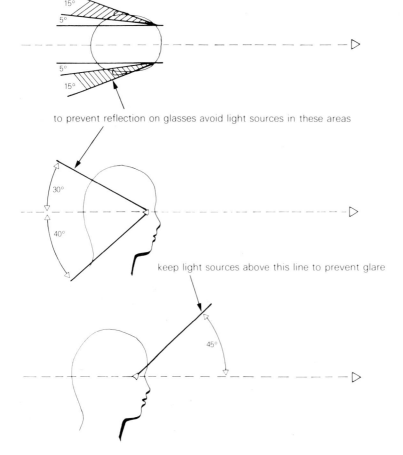

Figure 8.6   Reflection and glare.

Diffuse lighting can cause reflections that impede vision. Accent lighting is likely to cause glare, which at best makes it difficult to see detail (discomfort glare) and may make it impossible to see anything (disability glare). Glare is not exclusively the result of direct light, and can be caused, for example, by the reflections of a spotlight on shiny surfaces such as glass, metal and printing ink. All these tendencies are more marked with external lighting (Fig. 8.7), but internal lighting is not always feasible (Ch. 11).

The eye tends to be attracted to a source of bright light, so it is important to ensure that this fact is turned to advantage. 'Visual fatigue' is caused by the eye being asked to **adapt** to widely different or rapidly changing levels of illumination. For example, a graphic panel illuminated from an external, diffuse source is a lot less bright than a back-lit transparency, and if the eye has to adapt too rapidly from one to the other, the visitor will be distracted and suffer physical discomfort. Levels of illumination should vary gradually between exhibits. If differentially lit exhibits *have* to be placed together, the amount of illumination should be modified or the area of contrast reduced, or both, until satisfactory results are obtained.

The backgrounds of exhibits should also be considered from the point of view of contrast with their contents and with the general level of lighting in the gallery. In darker areas, white type on a dark background is to be preferred; at higher light levels, black type on a light background. Lighting should also relate to the visitors' needs. In general, younger people can manage at lower light levels than older people or the partially sighted.

Sequence

If function is basically about the way things work, sequence, i.e. the order in which things are best seen or done, is closely related. A straightforward example is provided by the instructions on an interactive device, which should obviously reflect the order in which the various actions are carried out.

People in Western cultures read from left to right and from top to bottom, and this tells us to arrange our displays on the floor of the gallery so that they can be read in a left to right sequence; headings and text should be arranged so that they appear in top-to-bottom order. Functionally,

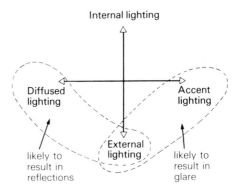

Figure 8.7   Problems caused by different types of lighting.

exhibits *can* work in other arrangements; many have been organised in a right to left sequence and many have display panels with headings in the middle or to one side. The point is that they would function better in a sequence that was both obvious and related to the previous experience of the visitors. Conventions should only be broken when there is some good reason for doing so.

When a display is badly planned, the visitor may attempt to organise the information and make sense of it for himself. This person is quite likely to come away feeling irritated and with a message different from the one intended. It is therefore worth asking a number of questions once a particular layout has been proposed.

(a)   If I use this layout or this piece of equipment, what am I saying and what am I asking the visitor to do?

(b)   Is this what I intended to say and should I be asking the visitor to do it this way?

(c)   Is there an alternative way of designing this display to say what I intend and can I change the corresponding task to one that the visitor can do more readily?

(d)   Have I an alternative to this display from which the visitor could learn more effectively?

In giving emphasis to displays, and in planning the order in which they are to be seen, the designer has a wide range of means at his disposal.

(a) *Size*. We can give a greater emphasis to an element in an exhibition by increasing its size. A photomural will seem more important than a small print. Alternatively, things can be made to appear related by keeping them all the same size, e.g. by not varying the height of plinths. Sequence can be indicated by varying the sizes of panels, so that the first image to be seen is always the largest and the last the smallest (Fig. 8.8).

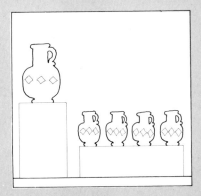

Figure 8.8 Emphasis obtained by size.

(b) *Isolation*. Exhibits can be placed apart from others or put into separate environments to give them emphasis. We can isolate displays to free them from distractions, or so that they can only be seen in a prescribed sequence (Fig. 8.9).

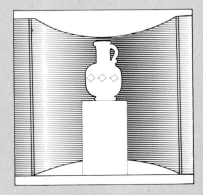

Figure 8.9 Emphasis obtained by isolation.

(c) *Colour*. Emphasis can be provided by colour or by colour contrasts, either in the objects themselves or between different back-grounds, or between each object and its background. For example, light backgrounds make dark things look smaller and dark backgrounds make light objects appear larger. Similar colours can be used to indicate that things are related, and colour contrasts to improve visual acuity. Bright colours can be used to stimulate, and restful colours to reduce, activity. Tonal changes, say from dark to light, can be used to indicate a sequence of ideas or objects (Fig. 8.10).

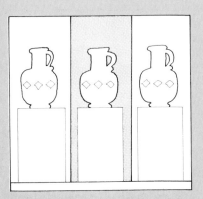

Figure 8.10 Emphasis obtained by colour.

(d) *Position*. Objects can be placed in front of other objects, or higher, or lower, to indicate relative importance. They can be placed in the best position to be seen or arranged in their original functional relationship. They can be arranged in the way they are to be used and also to encourage the orderly viewing of the exhibition (Fig. 8.11).

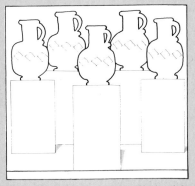

Figure 8.11 Emphasis obtained by position.

(e) *Shape.* Changes of shape can be used to give emphasis to parts of an exhibition (Fig. 8.12), but shape should also reflect the ergonomic requirements of the visitors. Shape can be used to create a smooth flow of visitors through an exhibition and also to suggest a correct path.

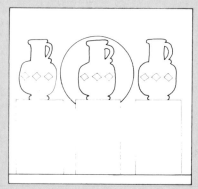

Figure 8.12 Emphasis obtained by shape.

(f) *Texture.* Textures can be used functionally as in a pebbled surface to discourage visitors from walking over a particular area, or to identify a path for the blind and partially sighted. They can also be used to give emphasis, e.g. in the use of tarred ropes and wooden floors to emphasise the theme in a maritime museum, or different backgrounds for displays (Fig. 8.13).

Figure 8.13 Emphasis obtained by texture.

(g) *Light.* Light enables things to be seen and can be used to express the things that matter by enhancing form, texture and colour. It can be used sequentially to determine the order in which things are to be seen, and spotlights can be used to emphasise a particular display, or separate a group from the surrounding environment (Fig. 8.14).

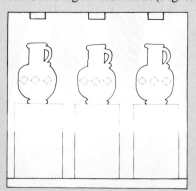

Figure 8.14 Emphasis obtained by light.

Maps and signposts

There is generally a need for devices to help visitors find their way around an exhibition, or indeed an entire museum. In fact, the principles are the same in the two cases, and they are particularly important in a museum, where the visitor has almost complete freedom. The subject is usually discussed under the heading of **orientation**; and it is important that the various elements of orientation – signposts and organizers such as maps, exhibit numbers and signs – fit closely together and work as one. Here we shall discuss maps and signposts, and in the next section take up the subject of exhibit numbers.

It seems obvious that the organisational structure of an exhibition should be clear to visitors, because otherwise they are likely to become lost in a meaningless mass of displays and give up. In other words, the visitors need to know at the outset what is going on (Ch. 3), and as they go round the exhibition they need to know where they are, in relation to both where they have been and where they are going. It is useful at this stage to draw a distinction between *topographic orientation*, which relates to the physical structure of the exhibition, and *conceptual orientation*, which relates to the organisation of the subject-matter (Ch. 6). In our experience these require separate treatment. Visitors will not, for example, look to maps and signposts for conceptual orientation; it is often difficult to present a preview of concepts at the beginning of an exhibition – say on a map of the exhibition – if the concepts, or the objects that are used to illustrate them, are strange or unfamiliar. It seems that conceptual orientation must, in general, be part of the connecting narrative that holds the individual displays together, though this does not rule out the need, at the entrance, for:

(a) an intelligible title, with an elaborating sentence if necessary (e.g. Origin of species – an exhibition about Darwin's theory of natural selection);
(b) a statement that the exhibition is trying to tell a story, if this is the case;
(c) a brief summary of the story giving its major components and the interrelationships of these components.

Turning to topographic orientation, there is a need with exhibitions of any complexity to:

(a) provide a ground-plan at the entrance, which shows:
    (i) the overall physical arrangement of the exhibition and, if thematic, the intended route through it;
    (ii) the correspondence between physical and conceptual structures (e.g. if sequences are numbers the plan should carry large and clear numbers accordingly);
    (iii) major landmarks;
    (iv) choice points in the intended sequence;
(b) reinforce this information throughout the exhibition (Fig. 8.15);
(c) explain at choice points the consequences of any one decision (e.g. to leave the exhibition, to skip part of the story and so on);
(d) orient maps so they are in the correct topographic relationship to the physical features of the exhibition or gallery from the visitor's point of view.

Our experience has also shown that orientation devices must be developed at the same time as the exhibits and not tackled as an afterthought at a later stage. And they must be developed so that they are clear and usable for the visitor rather than for the benefit of the curator or designer (Fig. 8.16).

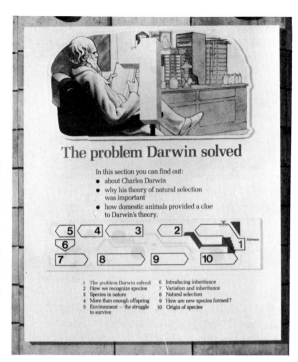

Figure 8.15 Orientation panel from the 'Origin of species' exhibition, British Museum (Natural History), 1981.

Numbering exhibits

In traditional exhibitions, numbering has never been regarded as a problem because there is rarely a narrative structure to follow. The subject has to be considered here because educational exhibitions do have a narrative structure, perhaps based on a chronological or geographical sequence or on some less obvious thematic basis. Designers should aim to make the structure of the subject-matter of the exhibition obvious to visitors. With the variety of media and constructions used in an exhibition, such clarity may not always be possible and the visitor will probably visit exhibits according to their physical proximity, i.e. what comes next. By numbering exhibits one is identifying a sequence in the belief that it will give the visitor a better understanding of the subject-matter. Whether or not visitors follow that sequence is up to them but it is a matter of importance that visitors should be aware of the sequence and the means of following the narrative from beginning to end. Awareness will depend first on visitors being able to locate and read the numbers and secondly, on their understanding of them.

Figure 8.16

numbers and secondly, on their understanding of them.

Most exhibit developments begin with a numbering system as a means of reference for the designers. Problems arise when these numbers are carried through to the final designs. First, the numbers might be based on a specialist's classification that is not reflected in the final form of the exhibition. Secondly, the numbering system may be fixed before the content is determined, so that additions and omissions occur leaving the visitor with puzzling sequences such as:

1, 2, 3, 5, 6, 7, 9, 10
1, 2, 3, 4a, 4b, 5a, 5b, 6, 7, 8, 9, 10

A further complication arises if there is a need to indicate subdivisions. Sometimes letters are used, e.g. A1, A2, A3, B1, B2, B3 and sometimes decimals, e.g. 3.1, 3.2, 3.3, 4.1, 4.2, 4.3. Such subdivisions can be carried to extremes, e.g. 3.1.1, 3.1.2, 3.1.3, which are difficult to read in an exhibition and confusing.

One must also remember that numbers not only describe sequence but status as well, e.g. 3.1 and 3.2 are part of a larger group 3. This system can also imply that 3.1 is more important than 3.2.

A numbering system must be developed with the needs of the visitor in mind and there are a number of points to remember:

(a) Numbering systems are cryptic. When explaining the organisation of an exhibition, tell visitors that numbers are used to indicate a sequence and, where necessary, the sub-divisions of the subject-matter.

(b) No numbering system can work if the numbers are hard to find or illegible at the normal viewing distance. A space for the number should be allowed on each display and should be in the same relative position each time.

(c) Numbers should not conflict with sequences in the narrative structure or with the physical organisation of the exhibition.

(d) Visitors find straightforward numbering systems easier to understand, e.g. 1, 2, 3 . . . n exhibits. Where subdivisions have to be used in large exhibitions, visitors find it easier to understand letter-based systems, e.g. A1, A2, A3, B1, B2, B3, rather than decimal-based systems, e.g. 3.1, 3.2, 3.3, 4.1, 4.2, 4.3.

(e) Numbers should be removable to accommodate changes in the exhibition at some later date.

Housing the exhibits

So far we have looked at the kinds of factors that determine the final form of an exhibit, and have seen that the designer can use a variety of *means* to solve the problems that these factors raise. These means combine with the specific demands of each medium (Ch. 9) and are reflected in the final form of the exhibit, i.e. its three-dimensional structure. But there is more to the origin of an exhibit structure than this; it is subject to the practical demands of economics and availability, and also to the need for change as a result of evaluation and continuing maintenance.

Economic considerations are closely associated with those of availability. Materials are usually only available in series of standard sizes and the objective in designing a structure should be to make the best possible use of them. So whatever the importance, function and sequencing of an exhibit, its structure will have to conform to predetermined norms that have little to do with these demands. But, even within these limitations, considerable variety is possible. For example, chipboard panels 2400 mm by 1200 mm may be an economic choice of construction material. It would be possible to use

them uncut or cut them into a series of modules that reflect the organisation of the intellectual content of the exhibit.

From this it can be seen that four qualities form the basis of economic and practical structural design: standardisation, modularity, flexibility and demountability.

Standardisation

Standardisation means the repetition of components to simplify production. If properly used, it can reduce cost in terms of both time and materials and has the added advantage that the structural performance of components can be tested and improved. The increased knowledge resulting from standardisation encourages a positive attitude to change in that one can assess the necessary resources and it allows for the possible reuse of materials and components. The disadvantage is that standardisation can be used for its own sake, predetermining the sizes of displays irrespective of any particular needs the subject-matter or the visitor might have.

Standardisation can result from ergonomic, production or learning requirements. For example, the heights and positions of displays will be governed by the physical and perceptual characteristics of the visitors, irrespective of the style of the exhibits; graphic **sandwiches**, electronic circuitry, and show-case details need not be redesigned every time they are required; and the content and layout of signposting materials can be repeated.

These are arguments for a high degree of standardisation, but they only apply if a strong case can be made out for their acceptance. The reason for taking this stance, rather than insisting that designers fit their exhibits into pre-determined structures, is the need for exhibits that match their objectives and look interesting to the visitor. It also ensures that designers have the opportunity to produce exhibits that are *seen* to reflect the arguments that underlie a thematic exhibition.

Modularity

Modularisation is a process of partial standardisation. It facilitates production, assembly and replacement by reducing variety but at the same time allows considerable flexibility to be retained. As Alexander (1964) puts it:

'No complex adaptive system will succeed in adapting in a reasonable amount of time unless the adaptation can proceed sub-system by sub-system, each sub-system relatively independent of the other.'

These sub-systems are conventionally called modules, but this same name is often given to a secondary unit which is some multiple of the primary one. For instance, it simplifies things considerably to restrict linear dimensions to multiples of 100 mm, a module which effectively bridges the gap between the metric and imperial systems because it closely approximates four inches. Thus timber is now sold in lengths which are multiples of 300 mm, near enough to one foot for most practical purposes. As a general rule a module should not be so small as to be trivial nor too large as to be impracticable in relation to the circumstances in which it is to be used.

The coordination of dimensions is justified for both visual and practical reasons. A module helps the designer achieve consistency, clarity and order. It is aimed at reducing the overall visual noise of an exhibition and there is some evidence that this works to the benefit of the visitor. A module helps simplify specifications and thus misunderstandings are avoided. It promotes the standardisation of material dimensions and components, and thereby simplifies construction. The coordination of dimensions also assists change through the matching of components.

Flexibility

Flexibility allows structures to be changed or moved. Basically, this requires exhibits to be structurally independent so they do not rely on one another for support. It means that finishes around displays should be continuous as should be the carpets beneath. No display should have its dimensions determined by holes left by previous exhibits.

The density of displays on the floor of the gallery is critical in determining the amount of flexibility. If there is no room to move displays into a new configuration, it makes little difference what form the exhibits take. An entire exhibition would have to be found wanting to justify the cost of changing it, even assuming the resources were available to do so. On a smaller scale, individual displays or their components can only be modified to a small degree if displays are packed side by side. This suggests that wherever a display is thought likely to be changed, it should be given sufficient space to allow for possible modification.

These factors sometimes vary in importance within one exhibit. For example, an exhibit of varied objects can be seen as comprising two elements: first, the objects themselves and their labels, and secondly, the information that explains their arrangement. The former is not likely to change much because the arrangement of the specimens is based upon generally agreed principles. The latter, on the other hand, is liable to change depending on our ability to make clear to visitors the arguments that determine the arrangement. In this example, the display of objects can be regarded as more or less permanent and advantage can be taken of those aspects of case design that will aid conservation. The information part of the display should ideally be structurally (but *not* perceptually) independent of the display case, and therefore easily replaced.

When designing graphics it is necessary to allow for inaccuracies in the exhibit structure. Space should thus be left around graphics where they are adjacent to frames and the accuracy of fit should never be crucial. Flexibility can be made more economical by ensuring that elements, such as photographs and text, are not combined. This makes it possible to change the text while retaining a perfectly good photograph.

Demountability

Demountability ensures that displays can be taken down and modified. It is an essential quality of educational exhibits for change is always probable. All display contents, but principally instructions and text, should therefore be easily replaceable. Text panels can inadvertently include mistakes or need updating, so they must be removable. This in turn may determine the form the panel will take. With in-house screen-printing facilities it is possible to print text onto a hard, non-porous surface such as plastic laminate and wipe it off. If this is not possible, photographic panels can be produced by a contractor and simply replaced on site.

Demountability should be taken into account in fixing the size of structures. The larger the structure, the more difficult it is to take down, and no component should be so large that it cannot be moved by two people. This imposes a limit of

2400 mm on the maximum dimension and about 60 kg in weight. It further ensures that components can pass through most doorways and passages in a public building. Where exhibits need to be larger, it may be possible to design them so that they reduce down to manageable components.

All displays are subject to evaluation of some sort or other, e.g. in terms of their appearance, attendance, and so on (Ch. 15). If the evaluation is to be of any practical use, the displays must be capable of being changed or removed, and all the factors discussed above become important. A further factor that relates to them is cost. All displays should be economically sensible and produced at the minimum cost necessary to answer the problems defined in the brief and raised by the need for maintenance. Exhibits should never be designed at such expense, in time and money, that all change is prohibited. If there are serious doubts about the possible success of an exhibit, it should be tested (a) before production to check the intelligibility of the message, and (b) after installation to check its appeal to visitors. Even if the design appears to work there is no guarantee that it will do so in the gallery. Such an exhibit should be installed cheaply until there is reasonable certainty that it works and then, if necessary, it should be built more substantially.

The above points can be summarised as follows:

(a) structures liable to change should be identified;
(b) where there is a high probability of change the exhibit should be tested, first to check the intelligibility of the story and secondly to check its appeal to visitors in the gallery;
(c) the structure should be rationalised to take advantage of

  (i) standardisation,
  (ii) modular components and dimensions,
  (iii) flexibility,
  (iv) demountability;

(d) the exhibits should be

  (i) ergonomically sensible,
  (ii) economical in the use of resources.

Travelling exhibitions

The problems of organising, scheduling, insuring, packing and publicising travelling exhibitions have been well documented elsewhere (Tyler & Dickenson 1977, Danilov 1978, Pugh 1978, Gleadowe 1979, Witteborg 1981) and the reader is referred to these works. Many of the things discussed so far also apply to travelling exhibitions, but these do present their own particular problems. First, when several locations are involved, each will have its own structural and statutory limitations which may, or may not, be known in advance. Secondly, the exhibits will have to be transported, not once but several times when moving from one location to another; and thirdly, there is the problem of building and maintaining an exhibition that, during its life, will experience a variety of climates and uses.

Locations

Travelling exhibitions are displayed in a variety of spaces so, if visitors are to see them in an orderly way, they must be sufficiently flexible that they can be arranged in different configurations without disrupting the natural sequence. It helps if the structural characteristics of each location are known in advance, particularly if large or heavy exhibits are involved, e.g. the area and height of rooms, loadbearing capacity of floors and walls. Dimensions of doorways and passages are particularly important as an exhibit may well fit the exhibition space but be too large to go through doors or up stairs to get there. Fire regulations also affect the organisation of the exhibits on the floor and may even determine the materials used if a high resistance to fire is required.

On a different level, the location may influence the designer's choice of colour or finishes. Colour contrasts or materials that clash with the surroundings can detract from an exhibition, as can the poor decorative state of either the exhibition or the room in which it is located. The quality and quantity of illumination may determine the need for additional light and the power required. Climatic conditions will vary and these can affect the exhibition, e.g. unsealed, hardboard buckles in humid conditions. The nature and availability of security, and pest control, will determine what is needed in the way of special show-cases and other protective devices. Variations may also be experienced in the voltage of the power supply and in the formats of audio-visual hardware.

Transport

Travelling exhibitions not only have to fit exhibition rooms but also the interiors of vans and lorries. The transport costs of an exhibition can be considerably reduced if it is designed to fit the most economical vehicle. The way the exhibition is packed and constructed should take into account the people assigned to move it, and one should never rely on manufacturer's packing because it is not usually designed for repeated use. Packing may also have to ameliorate the effects of changes in climate, e.g. in moving an exhibition from Europe to the Indian sub-continent. All packing cases and structures should be clearly labelled and easily placed in the correct sequence for installation and, although carriage instructions should be clear, it is advisable not to be too explicit about contents that might attract unwanted attention while in transit. Some form of checklist or key should be provided so that recipients can identify all the cases and their contents. It is also worth informing recipients of the amount of space needed to store the packing, which may be considerable.

Installation

Travelling exhibitions are not only subject to the rigours of daily wear and tear but also those of continuous handling by staff during installation. One cannot rely on the skill and experience of such staff unless they are well supervised, so every exhibition should be accompanied by clear instructions for putting the exhibition together, for packing it away and for maintaining it. A schedule should be incorporated, perhaps linked to the numbering on the packing, to determine the correct order of installation, e.g. completing the electrical work *before* the displays are unpacked. A set of photographs showing the original installation may be of great help to the recipient.

Instructions should tell people what to do and what *not* to do, and refer them to experts in the institution owning the exhibition should problems arise. Maintenance begins with the unpacking of the exhibition. All damage should be recorded as should any that happens during installation. Reports should be returned to the parent institution so that it can monitor wear and tear. If possible, the design team should retain control over any repairs, repainting and replacement. The same standards of presentation cannot otherwise be guaranteed at each location. Finally, the parent institution should obtain feedback on the success or otherwise of the exhibition by the regular receipt of comments and attendance figures.

9 Choosing media and their modes of use

Although the overall plan of the gallery provides guidelines along which the exhibition can be organised, it is the information to be communicated and the needs of the visitor that are the main considerations in developing the exhibition in detail. The objectives and story-line provide some guidance in this, and it helps to use **story-boards**, rough models and so on to give a preliminary idea of what the exhibits will look like. This means that early decisions have to be taken about media and modes.

To clarify the distinction we draw between medium and mode, we remark that the medium is the vehicle that carries the information the designer wishes to communicate to the visitor, and the mode is the way in which the medium is used. The relationship between medium and mode can be seen in the following examples.

(a) In the audio *mode* the medium may be a sound track on a cine film, a magnetic tape, a gramophone record or a compact disc.
(b) A diorama is a *medium* which itself comprises simpler media (e.g. real things, models, photographs), and it can be used on its own in the visual mode, or with a sound recording in the audio-visual mode.
(c) Various print *media* (e.g. photographs, diagrams, drawings) may be used alone in the print mode, or in conjunction with an audio medium of some kind in the audio-visual mode.

The term audio-visual is sometimes used as a noun and sometimes as an adjective. As the above examples show, in addition to being used to define a type of presentation, it may be used to describe either the mode of presentation or the medium that it uses. An audio-visual medium may be an indivisible unity (e.g. a sound film), or it may be divisible into simpler component media (e.g. slide-tape).

Selecting the medium

Selecting the *right* medium is one of the key activities in exhibition design. This is not a straightforward matter, however, and there are few rules to guide the selection process. Moreover, the exact meaning of the word *right* may be open to doubt, because the designer has often to try and reconcile conflicting demands, such as capital costs, running costs, size of user groups and different learning styles. As it is, most discussions of media and exhibit problems are centred on the technology. This approach is unfortunately all too typical of the present-day attitude to problems – ignore the real problem, which is too difficult, and concentrate on one that you can solve. In the present instance, this amounts to ignoring the visitor as a factor influencing the choice of medium and misapplying the McLuhan adage 'the medium is the message'. Media are a means of attaining the end of effective communication, not an end in themselves. Most of the literature, therefore, is unhelpful, comprising as it does a paragraph of introduction and an extended discussion of screen size, the best projector, and so on. All valuable stuff, but only if the medium is correctly used. It does not matter how well a film is projected if film is not an appropriate choice in the first place. Appropriate choices must be made by looking at the characteristics of both (1) visitors and (2) exhibits.

Research in formal education strongly suggests that the use of one particular medium, rather than any other, does not directly influence the learning that takes place. However, the choice does influence the cost and efficiency with which the information is transferred. Thus, for example, we could design an exhibit to teach visitors to discriminate between the songs of a group of related birds as:

(1)   a graphic panel using musical notation, or
(2)   with computer simulations, or
(3)   with recorded sound.

There seems little doubt that, for most visitors to an exhibition, method (3) is the most efficient way of communicating the message, though the setting-up costs may be high if recordings are difficult to obtain, and the maintenance costs are probably going to be higher than in the other two cases. Method (1), on the other hand, will probably be the cheapest to set up and run, though it is doubtful if the message will be communicated efficiently to most visitors. Method (2) probably falls between (1) and (3) in terms of efficiency of communication and maintenance costs, but is likely to be the most expensive to set up when the costs of equipment and programming are taken into account. However, because computers are still novel to many visitors, method (2) might succeed over (1) and (3) in attracting an audience. All of this should show that there are no easy answers. In fact, the main conclusion must be that the selection of media is a creative act that relies, as much as anything, on the designer's intuition and flair. There are, however, a number of guidelines and constraining factors that should be kept in mind.

In approaching the problem of media selection it is useful to consider:

(a)   what the visitor should be able to do, after having experienced the exhibit;
(b)   the qualities inherent in the subject-matter of the exhibit.

Thus the teaching of dynamic processes such as continental drift ideally calls for the use of dynamic media such as film or videotape, whereas an attempt to communicate the way the joints of the human body work might employ some form of mechanical model for the visitor to manipulate. However, a further consideration is the need for variety. For example, interactive computer exhibits may be the best way of teaching a related series of concepts, but if they are used one after another, with no break or change of medium, the visitor will soon lose interest and cease to attend. This is, in fact, an aspect of the broader problem of pacing in exhibition design, a topic that was introduced at the beginning of Chapter 8.

Another way of looking at the need for variety is to consider different learning styles among the visitors. Although no exact data exist, we may safely assume that some visitors would prefer text and graphics to hands-on activity, or would like to see real things in preference to working models, while others will hold opposite views. Then again, some visitors will want to see many examples of real things, while others will want fewer, for fear of being overwhelmed with information. At a deeper level, some visitors will prefer to be given a general statement and *then* shown the objects and so on that illustrate it, while others will want to see the examples before the rules. As already suggested, these are difficult problems when we are dealing with a hetero-geneous and largely unknown audience, and it is therefore wise for the exhibition designer to build a range of opportunities and experiences into an exhibition, and to allow for a certain amount of redundancy by using different media to com-municate the same messages.

It is a reflection of our difficulties that common sense is often the final arbiter in choosing an appropriate medium. When two or more design solutions are in competition, all other things being equal, the solution thought to present the minimum production and maintenance problems should always be chosen.

Modes of use

Media can be used in a variety of different ways and, in discussing them, it is helpful to distinguish four basic modes of use. The primary distinction is between the static and dynamic modes. In the static mode the exhibit does not change state: for example, the traditional museum, where there is nothing on display except motionless objects and labels, uses only the static mode of communica-tion. Exhibits incorporating something that, in one way or another, is caused to change state from time to time function in the dynamic mode. Even the printed word, the commonest medium of communication, may be used either statically, as in a label for a piece of pottery, or dynamically, e.g. when built up letter by letter on a screen. Many museums use working models, moving pictures and diagrams, and in particular there is a growing use of computers to provide the element of dynamism.

In a dynamic exhibit the way in which the

change of state is brought about has considerable influence on the learning process: hence the further subdivision of the dynamic mode into automaton, operand and interactive modes.

In the *automaton* mode, nothing the visitor does can influence what goes on in the exhibit. Film is a medium that can be used in this way, as a loop which keeps running round and round, come what may.

In the *operand* mode, the visitor plays an active role but what happens is not influenced by the message that the medium carries. Thus a film or videotape can be started by pressing a button, or a model of a skeletal joint can be manipulated by the visitor. The visitor acts on the exhibit, but the course of subsequent events is predetermined: there is no interplay of action and reaction.

In the *interactive* mode, visitor and exhibit act reciprocally on each other. Because of the complexity of action and reaction there is almost always a computer behind the scenes, although this may not always be obvious. There are a great many possibilities in computer-assisted learning (CAL), but there are two distinctly different ways in which computers may be used: hence the further subdivision of the interactive mode into *tutorial* and *simulation* modes. The difference between these is that in the simulation mode the outcome is open-ended, whereas in the tutorial mode it is predetermined to a considerable extent. In other words, in the tutorial mode there is a preferred answer to every question asked of the visitor, whereas in the simulation mode there are no wrong answers.

The ends to be attained

Before examining in detail the specific media and the ways in which they are used in exhibits, it is worth examining in a general way what a medium has to do. How does it help visitors to learn about the subjects on display?

The ways in which it can help include:

(a) attracting the visitors;
(b) holding their attention;
(c) helping them recall knowledge;
(d) presenting them with information;
(e) activating their response;
(f) providing them with feedback.

Attracting the visitor

The power of an exhibit to attract visitors is indicated by the ratio of the number of visitors stopping at it to the total number encountering it. There are two main influences here – the visitors themselves and the other exhibits. Different visitors have different interests and levels of knowledge. People come to the exhibition with expectations and wishes that in all probability are very different from those assumed by the exhibition developers. Exhibits that inspire respect rather than comprehension may attract an audience, but are unlikely to do so again if they leave the visitor feeling inferior. Exhibits that can be understood and are challenging at an appropriate level are more likely to attract people than exhibits that make them feel stupid or bored. However, it must be recognised that different visitors will want different things: a knowledge-able visitor will perhaps want more than a casual visitor does. Thus the problem is that exhibits and displays might well have different levels of success, for not all subjects will be of uniform interest and not all media will succeed with all visitors.

The second factor concerns attraction within the exhibition. Obviously, certain types of display are more attractive than others, e.g. real things and participatory displays attract more attention than static graphic panels; in general, media associated with entertainment are more attractive than those associated with formal education. However, from a learning point of view, the spectacular kinds of techniques often found in exhibitions are not always needed, and may actually be distracting. If displays are regarded as being in competition with one another, then it is very easy to select the obviously attractive media and avoid the rest. But the selection of an 'unattractive' form of display may be perfectly justified from the point of view of the message to be communicated. To see things in terms of attraction might be appropriate for the market-place, where everything is shouting out in competition, but it is inappropriate for educational exhibitions where displays are intended to work together.

Audio-visuals are very attractive but the medium they use is one of the most distractive, both visually and acoustically. As Grandjean (1969) has pointed out, acoustic stimuli distract more than any others. The unexpected and discontinuous noise that emanates from audio-visuals is more disturbing than continuous noise. There is therefore a need to isolate such displays when they are in danger of distracting from those surrounding them. Sometimes an important point has to be made in an exhibit that is adjacent to one more likely to hold the visitor's attention. The two could be isolated from one another, but this is not always possible and the alternative of making that point within the more attractive exhibit should be considered.

Holding the visitor's attention

Holding power can be measured by the length of time visitors stay at an exhibit. The longer they stay in front of a display, the greater the chance that they might understand the message it is intended to convey. To increase the time visitors spend at a display, we must try to engage their attention by telling them:

(a)   what the display is about;
(b)   that it has something to do with them;
(c)   that it is organised in a particular way;
(d)   it will function (if dynamic) in a particular way.

Exhibit developers must appeal to the visitors' interests if they are to hold their attention. Try to put yourself in the visitors' shoes and ask what, in general terms, they feel about using a display. Do they feel coerced into using it? Will they find it interesting? Are they able to relate it to their own familiar world and use their own knowledge? Can they participate in their own way? Do they find it challenging?

Other factors also influence the time people spent in exhibitions: for example, there is some evidence that exhibitions with a clear organisation and in which concepts are linked together by clear themes are more interesting and more likely to hold the visitor's attention than unrelated facts and isolated objects.

Recalling earlier knowledge

In any complex mixed-media exhibition with an unfamiliar subject-matter, it is important to relate the message to the visitor's world and to what he already knows. It is also necessary to remind him of what has gone before, so that when he sees it in a different context he is reassured that the information can be understood. This also allows for the fact that the visitor may have missed something earlier in the exhibition that has a direct bearing on the later display. This is particularly important where audio-visuals or participatory displays are used. Visitors with little time or who are unwilling to wait around for their turn must be provided with the information elsewhere, either as a separate display or as an introduction to another, later display.

Presenting information

The medium conveys the message. Within this central purpose it may be called upon to:

(a)   explain things;
(b)   give examples (and counter-examples);
(c)   give emphasis;
(d)   show the visitor what to look for;
(e)   sequence and pace the information so that the visitor is not overwhelmed or bored;
(f)   encourage the visitor to respond.

Activating the response

Exhibitors are fortunate in that, whatever they do, visitors will in general respond positively in some way: the aim of the designer is to encourage the visitor to respond in a particular way. Active participation is associated with mechanical, electromechanical and electronic devices. Although well-designed devices can improve the response, there is always a danger of irrelevant activity. Pushing buttons or turning handles can become an end in itself, which does little to improve the quality of the communication and much to encourage small boys and girls to compete in starting all the devices in the shortest possible time. Push-buttons are a negative factor in exhibit learning when they do not permit the visitor to manipulate, experiment with or vary the demonstration.

Participation need not be overt (Fig. 9.1) and covert responses can be equally effective in improving the quality of the learning. Questions in particular are more likely to stimulate a response than factual labels. They can motivate visitors and attract attention to parts of a display that matter. However, we should avoid irritating

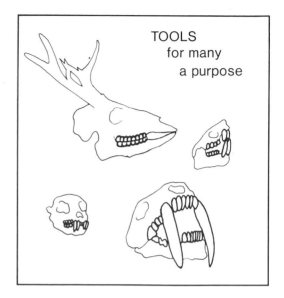

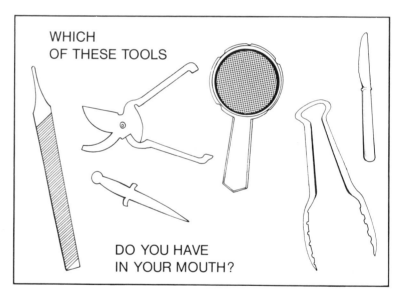

Figure 9.1 Two panels from an experimental exhibition on mammalian skulls. After Wittlin (1971).

the visitor by using questions that are trivial or too obvious.

Providing feedback

Communication between exhibit and visitor is an ongoing process involving action and reaction, although the 'reaction' of the exhibit is somewhat limited, except when it is an interactive device. Visitors should be allowed to check their understanding. Therefore, it is desirable to provide feedback in the exhibit because, if you are not there to answer questions, visitors may wonder if they understand you properly. When they are asked to choose one alternative among several, the wrong answers should be based upon the most frequent mistakes and misunderstandings. Questions that include trivial, redundant or obviously irrelevant alternatives should be avoided. When a wrong choice is made, the exhibit should not identify the right one but should encourage the visitor to think again. The

Figure 9.2 Models at increasing levels of abstraction.

feedback should be immediate, so that the visitor does not lose interest, and it should be concealed until the visitor has responded to the question or problem. If visitors are likely to see the answer before the question, or the solution to a problem too soon, it is probably better to give no feedback at all, although displays can be designed to limit the chance of this happening.

The range of choice

Objects

The fundamental importance of real things, or realia as they are sometimes called, has been noted in Chapter 1. This section looks at them, and at other forms of three-dimensional objects that are used in exhibitions, from a different viewpoint.

Models solve the problem of showing things in three dimensions, which in their original form are too small, too large or impossible to use for other reasons. They include everything from mounted

animal specimens to replicas (Fig. 9.2) and can be faithful representations, stylised reproductions (e.g. a generalised cell) or abstract constructions (e.g. a molecular structure). Models can be a highly flexible form of representation, because they concentrate the attention on features that are relevant to the purpose of the display and eliminate irrelevant detail that might distract the

Figure 9.3 Working model in the Science Museum, London in 1981.

Figure 9.4 Generalised cell model in the 'Hall of human biology', British Museum (Natural History), 1981.

viewer's attention. They can be used to show internal relationships, spatial relationships, texture, shape, and so on. For example, a working model of a steam engine can be used to demonstrate principles that would be hidden if the real thing were used (Fig. 9.3); a model of a molecular structure to show relationships that would be incomprehensible to the layman in a photograph; a scale model of a Saxon village to exhibit both the form of the buildings and their relationship to one another.

All scale models should be accompanied by something that indicates the true scale. In the case of a model of a Saxon village this might be a human figure, or for a human cell a pin-head. Models do appear to be popular and their ability to attract might be a useful way of drawing people towards a subject. However, a model will only be effective if visitors are told what to look for (Fig. 9.4). In the absence of this information, attention can become fixed on one thing and important features may be overlooked.

Mounted animals can be very close to the 'real thing'. Nevertheless, the specimens have to be modelled and this permits considerable room for interpretation by the taxidermist (Fig. 9.5). Thus a pose can be set up to make a particular teaching point about behaviour, or to emphasise a particular feature, such as wing span.

Dioramas originally consisted of back-lit illustrations. Later, in order to enhance the effect of reality, objects were placed in front of the pictures (Fig. 9.5). We shall expand the use of the term here to include both habitat groups and period rooms. Such exhibits are usually expensive to set up, though in the form of habitat groups they are one of the glories of traditional natural history museums. Their educational effectiveness has been questioned, particularly now that alternative media such as film and videotape are available. The advantages of dioramas are that they can present three-dimensional objects in a chosen context, and they can combine events that might not occur at the same time in the real world, e.g. the events in a series of food chains as shown in the exhibit in Figure 9.5.

Replicas can be defined as models in which no details have been suppressed: in other words, exact models. They are used where 'real things' are not available, or where they are too fragile or too valuable to be displayed. Two problems occur with the use of replicas. First, there is the problem of accuracy. How close to the original should a replica be to avoid misrepresentation? Secondly, there is the problem of display. Care should be taken not to imply that a replica is the original object, e.g. by introducing plinths or glass cases. Visitors do not seem to mind replicas in the right context, but they might object if the replicas were invested with greater value than is justified.

Replicas are excellent where the message to be communicated involves tactile instruction or discovery. One such problem faced us in developing an exhibition in the British Museum (Natural History) on 'Man's place in evolution'. We wished visitors to identify a small dent on the back of a fossil skull, of which only three pieces were available and these were too valuable to be put on open display. Further, in a display case the small dent would not have been visible. A

Figure 9.5 Diorama illustrating oak woodland – marine food chains in the 'Introducing ecology' exhibition, British Museum (Natural History), 1978.

reconstruction was necessary to show the original pieces in the context of the complete skull. This was cast in plastic and mounted on a swivel joint so that visitors can now manipulate the skull and identify the dent (Fig. 9.6).

Although replicas have many uses, there will be occasions when their use would be almost unthinkable. Given a choice between exhibiting a replica, and exhibiting the 'real thing', few museums would be happy to opt for the former.

Audio-visuals

In the audio-visual mode, strictly speaking, two media are used – sound and vision – as is normally the case with slide-tape programmes, films, videotapes and videodiscs. However, many of the following remarks relate to one or other of the two media when used alone. There are a number of aspects to consider. Furthermore much of what is said later in this chapter about typescript applies to spoken commentaries in audio-visuals.

Acceptability. Audio-visuals are often regarded as gimmicks or a passing fad. They are often seen as a threat to the display of real things and there is a commonly held belief that they are mechanically unreliable. They are indeed gimmicks if not used appropriately, i.e. to enhance the visitor's experience, and they are unreliable if the resources to maintain them are not made available.

Appropriateness. Audio-visuals are very attractive and can, in the right conditions, hold the visitor's attention. They are very good for movement, real events, things that for geographical, historical or practical reasons cannot be shown, and change over time. A moving camera can make spatial and three-dimensional form clear, and cope with both very large and very small things. Sound can be used to illustrate real events and to create an atmosphere reflecting the subject-matter of an exhibition. Nevertheless, exhibitions are places where people can choose what they want to see and when they want to see it; they are free to linger over things that interest them and skip those that do not. Unlike interactive videodiscs, which are considered elsewhere in this chapter, audio-visuals do not normally allow this.

Effectiveness. There is no evidence to suggest that

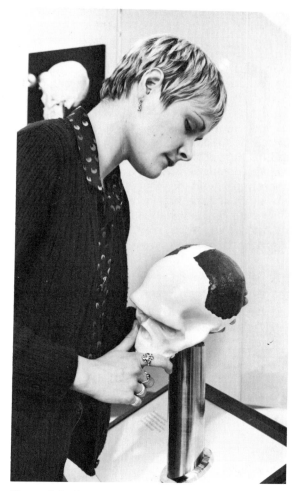

Figure 9.6 Reconstructed fossil skull in the 'Man's place in evolution' exhibition, British Museum (Natural History), 1980.

audio-visuals facilitate learning more than other media. There are, however, special difficulties in producing good educational examples for use in exhibitions. The production of audio-visuals often gets out of hand. For example, a film might be commissioned showing the life and habitat of an animal. The producer will, of course, wish to make a good film in his terms and the beauty of the photography may become an end in itself. In these circumstances it is very easy to forget why the film was wanted in the first place, and the commentary may well get written around the images to be shown. Once questions are asked about the programme the answers often prove inadequate and quite arbitrary. The film may well be attractive and entertaining, but what will it add to the communication? Exhibit developers must keep professional control over the content of audio-visuals – they must not relinquish it to an independent producer. The visual images in an educational audio-visual are a means of emphasising the messages, not an end in themselves.

Resources. Audio-visuals are expensive to produce and install, and difficult to revise and update. If they are to succeed, they must say what you want, and the equipment *and* the programme must be regularly maintained. Audio-visuals should be used with great care and only specified where they are likely to answer real needs. Resources must be available to do the job well, for a poorly produced audio-visual may be less effective than a well produced graphic.

Thus there are many points to bear in mind when developing audio-visual presentations.

(a) Be clear what you want to say and be clear about your **target audience**. Ensure that the commentary (content and style) matches the message and the target audience.

(b) Analyse your educational objectives and content into a series of small steps and describe them in the form of a story-board with preliminary ideas for text.

(c) Ensure that your target audience can understand graphic devices such as charts and diagrams, particularly if these are to change through movement or **dissolves**.

(d) Integrate your audio-visuals into the exhibition so that they have a better chance of communicating their message. They should be introduced in earlier displays and built upon by later ones.

(e) Make the content interactive by asking questions and directing the visitor's attention to the images and parts of images that matter. Do not waste time describing what the visitor can see for himself.

(f) Use music and sound to reinforce the points being made, not just to make a dull film or narrative more dramatic or interesting.

(g) Make sure that the quality of the images and sound is high. Poor images and sound will distract the visitor.

(h) Do not let sequences run on too long. Try to break the programme down into manageable sections.

(i) Arrange film shots to elicit the maximum relevant information. For example, show a manual skill from the operator's viewpoint.

(j) Remember that children have difficulty understanding techniques such as 'flash-backs' and symbolic representations.

(k) Present ideas at a pace that will suit your target audience.

(l) Avoid long presentations (more than 10 minutes) if possible. There is a limit to the amount of time visitors will spend watching an audio-visual and a limit to the amount they can take in from a paced presentation.

(m) Avoid short presentations (less than three minutes) if possible. There is a limit to how much can be done to make use of the medium in a short time.

(n) With slides, use dissolve sequences. These hold attention and avoid the blanks that occur between slides on a single projector.

(o) Avoid unfamiliar viewpoints and words, which distract visitors from the sequences following them. Allow time for consideration.

(p) Always relate diagrammatic or close-up shots to familiar images. When showing moving pictures of unfamiliar objects, make clear whether it is the camera or the object that is moving.

(q) Retain the same viewing position when changing from normal images or speeds to animation or slow-motion shots.

(r) When using artificial speeds, indicate that you are doing so by including an appropriate clock or similar device. This will ensure that visitors do not think this is the speed at which something actually happened. When using photomicrographs always show the scale.

(s) Leave captions on the screen long enough for them to be read; with stop-frame techniques leave the image on the screen long enough for the point to be grasped.

(t) Ensure that copyrights have been checked for images *and* sound when using existing material.

Audio-visuals should be carefully housed within the exhibition and the following points considered:

(a) the housing should be a self-contained, sound-proofed booth to avoid interfering with other exhibits;

(b)   seats should be provided to encourage visitors to stay for the full programme;

(c)   presentations should be visitor-activated (by press-buttons or automatic sensors);

(d)   a light-up panel linked to the presentation should tell the visitor about to enter the booth what the programme is about, how long it is, what point the programme has reached (if it has already started) and how long the interval is between shows, some of the information should also be provided permanently inside the booth and there should be a clock to tell the viewer how much of the programme is completed;

(e)   a summary panel should be provided carrying the same basic points as the audio-visual, so that visitors unable or unwilling to follow the programme have access to the information;

(f)   people should be told if the audio-visual has broken down, or if there is a delay before the programme starts;

(g)   back projection should be used rather than front projection for slide-sound because:

  (i)   the equipment is more accessible for maintenance and out of the way of visitors;
  (ii) the visitors cannot get in the way of the beam;
  (iii) the presentation can tolerate a higher ambient light level;
  (iv) the equipment and the noise it makes are less apparent;
  (v)   it is easier to disguise distortions in the projected image.

(e)   Is the content logical and well organised?

(f)   Are the important ideas appropriately emphasised? Are unimportant ones given too much emphasis?

(g)   Does it present too much in the time? Are new facts and terminology introduced and explained at the appropriate point?

(h)   Are the pictorial presentation and commentary appropriate for the target audience?

(i)   Is the film clear and the sound-track audible and free from interference?

(j)   Is the commentary properly integrated with the visuals?

(k)   Is the content up to date and technically accurate?

(l)   Is the content sufficiently specific?

(m) Can it be edited?

(n)   Can it be copied?

(o)   How much does it cost?

(p)   Are there copyright problems, especially if the exhibition has an accompanying publication?

A problem faced by exhibit developers who cannot have programmes made to measure is that of selecting off-the-shelf presentations. Ready-made audio-visuals are often not explicit in their objectives. Their suitability should be carefully examined. Questions to be asked include the following:

(a)   Is the subject-matter appropriate for the exhibit?

(b)   Are the objectives clear? Do they relate to those of the exhibition?

(c)   Will the target audience find it interesting?

(d)   Does it build on the audience's existing knowledge or on knowledge given in the previous sections of the exhibition?

Figure 9.7   Different ways of representing a rabbit.

Graphics

The word graphics is imprecise, but it is one with which most people are familiar. It covers all the two-dimensional elements of an exhibition with the exception of prose. These are either (i) illustrations or (ii) diagrams for presenting financial and statistical data and so on, such as graphs, tables, bar charts, pie charts and pictorial charts (e.g. Isotype diagrams).

Illustrations include a wide range of representations, such as photographs, full-colour drawings, line drawings, cartoons, maps and symbols (Fig. 9.7). Like three-dimensional models, they form a continuum in the degree of abstraction, both in the way in which they depart from reality, and in the way they become more generalised as the information content is increasingly controlled by the designer.

Photographs are the most realistic form of illustration. They can be used in a wide variety of circumstances, are relatively cheap, and can show things that would not otherwise be accessible. In exhibitions they can be used to show anything from a single object to an entire environment; they can convey three dimensions and are convincing – 'photographs do not lie!' Like 'real things' they are immediate and easily understood.

There are, however, four problems associated with the use of photographs.

(a) They often include more information than is needed, e.g. a photograph of a man standing in a room will show all sorts of things that are irrelevant.

(b) They cannot convey abstract meaning, e.g. a photograph can illustrate two people struggling, but it cannot give the significance of the fight.

(c) They can give a false idea of scale because:

(i) the object is unfamiliar and the visitor will not know exactly how big it is;
(ii) the object is familiar as a general concept, e.g. a vase, but is photographed from an unusual viewpoint so that it appears larger or smaller than it really is.

(d) They can distort reality, e.g. a photograph of figures on a Greek vase may tend to flatten the figures and distort proportions originally designed for a curved surface.

The way a photograph is taken and how it is used to illustrate a particular teaching point have to be carefully considered. Photographs can be effective when used to provide a general context,

Figure 9.8 Events presented simultaneously. A page from *Nature at work,* British Museum (Natural History), 1978.

i.e. when all the detail is relevant to the point being made. People in photographs, however, can be problematic, as photojournalists have discovered. Thus:

(a) a photograph can say as much about the relationship between the photographer and the subject as about the point being illustrated;
(b) an unposed photograph can show complex relationships between people in a way that is open to different interpretations, depending on the viewer's own background;
(c) people's facial expressions do not always represent what they feel and may therefore be misleading.

Photographs should always be captioned to make their purpose explicit. Colour photographs only rarely match the real thing in hue, and it is best to avoid combining photographs of objects with the objects themselves. It is also difficult to match a colour transparency with a colour print of the same object. Colour prints mounted on 'jazzy' black and white backgrounds are difficult to see, and this form of presentation should be avoided.

Other illustrative forms suffer from these same problems the closer they get to photographic reality. However, they are important as teaching aids in that we can encode only what is necessary for the teaching point and make images of 'things' that may not occur, or not occur together, in the real world (Fig. 9.8).

When specifying large illustrations, remember that illustrators may have difficulty in scaling up. The designer should supply detailed references to ensure that the final product is accurate, as small illustrations do not enlarge well. The type of illustration must match the way it is to be displayed, e.g. an illustration suitable for front-lighting may be unsuitable for back-lighting. Back-lit illustrations need to be strong and bold, with dense colour to ensure they do not look washed out.

The following points refer to illustrations in general:

(a) illustrations of things (especially line drawings) appear to be remembered more readily than their names, but captions aid subsequent recall;

(b) comprehension can be reduced both by oversimplification and by excessive detail;
(c) illustrations of a process involving a number of separate steps or actions should have at least the same number of individual pictures or frames;
(d) educational background is more important than age in comprehending illustrations, especially those dealing with abstract or unfamiliar matters;
(e) illustrations should be integrated with the text to maximise attention, rather than separated and linked by a key.

Pictorial symbols are useful for signposting as well as for making teaching points. One of their useful features is that they can be colour coded. They are only really successful when they are self-explanatory, so check that they are familiar to visitors and, if not, explain what they represent. Keep them as realistic as possible, especially for children, who have difficulty in understanding their meaning. Symbols provide a simple way of saying things that have to be repeated from time to time; each referent should have its own unchanging symbol and different referents should be given distinctive symbols.

Simlinger (1980) makes the following points:

(a) Only invent a new symbol when there is no alternative, and wherever possible use one that is already accepted internationally.
(b) Solid forms are generally to be preferred – psychologists agree that boundary contrast is more effective than line contrast; outline forms, however, should be used to represent objects or elements of glass, paper or other translucent materials.
(c) Directional characteristics should be avoided where they might conflict with directional motifs (such as arrows) in graphics (Fig. 9.9).
(d) Symbols should be designed so that they can be scaled down, or enlarged.
(e) A symbol should be considered in the light of possible future uses.
(f) Elements dependent on fashion or on foreseeable technical change should be avoided.

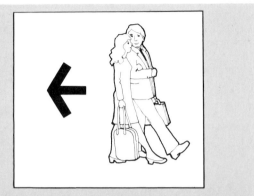

Figure 9.9 Arrows and directional characteristics in conflict.

(g) The design and scale of a symbol should be related to that of other symbols being used.
(h) Symbols should always be evaluated in their final context.

Diagrams, i.e. line drawings, are much used to present numerical data, of which there are two main sorts, (i) basic data and (ii) general trends and comparisons. Basic data will rarely be needed in exhibitions, so it will be sufficient to note that they are generally best presented in tabular form. For the second function, of presenting trends and comparisons, there are several familiar devices, some better than others. For instance, many visitors are put off by line graphs because they *seem* to be difficult to understand. And it is true they are often badly done. Therefore it is better, if possible, to use bar charts, because they are more easily read. Research also suggests that horizontal bars are better than vertical ones. The position with segmented bar charts and pie diagrams is less clear cut, but these are perhaps best avoided with a general audience. The more obscure methods such as segmented graphs (which use one curve as the base of another), which are often mis-interpreted, should not be used at all, nor should three-dimensional forms (which use volume to represent quantity). All diagrams should be accompanied by a verbal explanation of the data and their significance.

Pictorial charts are less abstract than the devices discussed above, and therefore are more appealing to many visitors. Isotype charts (Ch. 1) are particularly effective, though far more difficult to do well than appears at first sight (Fig. 9.10). The main principles of the Isotype system are:

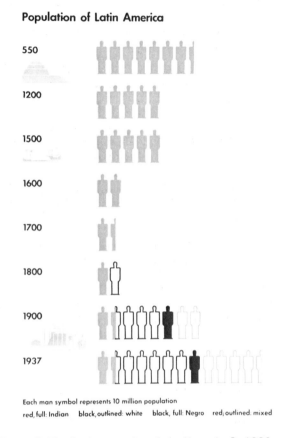

Population of Latin America

Each man symbol represents 10 million population
red, full: Indian   black, outlined: white   black, full: Negro   red; outlined: mixed

Figure 9.10 An Isotype chart from Neurath, O. 1939. *Modern man in the making.*

(a) the subject-matter is represented by standard iconic signs;
(b) each sign stands for a given quantity;
(c) larger quantities are shown by using more signs (not larger signs);
(d) the signs are arranged to make a 'visual argument'.

Graphics embodying movement. We refer here to back-lit graphics in the automaton mode. An example is the use of polaroid filters to suggest movement such as the flow of gas (Fig. 9.11). Such graphics have, in general, few of the advantages of film and most of the disadvantages – in particular, that of pace.

Flip panels. These work on the same principle as flip charts and are better when operated by the visitor than when they function automatically. A similar device is a hinged flap, which the visitor

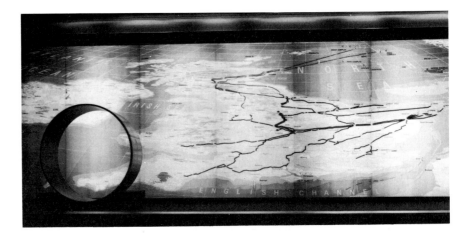

Figure 9.11 United Kingdom gas transmission system in June 1976, Science Museum, London, 1981.

can lift, used to obscure answers to questions, further information and so on (Fig. 9.12). Screven (1986) has done much to develop this medium, and finds it a simple, inexpensive way to capture the visitor's attention. Sliding panels can be used as a slightly more elaborate alternative.

Colour graphics. Colour represents an important element of the graphic medium and can be used in three ways:

(a) to represent the real colour of things;
(b) as decoration;
(c) functionally.

The last of these is the most important and the following should be borne in mind:

(a) Colour can be used to differentiate alternatives; difficulties will arise when there are (i) too many colours or (ii) too few (e.g. two colours to denote more than two functions).
(b) Research suggests a positive correlation between preference for coloured images and age, education and intelligence.
(c) Colour can assist discrimination.
(d) Where colour is used to encode information it should be used consistently.
(e) 8.5 per cent of males and 0.5 per cent of females are to some extent colour blind.
(f) A pale colour, visible in large areas, might be invisible in print or in fine lines.
(g) A dark colour will appear almost black when used in print or in fine lines.
(h) Bright colours can dazzle when used in print or in fine lines.

Figure 9.12 A flip panel in the 'Hall of human biology', British Museum (Natural History), 1986.

Typescript

Printed text is a multipurpose medium essential to any exhibition, and is used both alone and in conjunction with every other medium. Its importance cannot be over-emphasised. It may be used:

(a) to inform, to give a clear presentation of the facts;
(b) to instruct, to tell visitors how to operate an exhibit;

(c) to explain, to describe why something is like it is;

(d) to persuade, to encourage visitors to take a point of view;

(e) to entertain, to make a visit enjoyable.

Failure to integrate text with the rest of the display throughout the design process can lead to all kinds of problems. Text should not be an afterthought, although it is often treated as such – something to be *applied* once an exhibit has been designed. When this happens, it often transpires that the amount of text needed was under-estimated at the outset, and later proves difficult to fit in. Hence the preponderance, in many exhibitions, of panels of text unrelated to other exhibits. If the text is written last, the objects already chosen to illustrate a point may not, after all, turn out to be the best for that purpose – the emphasis can change during the course of the work and irrelevancies can creep in, which only serve to confuse the visitor.

The printed word must be considered as part of the design and developed alongside all the rest of it. The relationship of text to the remainder is functional, not just aesthetic. Text and the other components of the display must work together, each making its full contribution to the process of communication, and each making it easier for the other to fulfil its role (Fig. 9.13). Not only does this working together make the communication more effective, it can also stimulate ideas about the ways in which things might be displayed (Fig. 9.14).

The position of text is important. Exhibitions are not books; visitors are usually moving around, and text is competing with all the other things on display. There can be no guarantee that it will be read. It is necessary, therefore, to pay careful attention to the physical location of text, and to the need for recapitulation and cross-reference. Visitors should always be able to find information where they want it and it should make clear where they are to go next. The implication is that text should be closely related to the activities of the visitor, e.g. instructions should be placed next to press-buttons.

Figure 9.14 Text influencing the way in which things may be displayed. From 'Origin of species', British Museum (Natural History), 1981.

The designer should not try to overcome design problems by using text – this never works. Rather, an idea should be relinquished if it requires too many words of explanation. What kind of text, then, should be written for an exhibition? Text must always be written with the real audience in mind. It cannot be assumed that text suitable for colleagues, e.g. other exhibit designers, will be suitable for visitors, who will themselves vary in their knowledge and reading ability. Clearly the vocabulary and previous knowledge of the target audience will play a large part, but everyone – no matter what his experience and ability – is more likely to pay attention to text that is easy to read, lively, clear and correct.

Figure 9.13 Integrated design.

Some dinosaurs have hips like this . . .

A checklist of points includes:

(a) Is it straightforward? – visitors should not have to struggle through long or complex sentences containing many ideas.
(b) Is it active? – text written in the form of an academic report is very dull.
(c) Is it positive? – it is easier to understand what *is* than what *is not*.
(d) Is it familiar? – use everyday language, avoid unnecessary terminology.
(e) Is it relevant? – few visitors are likely to read texts containing a lot of irrelevant detail.
(f) Is it accurate? – generalising for the benefit of the non-specialist can lead to inaccuracies.
(g) Is it ambiguous? – check that the text means what you intended.
(h) Is it interesting? – questions used as headings or humour give variety to text.

Finally, when writing text, it is useful to ask yourself the following questions:

(a) What do I want to communicate?
(b) How much of this is likely to be in the form of words?
(c) Who am I saying it to?
(d) Where will they read it?
(e) What is the best way of saying it?
(f) What is the best way of presenting the text?

Basically the same typographic rules apply as in book design, though perhaps less rigidly. Most exhibitions use one of four ways to produce type-script: photography, **silk-screen printing**, hot metal and dry transfer lettering. Some of these require no **artwork**; photography and silk-screen printing do. The two main criteria of choice are normally the resources available and the amount of maintenance required, e.g. in exposed positions, silk-screen printing might be a better choice than dry transfer lettering. Other things to bear in mind when choosing include:

(a) What typefaces are available?
(b) Is the range of sizes and weights sufficient?
(c) Are all the required signs and symbols included?
(d) Is the type design suited to the method of reproduction?

And remember:

(a) Black on white is highly legible, white on black less so, black on a colour worse, and colour on a colour worst of all.
(b) A combination of upper and lower case letters is more legible than upper or lower case letters on their own.
(c) Text becomes less legible the more the line of sight diverges from the perpendicular.
(d) The surface of the display and the way it is lit affect legibility, e.g. glossy surfaces and inks glare when spotlit.
(e) Text printed on a broken ground (e.g. a photograph) or on a transparent surface (e.g. glass) is less legible than when the ground is solid.
(f) Individual factors may not be a problem but in combination can cause illegibility.

There are also a number of things to avoid.

(a) Typefaces with an unusual character that may reduce legibility when used in a display.
(b) Typefaces that are likely to break down in production, e.g. those with fine lines that disappear in silk-screen work.
(c) Typefaces with small internal spaces, which are likely to fill with ink.
(d) Typefaces with strong contrasts between thick and thin strokes, which are likely to set up an optical movement on a white surface.
(e) Letters that are so close together that they blend when printed.

Striped skunk
Mephitis mephitis

These skunks eat mice, eggs, berries and the bodies of dead animals, and also benefit man by eating harmful insects. They are still hunted and trapped for their fur. They live in burrows under rocks, logs, and abandoned

Figure 9.15 The use of bold and italic type.

Bold type emphasises, and italics are useful for unfamiliar or previously unused terms, or for other special purposes such as the Latin names of animals and plants. To avoid changing the character of the text, all fonts should be of the same design (Fig. 9.15). If the reason for a typographic change is not obvious, visitors, especially children, should be told why the change has been made.

Television

Graphics and typescript for television presentation present additional problems, some of which can be avoided by following some simple guidelines:

(a) Use single-column layouts of text (the possible line length of 40 characters available on the screen is already less than the ideal of 50–60 characters preferred in print).
(b) Keep within the central 'safe area' on the screen to avoid cutting off the edges of the picture.
(c) Avoid large blocks of solid text, but beware of disjointed text; paragraphs of three to six lines of text are best; separate them with a break.
(d) Range text left as it is easier to read than when centred.
(e) Integrate images with the text.
(f) Keep graphic techniques simple.
(g) Keep the lines in graphics horizontal or vertical as diagonals tend to be disjointed; bar charts are particularly suitable.
(h) Use solid colour in the design of maps, and ensure that boundaries between colours are well defined.
(i) Compensate for poor definition by using large type, and bigger spaces both between characters and between lines.
(j) Avoid serif faces, because they are often too fine.
(k) Avoid bold or condensed faces as they can fill in.
(l) Make the screen 'blink' to emphasise points, but this should only be done with care.

Finally, in using colour for text and graphics on screens, it should be noted that green is probably the best colour for large areas, followed by white, yellow and dark blue (cyan). Strong colours such as reds and oranges, which tend to bleed into the screen, should be avoided. And not more than three colours should be on the screen at one time.

Interactive exhibits

A visitor is more likely to learn from an exhibit that involves him in physical activity than from one that limits him to looking at objects and reading labels. This is the fundamental reason why science museums have for some time built participatory or 'hands-on' exhibits incorporating mechanical or electrical mechanisms. Unfortunately, this has led to the frequent misuse of the word 'interactive' in museums. To interact is to act reciprocally, to act on each other. Some exhibits give a simple fixed response after a simple fixed input from the visitor. A model railway engine that starts to move at the touch of a button, back-lit text which is illegible until a light is switched on, or a simple multiple-choice quiz based on push buttons and back-lit text may make an exhibit dynamic, but it is merely a machine that the visitor operates and not truly interactive at all.

On the other hand, such exhibits need to be distinguished from entirely static objects. There are many of them, displays which, at their best, are available for free exploration by the visitor in science museums and science centres, as well as simple question-and-answer quiz games. Many so-called interactive exhibits are certainly dynamic, in that they incorporate mechanical, electrical or electronic elements, but actually function in the dynamic or operand mode: such is their diversity that it is difficult to find a good name for them. 'Non-interactive mechanisms' perhaps sums them up adequately. At their worst they make no intellectual demands on the visitor and provide no feedback, so they have little educative value. All they do is require visitors to turn a handle or press a button to make something happen, e.g. so that a wheel revolves or an engine starts. The designers of such displays make all kinds of assumptions about the visitor's previous knowledge and abilities, and the failure to explain the principles involved or to build upon the experience reduces the whole thing to a trivial level or leads to serious misconceptions.

The word interactive is used in another context

Figure 9.16 Combined computer and random access slide projector exhibit in 'Introducing ecology', British Museum (Natural History), 1978.

to define a particular learning process – the induction of events in the real world that make things real to us (Ch. 3). This is the traditional way of teaching apprentices their trade: museum examples are free exploration of natural history specimens in special discovery rooms and the use of replicas or simulacra to allow the same sort of activity in exhibitions. In these situations the exhibit is static – it has no element of reciprocal behaviour. Because such exhibits are not dynamic they are excluded here from our category of interactive exhibits.

Computer-based exhibits

The only truly dynamic exhibits that can legitimately be described as operating in the interactive mode are those that vary their presentations according to the designer's perception of the responses and needs of the visitor. Examples of such exhibits based on purely mechanical or electromechanical devices are difficult to find. It is only since the advent of cheap, readily available microcomputers that it has been possible to incorporate enough flexibility to make an exhibit truly interactive. Here are three examples from the British Museum (Natural History):

(a) 'Solving a real ecological problem' (Fig. 9.16). The computer is linked to a random-access slide projector and the visitor draws on concepts dealt with in the exhibition to enact the role of the ecologist.

(b) 'How are these dinosaurs related?' (Fig. 9.17). Visitors here enact the role of the scientist solving this problem. The computer programme is linked to a spoken commentary to guide visitors' observations and

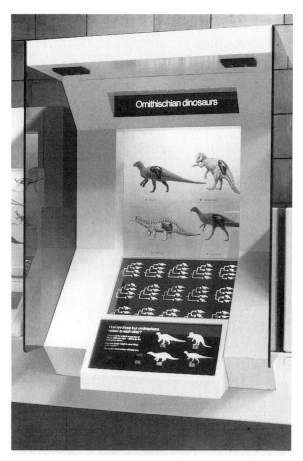

Figure 9.17 Computer-controlled commentary and back-lit diagrams in 'Dinosaurs and their living relatives', British Museum (Natural History), 1979.

elicit their responses.

(c) 'Impostors!' (Fig. 9.18). This exhibit teaches some basic human genetics by analogy with Martians (who suffer fewer exceptions to genetic rules than humans!). Our approach is based on research done by Malone (1981) on what makes a computer game successful. Thus the programme has an element of fantasy, uses computer graphics, colour and sound, and incorporates a definite target for visitors to work towards (Table 9.1).

All these exhibits operate in the *tutorial* mode. They are based on the provision of information and the asking of questions. They model the behaviour of a teacher, but they deal with systems whose parameters are controlled by the designer not the visitor. Where the converse obtains, the exhibit operates in the *simulation* mode.

As an example of an exhibit using the simulation mode we may cite 'Staying alive' (Fig. 9.19). The programme here models the process of homeostasis (in which internal conditions are maintained constant in a changing environment),

Table 9.1 Checklist for enjoyable computer exhibits

Challenge
(a) Goal
   (i) Does the activity have a clear goal?
   (ii) Is the goal relevant for the visitor?
(b) Uncertain outcome
   (i) Does the programme have a variable difficulty level?
   (ii) Does the activity have multiple goal levels?
   (iii) Does the programme reveal hidden information selectively?

Fantasy
   (i) Does the programme include an appealing fantasy?
   (ii) Is the fantasy related to the learning tasks?
   (iii) Does the fantasy provide a useful analogy?

Curiosity
(a) Sensory curiosity
   Are audio and visual effects used
   (i) to enhance fantasy?
   (ii) as a reward?
   (iii) as a representation system?
(b) Cognitive curiosity
   (i) Does the programme include surprises?
   (ii) Does the programme include feedback?

Figure 9.19 A simulation programme, 'Staying alive', in the 'Hall of human biology', British Museum (Natural History), 1982.

Figure 9.18 'Impostors' computer exhibit in the 'Hall of human biology', British Museum (Natural History), 1983.

and the visitor plays the role of the human brain, monitoring and adjusting certain key physiological processes while the body is walking, running, sprinting and so on. However, there are problems in using simulations. People, perhaps corrupted by school, tend to want to be told what to do, and to be told when they have got the one, approved right answer. And this is alien to the simulation approach.

Whatever the mode, one major difficulty is that most real-life systems are extremely complicated and, therefore, modelling them in a computer programme is far from easy. If variety is reduced by over-simplifying the model, realism may be lost. If too much detail is included, the programme may be too big to run on a microcomputer. Apart from this, few people are able to bring systems under control when they have to cope with more than two or three variables simultaneously.

Computer-based exhibits are undoubtedly popular. It is helpful therefore to provide two or three consoles for each programme, and to restrict the length of programmes to 5–10 minutes. However, interaction is not limited to individuals operating the console, and often discussion takes place among a group before the decision is taken to press a particular button, for example. When designing consoles a trade-off has to be made between the demands of group use, say five or six people, and the need to isolate them from the noise and distraction of other exhibits.

The remarks made above about television graphics and typescript apply to most computer-based exhibits, but computers are not, of course, limited to giving their output via television screens. An ecology exhibit, which uses a random-access slide projector to superimpose images on television text, has already been mentioned (Fig. 9.16). Other examples are the use of **LEDs** to form curves on a graph (Fig. 9.20) and taped commentaries, which are controlled from the programme (Fig. 9.17).

Videodiscs

The development of videodisc technology has added a new and exciting dimension to dynamic exhibits of all kinds, and in particular has opened the door to extreme sophistication in interaction, notably when videodiscs are used in conjunction with computers. However, videodiscs, like other powerful pieces of hardware, have their disadvantages: they are expensive to produce and therefore to amend, which means that it is only worth developing a videodisc-based exhibit if it is one for which the medium is both appropriate to the learning objectives and exploited to the full.

The unique characteristic of the medium is that it combines the attributes of its two precursors – videotape and data storage discs (the latter being themselves developed from audio tape), the most significant step in the whole process being perhaps the change from analogue to digital recording.

For any kind of recording, be it audio or video, discs have the great advantage over tape of what is conventionally called random access, though this is something of a misnomer because there is nothing haphazard about the process of getting at the information on a disc. To find a particular piece of information on a tape you must work along the tape to the appropriate spot, which takes a long time. The corresponding operation on a disc involves moving radially across the disc while it is spinning rapidly, which is many times quicker. Think what it would be like if, every time you wanted to look up a word in the *Oxford English Dictionary*, or to find something out from the *Encyclopaedia Britannica*, you had to read the book from the beginning! It is hardly surprising that discs have almost completely ousted tapes as data files for computers.

For some years data have been recorded and read from computer discs via a head that is extremely close to the disc. It needs to be close to pick up a strong enough signal, which calls for great precision when manufacturing discs and heads. A comparatively recent development, that of laser technology, has brought with it two advantages. It is no longer necessary to have an infinitesimal gap between disc and read–write head, and once the information has been put on the disc it can be given a durable protective coating, which keeps the information intact. The record is then permanent, which is fine for some applications, e.g. recording music, but a dis-

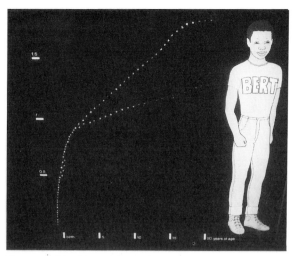

Figure 9.20 Use of LEDs (light emitting diodes) in an exhibit from the 'Hall of human biology', British Museum (Natural History), 1983.

advantage when a file of information needs to be amended or brought up to date.

One of the impressive features of videodisc technology is the vast amount of information that can be compressed into a small space. The entire *Encyclopaedia Britannica*, 43 million words and 30 thousand illustrations, could be recorded on a single 12-inch disc. More relevantly, 'Treasures of the earth' in London's Geological Museum has 16 videodiscs on important minerals. These each store encyclopaedic amounts of information and operate in the interactive tutorial mode. However, care needs to be exercised when utilising the enormous information storage capacity that videodiscs provide, because most visitors are not prepared to take more than one or two steps to arrive at the information they want.

The software required for a videodisc-computer exhibit should be thought about carefully before deciding to go ahead with developing the exhibit, just as it should with any other type of computer-based display. It is very expensive, like all bespoke software, but there is usually little prospect of covering the development cost by selling a great number of copies – the usual solution in the computer industry, hence the widespread use of 'packages' with all their disadvantages. The expense of design and manufacture thus tends to limit the use of videodiscs to the lower levels of sophistication, such as the straightforward transfer of videotape programmes (which fails to exploit the 'random-

Figure 9.22 Participatory exhibit in the 'Hall of human biology', British Museum (Natural History), 1977.

access' capability of discs) or to exhibits in which all the visitor can do is to select and play a particular segment of the disc (which exploits the 'random-access' capability but may lead the visitor to abandon his interaction with the exhibit in mid-stream because, as noted above, he is impatient with the number of steps he has to take to reach the information he is seeking).

Helping the user

The incorporation of keyboards, press-buttons, levers, dials, and so on, in displays poses problems because it is human nature to want to work them before reading the associated text. Large colourful press-buttons and levers do a good job in varying the form of exhibits, but their function is so obvious that any explanation is likely to be ignored. Touch-sensitive plates are less obtrusive and it seems that visitors are more likely to notice them *after* reading the instructions (Fig. 9.21).

Unfamiliar hands-on devices can be intimidating, and so it helps to tell the visitor what the exhibit does and how it is likely to respond. Some machines do not appear at first sight to have any logical connection with the subject of the exhibition (Fig. 9.22), so it is important to ensure that the visitor knows why he is playing the game or using the machine. Visitors come with their own ideas of how things operate. The designer should try not to confound these expectations, for example, with levers that when pulled back or pushed forward move parts of the display sideways. Such designs can only confuse and distract from the point being made.

Exhibit developers commonly forget the perceptual and physical limits of the human body. Things should not be placed too high or too low, as physical effort distracts and reduces concentration. Instructions should not be placed so they become obscured by the visitor who is operating the machine. The visitor cannot be expected to remember instructions, so they should be available when needed, e.g. by being linked to the operating device. Further, instructions should be recognisable as such, and perhaps emphasised by a change of colour or by their position. They should not be hidden in explanatory text; finding the instructions should not be a game of hide and seek.

Displays that are in the form of a quiz should not belittle the visitor because he cannot remember what is in the exhibition; revision displays should be provided around the quiz so that at any point the visitor can refer to them.

When an operand device is first developed, the text for the instructions should be written as part of the specification (Ch. 12). But as the device is developed further, the specification is liable to change: sometimes the technology advances, or maybe the engineer gets a better idea, or then again a better method of operation may be devised, or even the intellectual content may change. Instructions must therefore be tested when the exhibit is constructed, and again when the exhibit is functioning. Its operation may be obvious to the designer, but is the same true of the visitor? The implication of this is that the instructions may need to be improved, which involves change, so all instructions must be removable and replaceable.

When writing instructions, particularly for hands-on displays, two points must be considered: (i) what should the visitor be able to do after reading the instructions, and (ii) in what order will he carry them out? Instructions must be composed to get the right results in the right order. To do this they must be expressed in the order they are to be carried out, and they must be specific. Do not ask the visitor to 'identify the red triangle' if asking him to 'identify the red triangle in the top left-hand corner' is more precise.

Instructions should be written in short, simple, direct, positive statements. Too much text will make the device seem complicated and put people off. However, if long instructions cannot be avoided, headings and subheadings should be used to break down the prose into manageable chunks. One should not be afraid to use phrases like 'How to play the game' and 'What to do next'.

For a more detailed view of what is achievable with operand dynamic exhibits at their best, the reader can do no better than study the examples in Bruman (1984) and Hipschman (1980).

Even today, people using computer-based exhibits are unlikely to have much experience of computers or even of typewriter keyboards. It is therefore wise to:

(a) arrange that any button will start the programme;
(b) use a simple, purpose-built panel with as few controls as possible;
(c) label the controls clearly and simply with short, commonplace words such as 'Yes', 'No', 'Continue', 'Help' and so on, or familiar symbols such as numbers;
(d) use single-key input, which avoids the need for a special 'Enter' key;
(e) confirm the visitor's choice on the screen (e.g. by boxing round the item), when he makes a selection from a list, so that if the wrong key is accidentally pressed he is not misled by the computer's output;
(f) generate text on the screen gradually, not all at once (unless it is already familiar), either character by character at a reading speed (10–15 characters a second) or line by line;
(g) hold completed frames on the screen until the visitor presses a 'Continue' button, so that he can proceed at his own pace;
(h) give visitors the opportunity to skip one or more frames if they so wish;
(i) incorporate a restart button to enable the visitor to go back to the beginning;
(j) automatically reset the programme after a suitable interval (30–60 seconds) and give an appropriate warning if no response is made at the end of a frame, to avoid confusing subsequent users;
(k) encourage visitors to give way at the end of a programme with, for example, 'We hope you have enjoyed (name of programme). The programme will now start again for the next visitor';
(l) limit the number of times an individual section of a programme can be repeated without going all the way back to the beginning (like (k) this discourages young visitors from unfairly monopolizing computer-based exhibits).

Postscript

So far, in Chapters 7, 8 and 9, we have concentrated on the principles of organising and designing exhibitions, and in doing so we recognise that much more could be said about some topics, particularly those concerned with the physical components of the displays. For those seeking this more detailed information there are already many publications and periodicals, notably the Museums Association *handbooks* and *information data sheets*, which cover a wide range of topics from copyright to floor-coverings. Other publications include:

Gardner and Heller (1960), Neal (1987, 1976), Lord and Lord (1983) and Hall (1987) on designing and building exhibitions; Wright (1970) on producing audio-visual materials; Rowley (1925), Grantz (1969), McFall (1975) and Metcalf (1981) on taxidermy; Browne (1896), Lanteri (1902–11), Toft (1970) and Olschki (1977) on modelmaking, and Swann (1969) and Hartley (1978) on typography and graphic design. A number of periodicals regularly include articles relevant to museums and exhibition design, e.g. *Curator* (American Museum of Natural History, New York), *Museum* (Unesco, Paris), *Museums Journal* (Museums Association, London) and *Museum News* (American Association of Museums, Washington), *The International Journal of Museum Management and Curator-ship* (Guildford, England) and *Museum Studies Journal* (San Francisco).

A final word on interactive devices, and hands-on exhibits of all types, concerns the Health and Safety at Work Etc., Act 1974. In Britain, the Act covers both employees *and* visitors to an institution. Sections 3 and 4 state that an employer must conduct himself:

with a view to protecting persons other than persons at work against risks to health and safety arising out of or in connection with the activities of persons at work.

Hence all designers should be conversant with the Act and do all they can to ensure that the legal requirements are met.

10   Disabled visitors

In developing exhibitions there is a tendency to think in terms of a relatively homogeneous audience, in the sense that visitors are expected to behave rationally, exhibit no perceptual problems bar those created by the designer, and to be physically unimpaired. However, visitors do potentially include many people that do not fit this description and, if disabled people are missing among the visitors to an exhibition, the chances are that they have been deliberately or inadvertently excluded. For example, in Britain it is estimated that some 10 per cent of people, about 5 million, are permanently disabled. As significant is the fact that 95 per cent of people are likely to suffer some form of disablement during their lifetime. Most disabled visitors want to visit exhibitions as much as anyone else and even those with the most severe disabilities are likely to get something from a visit. The fact that little attention is paid to the disabled is evident from the paucity of information in the museum literature.

The need to provide for the disabled is fully recognised in the USA where it is embodied in Section 504 of the Rehabilitation Act of 1973. The Act prohibits discrimination against any person, by reason of handicap, by any organisation receiving federal support. The Act further provides that any institution that discriminates against disabled persons shall be deprived of all federal funds.

It is not within the limitations of this book to discuss all the social and architectural implications of providing for the disabled but only those directly pertaining to the development of educational exhibits. The provision of staff and special facilities to assist the disabled is already well documented in a number of publications (Snider 1977, Kenney 1979) and is covered by the *British Standard code of practice 5810* (1979). Designing exhibitions with the disabled in mind will benefit visitors in general, and there are a number of points that have a direct bearing on exhibit development both for the provision of learning opportunities and for physical access.

Accessibility for the physically disabled

'To the disabled visitor, the greatest handicap is the museum itself. Although in recent years the purpose and function of most museums has been seen to alter, the buildings in which they are housed and the displays themselves are in many cases part of the legacy of the past, unaltered and unalterable. It seems unfortunate that through this very legacy which museums are trying to preserve, a significant percentage of the population should be denied access to, or a full appreciation of the collections, merely because they happen to suffer from some disability – the loss of a "limb or sense".' (Callow 1974)

The problems are not only those of physical access. Attitudes, particularly the feeling that special environments are needed for the physically disabled, are also harmful and likely to deny such visitors direct experience of the exhibition environment. The physically disabled have the same reading level, curiosity and interests as more able-bodied visitors. In addition, the provision of facilities for the physically disabled can also benefit others, e.g. those with heart conditions, old people, pregnant women, people with heavy parcels, parents with small children *and* museum curators carrying fragile objects or trays of specimens.

Snider (1977) has made the excellent suggestion that exhibit developers should tour their exhibitions in wheelchairs to gain insight into the problems of the wheelchair user. This might result in a reassessment of the position of furniture or in the angling of textual materials above, say, 1800 mm.

Callow (1974) has suggested that if access to the upper floors is not available to the disabled, displays indicating the scope of the exhibits and suitable literature should be available at an accessible level.

There are a number of standards for physical accessibility and usability relevant to the physically disabled (Fig. 10.1) that should be followed in developing any exhibition.

(a) Ramps should be used where level access is not possible. The location of ramps and accessways is important, disabled visitors should not be made to feel like 'back-door citizens' (Snider 1977).

The gradient of a ramp should not exceed 1:12; the optimum is about 1:20. Where the gradient is more than 1:20 there should be a level platform of 1200 mm squared at the head of the ramp; and where greater than 1:15 handrails should be provided on both sides. However, if the ramp is more than 2000 mm wide. a central handrail can be substituted. Where the edge of a ramp is exposed, e.g. alongside a stair, it should have a lip of not less than 50 mm along that edge. And if long ramps are necessary, suitably sized and appropriately located level rest areas should be provided.

(b) Steps are sometimes unavoidable. Where included in addition to ramps, 'treads' should not be less than 280 mm, 'risers' should not exceed 150 mm. The vertical rise of a flight of steps should not exceed 1200 mm and handrails should be provided at both sides or in the centre if the stair is wide enough. The top and bottom steps should be clearly indicated.

(c) Changes in level should always be signalled either by a contrast in colour or by texture.

(d) Entrances should be level. If mats are used,

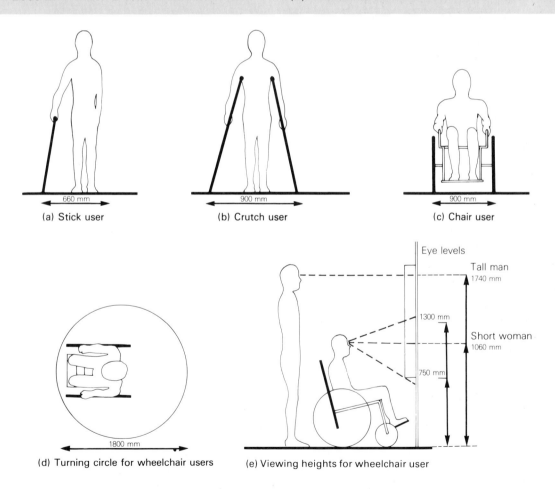

(a) Stick user (b) Crutch user (c) Chair user

(d) Turning circle for wheelchair users (e) Viewing heights for wheelchair user

Figure 10.1 Ergonomic standards for the physically disabled.

they should be recessed and of short pile so they do not inhibit movement of a wheel-chair.

(e) Doorways should never be less than 775 mm wide and passageways should be a minimum of 1200 mm wide but only over short distances because an independent wheelchair user might require up to 1800 mm to turn around.

(f) Surfaces should be level and smooth to the extent that they should not inhibit the movement or turning of wheelchairs. Carpets should be of a close, short, non-directional pile. Finishes, particularly on ramps and handrails, should be non-slip.

(g) The design of lifts to accommodate the physically disabled is covered by many standard publications; however, it may happen that lift access exists within the exhibition space, in which case a clear area of at least 1500 mm squared should be allowed in front of the lift doors.

(h) Rest areas should be provided.

Accessibility for the blind and the partially sighted

For the blind and partially sighted, accessibility has little to do with the removal of physical barriers except where they overhang or protrude from structures above floor level. Apart from indicating changes in level, an exhibition that is safe for the ordinary visitor will be safe for a blind person. The problem is rather one of accessibility to the educational opportunities provided, which will be non-existent if the sole means of presentation is visual. This does not mean that all exhibits should be touchable or audible, but it suggests that greater efforts should be made to provide some alternatives, e.g. braille captions, cassettes, low-relief diagrams, replicas and, for the partially sighted, reasonably large typesizes in textual materials. There already exists a vacuum-forming device that produces plastic braille captions and low-relief diagrams (Snider 1977).

It should not be assumed that all blind people are touch oriented. The age that a person became blind will make a considerable difference. Those blind from birth will have learnt to use touch as an alternative to visual perception; those blind through illness or accident tend to rely more on memory (Kenney 1979). One cannot rely on the blind or partially sighted being any more gentle with the objects they touch than any other visitors.

Accessibility for the deaf

Providing access for the deaf is easier because most exhibits are based on visual presentation. The problem then is to ensure that any audible information is also available in a visual form, either as subtitles in audio-visual presentations or in the form of supplementary graphic panels. An example from our own work in the British Museum (Natural History) concerns the comparison between chiff-chaffs and willow warblers, which look very similar (especially as mounted specimens) but have different songs. For most visitors it is sufficient to hear the two songs but, to make the point accessible to the deaf, diagrammatic representations are added. Like most disabilities deafness varies in degree. Some visitors that are hard of hearing may be quite able to hear commentaries if they are spoken clearly and are sufficiently loud.

Accessibility and the mentally disabled

This category ranges from those who are mentally ill or emotionally disturbed to those who are retarded or have learning difficulties. As visits can be in supervised groups, family groups, with normal school parties or alone, no single prescription will suffice and it is clear that within the scope of exhibit development only a limited amount of practical assistance is possible. Much of the work must be undertaken by teaching staff in the wider educational context. It may be true that some mentally disabled people would get little from a visit, but there are a great many who would learn from and enjoy visiting an exhibition. Moreover, certain misconceptions about mental handicaps could lead us to ignore the needs of those visitors who, through their disability, suffer more than their fair share of harrowing experiences.

One popular misconception concerning those who have difficulty with coordination is that a person who cannot speak intelligibly does not understand what is being said. Frequently, however, there is some physiological damage that interferes with speech but that does not impair the person's understanding.

> The belief that a mentally retarded person cannot learn has been one of the primary reasons the development of such people has been limited in the past. Recently, training techniques and philosophies have changed to take advantage of the long unrecognised learning potential most of them have. As a result, many are being helped to develop their fullest potential. (Beechel 1974)

Kenney (1979) suggests that concrete experiences of the kind found in exhibitions are valuable to mentally disabled people, particularly when related to everyday life through familiar activities.

Emotionally disturbed visitors are likely to be withdrawn, inattentive and easily distracted, while those with auditory or perceptual handicaps will see things in a very different way from most ordinary visitors, e.g. they may lack depth perception or find it impossible to put things together in sequence. Participation would seem an effective form of communication with these people when combined with demonstrations. Presentations should be short and simple and repeat key ideas and words preferably by relating them to familiar things.

Conclusions

Snider (1979) has offered a number of guidelines for establishing programmes for disabled visitors from which the following are derived.

(a) Disabled people wish to be integrated into existing educational programmes. They want to enjoy exhibits erected for the general public, rather than exhibits or programmes established especially for them.

(b) Disabled people possess different 'learning styles' (through the use of eyes, ears and hands) depending upon their particular disability. Exhibitions should try to incorporate all kinds of sensory experience so that visits can be enjoyed regardless of handicap.

(c) Disabled people and their teachers recognise that exhibitions can provide valuable learning experiences.

(d) Exhibition developers should contact organisations for disabled people and specialist teachers to identify the needs of the disabled and appropriate ways of helping them.

(e) The use of special exhibits is acceptable when inaccessibility precludes full participation in exhibits for the general public.

(f) Orientation is very important, particularly to the blind who have the most reason to feel insecure. Special facilities should be provided.

(g) Programmes or exhibits that are developed to include the handicapped should be advertised as such.

All of these provisions can be incorporated in an exhibition; but if the institution concerned is unwelcoming, does not provide adequate car-parking facilities or well planned toilets and so on, then all of the above is as nought.

11 Conservation

This chapter is not intended to be an exhaustive description of conservation and conservation techniques. For, although the difficulties encountered in displaying unique and valuable objects are a cause for concern, educational exhibits are directed more at achieving educational aims, and therefore alternative modes of presentation can be as appropriate as the 'real thing'.

Everything that is put on display, whether it be a valuable Greek vase or a photograph, is subject to deterioration over time by light, temperature, humidity, contamination in the air and contact by visitors. So even when specifying a photograph or model for display, it is necessary to ensure that it will survive for the time that it is needed, or at least a time commensurate with the amount of money spent on its production. Conservation in this sense includes not only preservation but also maintenance.

Undoubtedly the best review of conservation matters can be found in Garry Thomson's *The museum environment* (1978) which should be regarded as essential reading for anyone interested in preserving collections, particularly those on public display. It has an extensive list of references and is well organised, having sections for the layman and specialist. The Royal Ontario Museum's *Communicating with the museum visitor* (1976) also provides information on these matters, and a later report from the same institution (1979) discusses the problems of conservation in older buildings and the concept of microclimates for use in such environments.

Light

Of all the factors affecting things on public display, light is the most damaging, next to direct physical assault. However, because things need to be seen, it is the one problem for which there is really no effective solution. Light can only damage things it can reach, i.e. the surface of objects, given that they are usually opaque. All organic materials are at risk: animal skins, feathers, cotton, linen, silk, wood, hair, glues, and so on, but so are synthetic dyes, plastics, photographic materials and furnishings (Table 11.1). As Thomson concludes, 'Deterioration needs energy – either light or heat. Light is much more potent than heat in a museum.' Light is that form of radiant energy we can see, and whether from daylight, fluorescent or tungsten sources it can be split into a series of wavelengths. The most damaging are those with the shortest frequency, i.e. at the violet end of the spectrum. Beyond violet there is a non-visible radiation, called **ultraviolet**, which is more harmful because it causes chemical changes that lead not only to colour change but structural change as well.

There is a higher proportion of ultraviolet in daylight than in light from artificial sources such as tungsten lamps, and fluorescent lamps (with some exceptions) give more ultraviolet than tungsten. Thomson recommends that daylight and light from fluorescent sources should be filtered. Effective filters are obtainable in the form of rigid sheet, acetate and varnish, and these can be built into a display, mounted around fluorescent tubes or applied to glass.

Filtering out as much as possible of the ultraviolet and shorter rays is the most obvious way of limiting radiation damage, but the intensity of the incident light and the time the object is illuminated should be minimised. These last two factors are linked. What needs to be minimised is the amount of exposure, measured in lux hours, which is the product of the intensity

Table 11.1 Recommended illumination levels for museum exhibits.

oil and tempera paintings, undyed leather, horn, bone and ivory, oriental lacquer	150 lux
textiles, costumes, watercolours, tapestries, prints and drawings, manuscripts, miniatures, wallpapers, gouache, dyed leather and most natural history exhibits including botanical specimens, furs and feathers	50 lux

in **lux** and the time in hours – an exposure of 10 hours to 50 lux is equivalent to one of 100 hours to 5 lux (500 lux hours) and will do the same damage.

Lamps also give off heat, which is not in itself damaging but if the temperature rises sufficiently the relative humidity is affected (see below). The most likely sources of excessive heat are sunlight, over-bright spotlights and lamps inside show-cases.

Humidity and its effects

All organic materials contain a certain amount of water – man, for example, comprises some 65 per cent – and any alteration of its level is liable to cause structural change. They tend to shrink on drying and expand when moist. If too dry, materials such as wood will split or warp, paper will become brittle, and so on, whereas an excess of moisture encourages the growth of moulds and hence breakdown of the material.

Any given material behaves in a characteristic way when its moisture content changes, large objects tending to change more slowly than small ones. Objects constructed out of a variety of materials suffer particularly, because their components tend to move relative to each other.

Moisture content tends to settle at a value that depends on the state of the surrounding atmosphere, and the amount of water that a given amount of air can carry depends on its temperature. If saturated air is cooled, some of the water condenses – this is how mists form – but if it is heated, it will have the capacity to take up more moisture from objects with which it is in contact. It is the extent to which the air is saturated that affects the moisture content of organic materials in contact with it, not the actual amount of water in the air – i.e. the *relative* humidity, not the *absolute* humidity. The relative humidity at a particular temperature is the ratio of the weight of moisture actually present in a given volume of air at that temperature (the absolute humidity) to the weight that would be necessary to saturate it at the same temperature. Saturated air (100 per cent relative humidity) at 10°C contains 10 g water per m³, at 20°C 17 g and at 30°C over 30 g; air at 50 per cent relative humidity contains by definition only half these amounts.

To control the moisture content of an organic material it is necessary to control the relative humidity of the surrounding atmosphere. To keep wood at 12 per cent moisture, for instance, requires a relative humidity of 55 per cent, which is the norm recommended in Europe. A relative humidity above 70 per cent encourages the growth of mould and insect pests, whereas a relative humidity below 40 per cent causes fibres of wood, paper, leather and bone to become friable and break. Thomson (1978) has made a study of humidity problems and recommends that the relative humidity should be kept at between 65 per cent and 40 per cent.

Relative humidity can be controlled by regulating either absolute humidity or temperature or both, but compromise is often necessary. For instance, to maintain a relative humidity of 55 per cent during winter in a single-glazed building in England would entail excessive condensation on the cold windows and the danger of frost affecting the walls, so a lower value has to be accepted, but not one that is dangerously low for the objects in the building.

Air pollution

Air pollution in exhibitions results from solid particles carried in the air or from concentrations of gases. The solid particles of most concern are those that, owing to their small size, remain suspended in the air until trapped on some surface or other. Such particles can contain acidic materials derived from the sulphur dioxide given off from burning fuels. Visitors supply fragments of skin and textile fibres and act as agents by carrying contaminant particles into the exhibition. New buildings can give off harmful particles, e.g. new concrete gives off an alkaline dust that can damage silk, dyes, pigments and paintings.

The fuels burnt in buildings and vehicles produce two types of gaseous pollutant, those that are acidic and others that are oxidant. Acidic pollutants include sulphur dioxide and sulphuric acid, which is derived from sulphur dioxide, oxygen and water. The most dangerous oxidant pollutant is ozone, which is produced naturally in the atmosphere by the action of sunlight on vehicle exhaust fumes and by certain types of lamp and electrical fittings.

For a more detailed description of these pollutants and methods of overcoming them, consult Thomson (1986). All of them cause damage if present in uncontrolled amounts.

Microclimates

Creating microclimates is a means of protecting displays where wider architectural climate control is not possible, as in old buildings. The provision can vary in scale to suit anything from complete exhibitions to single display cases, though obviously the latter provide more opportunities for detailed control. To provide a microclimate for a single exhibit will require, on a smaller scale, much the same sort of equipment as that used on a full building. Most installations are concerned with relative humidity but the need to provide protection from air pollutants and ultraviolet light should also be considered.

The appropriate relative humidity can be achieved by physical means, such as sealed display cases either with or without the oxygen replaced by other gases; by the use of buffers, such as wood or silica gel which absorb and give out moisture and so ameliorate the rate of change, or by mechanical means, such as air conditioning or pressurising the cases so that any structural leaks permit air to escape but do not allow it back in.

The choice of buffers will depend very much upon the contents of the display case and the resources available. Although this method is more difficult to control and needs to be monitored, it is by far the cheapest and simplest of those available. Mechanical systems can be more reliable but are expensive to install and have to be regularly serviced.

Keeping pollutants out of the show-cases is always a problem. The ideal is a sealed show-case but this gives little or no access. Certainly with educational exhibits, this would be impractical in almost every instance. However, once access doors are incorporated they are never completely dust and air-tight, especially if the case is artificially lit. During the day, the case heats up and the air inside expands to escape through any ill fitting joints, whereas at night the air in the case cools down drawing in air from outside through the same joints. One simple way to alleviate the problem is to introduce breathers into the case structure. These take the form of holes covered by suitably graded filters which because of their greater size allow more air through than the ill fitting joints. The case can then 'breathe' air that has had at least some of the pollutants removed. A more expensive alternative would be the provision of a mechanical system to supply filtered air.

Some things must be protected but this should be done as inconspicuously as possible, the first concern being the educational objectives. This means providing visitors with as direct an experience as possible, even to the point of allowing them to touch things. If this is not possible, one should consider replacing the original objects with replicas. There is no doubt that some visitors experience deep disappointment when they discover that an exhibit is 'only a replica'. Even so, the idea that replicas undermine credibility is sometimes a poor argument, for the skeleton of the dinosaur *Diplodocus carnegii* in the British Museum (Natural History) is apparently a great attraction, yet it is made of plaster and painted black. If the 'real thing' is so important (to whom, one might ask?), perhaps it is better to include the real thing appropriately protected *and* a replica. An alternative would be to reconsider the use of something so fragile or valuable and ask whether the objectives are as well met by a less valuable or more robust example.

Our other concern should be to protect, secure and reduce maintenance in all exhibitions that include specimens, models and exhibits that are expensive, valuable, unique, fragile or difficult to maintain.

Specimens have to be protected from dust, damage and theft. Dust contains acids and salts that are harmful to skins, especially at times of high humidity. They should be protected from obvious damage from contact with visitors and from rapid atmospheric changes which cause skins to expand and contract. Many specimens also need to be protected from uncontrolled ultraviolet light which causes colours to fade.

Models are very attractive when displayed in the open and one should aim to do this wherever possible. However, certain factors have to be borne in mind when they can be touched or seen without barriers. A model on display must be sufficiently robust to withstand day-to-day contact with the public. It has to be constructed of materials that can withstand abrasion and maintenance by unskilled cleaning staff. A model of this kind can take longer to produce, and hence be more expensive, than one to be housed under glass. The choice is often between having more models in the exhibition, but under glass, or fewer, standing in the open.

Expensive, valuable, unique, fragile or difficult to maintain displays must nearly always be protected. The design should therefore take account of the following points.

(a) *Access.* Whatever form of protection is used, the display should be accessible to one but certainly no more than two people. It should not require any special expertise to get into it beyond the use of keys, and should not be designed so that it is likely to endanger the people entering the display or the display structure. Supporting devices should be supplied to hold accessways open.

(b) *Lighting.* No lighting should be fixed inside a protective container or display case, for electricians are not always appreciative of the display contents nor can they, in the nature of their work, avoid dropping things by chance. Further, some electrical appliances have been known to leak a variety of substances that have an adverse effect on the internal display materials. Lighting also creates heat, so the more lighting can be isolated from a display the less will be the effects of expansion and contraction of contents and air in the display (drawing in dust through ill fitting joints). If some form of barrier is used between the interior and the lighting, it too will need maintenance, particularly if lighting is close by, e.g. dust accumulates on **diffusers**.

(c) *Protection.* All forms of protection should be demountable to accommodate changes in the display. A protective barrier that determines the future contents of the display is a major handicap.

Security

Security involves the protection of displays from damage by fire and visitors and from theft. As it concerns buildings housing exhibitions as much as it does the individual exhibits within them, it is clearly not appropriate to go into the matter in detail in this book. There is, however, an excellent review written by Tillotson (1977) under the auspices of the International Council of Museums. It includes a detailed account of security problems and their solutions with an extensive list of references.

Security within exhibitions is usually provided by a combination of custodial staff and mechanical, electronic or electrical aids.

Custodial staff are employed to act both as a deterrent and a means of immediate apprehension. They may also help visitors by giving directions and answering questions. Theirs is a difficult task, particularly where educational exhibitions are concerned, for this type of exhibition is designed to encourage an enthusiastic response. It falls to them to judge when youthful enthusiasm becomes vandalism. Although the protection of valuable things is important, the necessity of dressing custodial staff in uniforms, and the fact that we in Britain call them warders, suggests that they have more to do with discipline than protection (Fig. 11.1). This is entirely foreign to the non-coercive nature of educational exhibitions (Ch. 3). If custodial staff have to be present, it is far better to present them as a resource to help visitors rather than as a restraint that detracts from the enjoyment of a visit. An alternative is to consider the use of technical aids.

Mechanical aids to security are the traditional means of protecting displays. They range from simple solutions such as screwing things down or putting them behind glass to elaborate locking systems on display cases.

Figure 11.1 A museum warder.

Electrical and electronic aids can also take many different forms, mostly resulting from an explosion in security activity during the 1960s. They include metal foil tapes around glass to signal entry; vibration sensors; pressure-sensitive mats; light sensor beams; and displacement sensors. Tillotson (1977) lists these and other devices, and discusses the advantages and disadvantages of each.

Maintenance

Maintaining exhibits is an important factor in ensuring that they continue to meet their educational objectives. Graffiti and litter attract more graffiti and litter. Damaged displays do not communicate or predispose the visitor to learn. The aim of exhibit developers is thus to design exhibits that will require the minimum of maintenance and make that which is necessary simple. Hence:

(a) materials should be able to withstand the predictable wear and tear of everyday use;

(b) it is often better to spend more on quality when the exhibit is constructed than to have a continuous maintenance problem through the use of inappropriate materials;

(c) all display elements should be accessible for replacement and repair; it is one thing to change a unit of equipment, but quite another to work on it *in situ*.

The following points should then be kept in mind in considering the maintenance of completed exhibits:

(a) daily checks should be made to ensure that exhibits are maintained at the same standard as when they were installed;

(b) records should be kept of all maintenance work, identifying the displays that break down, how often they do so, and how long they take to repair;

(c) preventative maintenance is better than cure, e.g. if projector bulbs have a limited life, specified by the manufacturer, they should be replaced regularly, not when they break down, for this always happens at the worst possible time;

(d) maintenance staff should be available throughout the open hours of an exhibition;

(e) it may be best to scrap displays that break down frequently, are difficult to repair, or take a long time to repair;

(f) detailed records should be kept for each display showing

   (i) the date the display was built,
   (ii) the colours used (manufacturer's name and code),
   (iii) the equipment (manufacturers' addresses and codes),
   (iv) a list of all objects, artefacts and specimens with curatorial codes,
   (v) copies of all text (and the original photosetting or artwork if possible),
   (vi) a list of references for all illustrations used and a record of copyrights obtained,
   (vii) a list of photographic negative codes,
   (viii) a list of the objectives for the display (in case radical changes are proposed);

(g) space must be provided in the exhibition for the storage of equipment and spare parts;

(h) spares must be available for all components;

(i) standardised components make replacement easier and quicker;

(j) electronic devices are more reliable than electromechanical and mechanical ones;

(k) it is better to use two videotape decks if possible – then, if one breaks down, the other can take over automatically (this also does away with the interval between showings caused by rewinding);

(l) sliding devices should be fitted with buffers and slip-clutches so that they are better protected from the visitors;

(m) the person who maintains a device should either build it or supervise its construction (this ensures feedback from project to project);

(n) programmes have to be maintained as well as the equipment;

(o) compartments containing audio-visual and similar equipment must be suitably fire-proofed and ventilated;

(p) audio-visual compartments must be kept clean and a filtered air supply should be considered; white backgrounds on slides should be avoided as dust shows up on them;

(q) plastic materials should be avoided as far as possible as they attract dust electrostatically.

12 The specification

The work of development is guided by the brief for the particular phase of work, which may cover one or more exhibitions, or only part of an exhibition. In general, it is convenient in a museum if each phase spans one to two years. This allows new exhibitions to be presented to the public at acceptable intervals, as argued in Chapter 6. Longer intervals are liable to lead to the criticism that the museum never does anything new, and so are very short intervals, because they will give the impression that no changes are ever made apart from minor ones.

With intervals of this size, each phase will require the production of a substantial number of exhibits. The development of an effective exhibit involves a great deal of soul-searching and, unless the resultant design is very closely specified, it is bound to be modified during production, which may well set at nought all the efforts of the development team. After all, the members of the production team have a different outlook from that of their colleagues in development. They are not as immediately concerned with the educational effectiveness of the exhibits; their concern is the hardware, not the software. It is, therefore, up to the development team to specify their requirements in considerable detail.

The specification, in the broadest sense of the word, is the sole output of the development team. It is a metamorphosis of the brief, just as a butterfly is a metamorphosis of a chrysalis. The input to the development process is the brief and the output is the specification; this in turn is the input to the production process, and the output is the exhibition and supporting items.

Everything in a well designed educational exhibit is there for a purpose, and everyone working on it during production, even if concerned with some minor aspect such as the preparation of a dormouse, should be aware of the educational and physical context in which it is to be seen, and should appreciate the intentions of the designers. Experience shows that the better people understand the intentions behind a design, the better they are able to suggest alternatives – or even improvements – that will make production easier and therefore more efficient. This is where the specification document comes in.

Many things need to be included in the specification but can easily be overlooked. It is best, therefore, to communicate the design requirements in the form of a standardised specification document (Fig. 12.1). This is produced jointly by the development team (Ch. 5) and aims to:

(a) explain fully the organisation and operation of exhibits;
(b) ensure that everyone involved in producing the exhibits has an opportunity to see his work in context;
(c) indicate the reasons for a particular choice of exhibit or type of arrangement.

The specification document

A *summary* section should include:

(a) the story, exhibit by exhibit;
(b) the objectives of each exhibit in turn;
(c) a brief description of the form of each exhibit and the number of displays it includes;
(d) itemised check-lists, with brief descriptions for graphics, photographs, models, specimens, objects, artefacts, dioramas, audio-visuals, and any mechanical, electronic or electromechanical devices for special effects.

The *details* that follow this summary are what actually defines the opportunities for further interpretation. Wherever possible all proposals should be confirmed with the people responsible for implementing them *before* the specification document is written. It should similarly be confirmed with the responsible sources that all required specimens, objects and artefacts are available and that the proposals entail no intractable conservation problems, also that all reference material is both suitable and available.

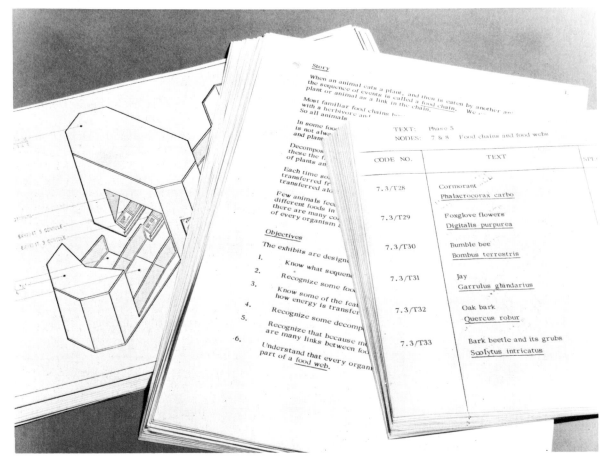

Figure 12.1   Specification document and drawings.

Each exhibit should be specified in turn, explaining exactly how it is to be arranged, how objects are to be displayed, what is to be included in graphics of the various kinds, and where text is to be placed. The reasons for the choice of each component and its arrangement should be provided if these are important. References for graphic designers, modelmakers and photographers should include:

(a)   a relevant view of the subject;
(b)   more than one close-up view;
(c)   the names of any potentially helpful contacts;
(d)   the locations of the source material.

The components of each exhibit, apart from text, will have been mentioned group by group in the *summary.* They need to be specified fully, and this is best done exhibit by exhibit after dealing with the more general matters covered by the preceding paragraph. For each component there should be:

(a)   a coded reference number (see below);
(b)   specific objectives;
(c)   a general description;
(d)   recommendations as to the style of presentation (e.g. stylised, realistic);
(e)   a statement explaining the detail needed;
(f)   comments on emphasis;
(g)   comments on references;
(h)   for films and audio-visuals, a story-board showing images, their relationship to the commentary and the effects proposed (e.g. **dissolve, snap-change**).

The use of coded reference numbers for the components facilitates:

(a) identification at all stages;
(b) location;
(c) recording and filing;
(d) progress chasing;
(e) linking components together;
(f) communication between the various specialists involved in setting up the exhibitions.

The code should not be too detailed or it will be cumbersome to use, but it must not be too general or it will fail to distinguish the components from one another. It should reflect the way each component is to be produced, and therefore take account of the different skills and disciplines involved. We have found it useful in the British Museum (Natural History) to number finished exhibits on view to the public (Ch. 8). But the drawings that are an essential part of the specification are numbered according to a different system which combines numbers and letters to provide the maximum flexibility.

The exhibits are numbered sequentially within the phase and grouped into sections. For instance, the number 06.02.04 would be that of the fourth drawing relating to the second display in the sixth phase of work. Components are characterised by a letter code which we have found to be both simple and effective:

AV   audio-visual, including both hardware and software;
G   graphic material, including diagrams, illustrations and anything else for which **artwork** has to be produced, also any photographs that require the attention of an artworker; graphics that include photographs are listed in the *summary* under both graphic and photographic headings;
P   photographs, excluding those used in audio-visuals;
M   models, machines and participatory devices; a model may include graphics and photographs which are separately coded;
D   dioramas; specimens and background are normally given separate code numbers, this code provides a short way of referring to the whole;
S   specimens, objects and artefacts;
T   text; normally each separate piece of text is coded, even if it is a single paragraph or even a single word;
TAV text for audio-visuals.

Thus the reference 06.02.04/P1 would identify the first photograph shown on the drawing referred to immediately above. In practice, this is usually abbreviated to 2.4/P1 because there is no uncertainty about which phase of work is being referred to. The next photograph in the same display would be 2.4/P2, the first photograph relating to the first drawing in the next display would be 3.1/P1, and so on. This system provides sufficient flexibility to enable code numbers to be updated without altering a whole lot of other ones for the same phase.

The third part of the specification is the *text*. It notes where bold, italic or capital letters are called for, includes any relevant comments on the text, and indicates any text that is subject to later confirmation, as when captions for specimens or text for audio-visuals are likely to be modified during production.

The fourth and final section of the specification document comprises the *drawings*. These include plans and elevations of all the displays, and should show the locations and fixing-points for models and machines, all access points and power outlets, and the locations and specifications of ancillary equipment such as lighting, text and graphic layouts.

Specifications should be checked by an independent critic before they are issued, then circulated to *everyone* working on the project. Layout drawings for graphics must correspond with the constructional drawings and should cover all relevant structural details, such as joins between panels. Before starting production, every producer should discuss the specification with the development team, and experience shows that it is essential to make a whole series of checks during the production period:

(a) text should be checked after it has been printed, before it is incorporated into artwork;
(b) illustrations should be checked before they are photographed;
(c) artwork should be checked to ensure that it

has been laid out as agreed and all text has been included;

(d) working drawings for constructional work should be checked for accuracy and to ensure that all necessary information has been included;

(e) models should be checked before casting;

(f) audio-visuals should be checked at appropriate production stages;

(g) all components should be checked before installation;

(h) mechanical, electronic and electromechanical devices should be rigorously tested.

It is essential to record every check, the checker indicating approval by signature. All reference numbers should run through, though additional information can be included provided it follows the original scheme. The supervision of the production team is the responsibility of the production controller, but it is important that he should have a counterpart in the development team who is personally responsible for the filing of all specification material, for circulating amendments, for recording decisions and for up-dating all copies of drawings.

13 Scheduling, monitoring and controlling exhibit production

The most precious resource in exhibition work is the group of people who create the exhibits, build them, and make them available for the use and enjoyment of the public who come to learn from them. The effectiveness with which resources are used is judged by the way members of the group spend their time. One of the most important and useful tools for managing the work of the team is a system for scheduling what has to be done and when, monitoring what actually takes place, and comparing the two. The necessary management action can then be taken to ensure that, despite the inevitable hiccups that disrupt the schedules in the short term, the exhibits are nevertheless ready on time in the end.

The system has three foundations. First, there is the chain of activities referred to in Chapter 5 in the discussion of the way in which the exhibition team is organised. Secondly, there is the definition of the unit that is processed through this chain of activities. It cannot be an exhibit because the chain starts with the transformation of the brief into a series of exhibits, and at the outset when the schedule is being drawn up nobody knows the number or size of the exhibits that will be needed to communicate the ideas embodied in the brief. In the beginning, the only way of defining a work unit is what can be accomplished in a specified period that is short enough not to cause too much trouble if things go wrong (as they always do) – say four to six weeks. This then has to be linked to the basic unit used to organise the intellectual content of the exhibition, i.e. a **node** in a concept hierarchy (Ch. 6). When setting up the scheduling and the monitoring and control system it is difficult to be confident about the correspondence between these two units, but this is easily overcome if we accept that very few things are perfect, including management systems. Just like exhibits, they should be regarded as trial solutions to the particular problem they exist to solve, not as the final definitive answer. Thus, in the early stages, each node is taken as calling for one unit of work, and in our case we allowed our first development partnerships four weeks per node. Then, as experience grows (in the drafting of briefs as well as in the development and further processing of exhibits), the one-to-one relationship can be modified in either direction. The units may be redefined too, but there is not much point in altering both the units as well as the relationship between them; only one need be changed. The node is a very fundamental unit and it seems best to leave it alone, but we found quite early on that it was more convenient to work to a unit of six weeks instead of the original four. Just as one phase may correspond to more than one unit of information (Ch. 6), or vice versa, it may sometimes be necessary to allow more than one stint of six weeks to a node and occasionally go the other way. The system exists for the benefit of its users, and it must above all be flexible.

Finally, the third foundation of the system is a series of precisely defined outputs, one for each activity in the chain. Unless there is a real identifiable output from each and every activity, something that can be passed from the person (or group) responsible for one stage to the one responsible for the next, the whole system is likely to prove unworkable. The handover of responsibility from one person (or group) to the next in the chain of activities needs to be a formal event involving the issue of a receipt, otherwise acrimony is liable to ensue when schedules slip.

Activities and outputs

The operation of mounting an exhibition calls for the exercise of a variety of skills and abilities, by either one individual, a handful of people or a larger team. Where more than one person is involved, these skills may not all be available within the group (e.g. a museum department) that carries the primary responsibility. The operation is likely to involve not only others within the same organisation (e.g. other museum departments), but also outsiders such as other official bodies and commercial firms. It is important for all concerned to know when they will be called upon to make their contributions and how much time will be available to them, so that the exhibition may open on time. For this reason the activity chain needs precise specification, and this is where the outputs serve a useful purpose. The output from one activity is the input to another, each activity being in essence the transformation of input into output. This takes time, whereas the reverse transformation, of output into input, which takes place at the formal handover of

responsibility from one person (or group) to another, is by comparison an instantaneous event, for which there is a scheduled deadline. Figure 13.1 is based on our experience in the British Museum (Natural History) and depicts the outputs/inputs, the transformation activities that they link, and the events with scheduled deadlines.

The activities are represented in this figure by rectangles, each of which bears a brief legend naming the particular activity. The oval boxes represent events; but only one handover is shown, that from the Development Section, to avoid complicating the diagram. The outputs/inputs are represented on the diagram by unboxed

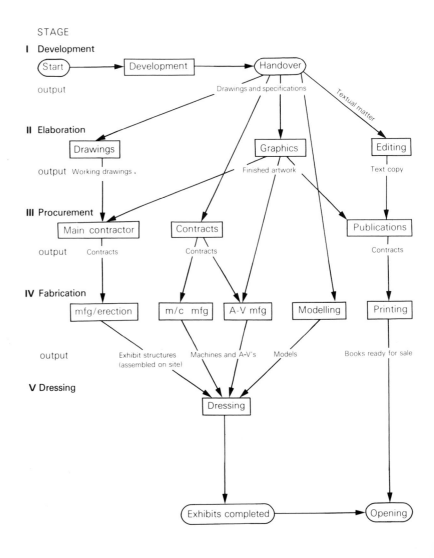

Figure 13.1   Output diagram.

legends, which are arranged in four rows. Each row identifies the transition from one stage to the next, each phase of work being divided into the five stages listed on the left of the diagram. The first stage is development, the output from which is a written specification plus a set of design drawings (Ch. 12). It includes the final text for all the exhibits and its function is to describe the physical and intellectual components of the exhibition in sufficient detail for them to be produced without further consultation. At hand-over, the responsibility for the various physical components passes to one of the other teams in the exhibition department (the Department of Public Services) – the Drawing Office, the contracts group, the Graphics Section or the Editorial Section, and so on down the chain. Thus the second stage is that of elaboration, i.e. the preparation of working drawings, finished art-work, and manuscripts for publication, from the specification and design drawings produced during development. The third is procurement, i.e. the placing of orders with the appropriate contractors. In our case, three different bodies are involved, the exhibition department itself, the Publications Section of the Museum (in the Department of Central Services), and an external, main contractor. The main contractor places contracts on the basis of competitive tender, a process that takes a minimum of 10 weeks. The fourth stage is that of fabrication. The fabrication of machines, audio-visuals, models and books is completed away from the actual exhibition site, either in the workshops of an external sub-contractor or elsewhere in the Museum if the 'subcontractor' is an in-house group. The structures that house the exhibits proper are usually assembled on site from prefabricated components. We call this installation, and the contracts for the structures have to be phased to avoid congestion on site, to allow the Museum to provide the necessary back-up services, and to spread the load on the main contractor, all of which complicates the scheduling process. The fifth and final stage is dressing the exhibition, i.e. bringing everything together in its final form prior to opening to the public.

For the purpose of defining the outputs in greater detail we use certain terms in a particular or restricted sense as follows:

(a) *Illustrations* are graphic items, all of which take the physical form of finished artwork.

They include all diagrams, drawings, pictures and photographs and are subdivided into two separate groups: (i) illustrations for dynamic displays, e.g. those included in the audio-visual scripts, and (ii) illustrations for static displays.

(b) *Audio-visual scripts* include not only the words to be spoken (previously approved by the editorial staff), but also a full specification of the objectives and other functional requirements of the item, as well as the illustrations just mentioned.

(c) *Models* are all representations other than graphics. They are three dimensional, graphics are two dimensional, and include the mounted specimens, dioramas, and so on produced by taxidermists.

(d) *Machines* include all other artefacts, mechanical, electronic or electromechanical. Any device with moving parts is *ipso facto* a machine.

Though the transfer of responsibility takes place at a particular instant in time, at handover, there is no question of the recipient group remaining aloof from the work of the donor until responsibility is transferred to it. For instance, the Editorial Section has a very close relationship with the development partnerships who together specify the wording and presentation of all textual material. It is the responsibility of the editorial staff, in conjunction with the relevant subject-matter experts, to prepare the copy for all publications. The text for this constitutes the output of the Editorial Section; the artwork for the publications is one of the outputs from the Graphics Section. Together they form the input of the Publications Section, which at the British Museum (Natural History) is not part of the exhibition department. There is constant consultation between the editorial, graphics and development staff during the elaboration.

The drawings and specifications that are the output from Development are also the input to the Graphics Section, which finalises the design of all exhibition graphics (including the art direction of in-house photography and the selection of photographs purchased from agencies) and produces the finished artwork which constitutes its output to the main contractor, more correctly to the graphics subcontractor appointed by the latter. This artwork comprises both that for the illustrations, in the broad sense of the definition above, and that for the text panels, and is incorporated in the structure of the exhibits. The Graphics Section has a permanent staff to finalise the design work, and it is also able to commission freelance work when its capacity in this respect is inadequate. In any situation of widely fluctuating demand, the most economical procedure is to meet the base load from internal resources and supplement these as necessary from external sources. In addition to producing the finished artwork for (a) exhibits and (b) exhibition books, the section has other responsibilities not shown by the output diagram. It designs and produces finished artwork for posters and leaflets (and liaises with the printers) and for various educational materials produced by the Museum. It also provides silk-screen facilities for maintaining existing exhibitions.

The diagram shows a further output of finished artwork from the Graphics Section, this time to the audio-visual subcontractor. Machines and audio-visuals, like the other physical components of the exhibits, are specified by the development partnerships. Their drawings and specifications provide the input to the contracts group, who engage specialist subcontractors to produce various items and also act in a liaison role for in-house production.

In summary, the output from the Graphics Section is finished artwork of one kind or another. All finished artwork is checked by the people who originated it, who indicate agreement by signature on the reverse. The Graphics Section is responsible thereafter for controlling the quality of the work of the subcontractors in the graphics field.

The drawings and specifications from Development also provide the input to the Modelmaking and Taxidermy Section, which is responsible for mounting all specimens and producing all models, but not usually machines as defined above (though they may be consulted before the contracts for these are placed). Like the Editorial and Graphics Sections, the modelmakers and taxidermists collaborate with the partnerships during development. It is their responsibility to acquire the specimens to be used in the exhibits and their advice on the likely availability of specimens during the development stage makes a valuable contribution to the efficiency of the whole operation. Nowadays all machines are fabricated in house, by the Special Effects Section of the Department of Central Services. This has

the advantage of making it possible for the same sort of liaison to take place during development in relation to machines as takes place in relation to models and illustrations.

Finally, the drawings and specifications from Development provide the input to the Drawing Office, where they are translated into drawings which are the basis of competitive tenders for the construction of the displays. As mentioned previously, these contracts are placed and managed by the main contractor. Like finished artwork, and the models produced in house by Modelmaking and Taxidermy, working drawings have to be approved by the Development Section and everyone else directly involved before being released to the main contractor. Copies of them go to the Graphics Section, Modelmaking and Taxidermy and, where appropriate, to the producers of machines, the work of the Drawing Office having defined the exact spaces available to these groups for their work.

The last set of outputs, those of the fourth row in the diagram, are much easier to define exactly than the earlier ones because they are all pretty obvious. Apart from the printed and bound books, which normally are not needed until immediately before the opening date, they constitute the input to the section responsible for supervising the dressing of the new exhibits and displays. The same section is responsible for supervising the on-site assembly of the exhibit structure ('installation'), and its subsequent maintenance. Putting all the bits together at the eleventh hour is a hectic operation and vital components, intellectual as well as physical, can all too easily be omitted or ruined at this stage, thus wasting all the effort that has been put into ensuring the effectiveness of the exhibits. Some variation is inevitable, and for proper control to be exercised it needs to be vested in one particular person.

Scheduling and monitoring

Once the activities of the exhibition team have been defined on the basis of the outputs that result from them, it becomes possible to schedule the operation of mounting an exhibition. The first thing that has to be realised is that the time available per year is considerably less than the 365 or 366 days which immediately spring to mind. In Britain, weekends and public holidays reduce the total by 115 days, so the working year is really only the equivalent of 50 five-day weeks. Even this potential can never be realised in practice because of annual holidays and the encroachment of training courses and conferences, to say nothing of absence through illness, so the safest thing to do is to plan on the basis of no more than 200 days of productive time per year, i.e. 40 weeks of five days each (Fig. 13.2).

We have defined a work unit (above) based upon, but not identical with, a node in a concept hierarchy. There is, however, a further scale of measurement that has to be taken into account, namely that of floor area. The floor area per node, like development time per node, is a variable quantity. In planning the work on the broad scale, an average value is perfectly adequate; variations around the average are introduced when planning the work of the development team with the object of drawing up the detailed schedules that are the basis of the management system. The figure we use is $33\,m^2$ per node, and the later variations range from 30 to $40\,m^2$.

The time required in the post-development stages also needs to be established, particularly in the chain that begins with the drawing office. This tends to be the critical chain, principally because it concerns the biggest component of the exhibit and the lengthy process of contract by tender to which we referred earlier. The other chains are less critical because the individual items are much smaller and additional resources are easier to procure when needed.

In our work we initially allocated three man-weeks per node in the Drawing Office, a figure that we checked against quotations from a commercial drawing office with many years of wide-ranging experience as a contractor for this kind of work. This allocation was later increased to four weeks by adding an extra week for additional tasks such as the costing of materials. Similarly, we allowed six weeks for the main contractor to place its contracts, but once the operation was fully under way the work began to build up and we had to increase the figure to the 10 weeks mentioned earlier.

In our experience it was even more difficult to decide how long to allow for fabrication and assembly of the exhibit structures, and this problem only really resolved itself after some juggling with contract size. The procedural steps take no longer for a big contract than for a small one, so there is an advantage in maximising contract size. On the other hand, if a contract takes more than six months, the contractor is entitled to payment in stages, which makes it difficult (though no less essential) to control costs. Furthermore, as already mentioned, contracts must be phased in order to avoid congestion on site and enable the installation and maintenance crew to cope with the flow of work. Taking all these factors into account, we eventually came up with a target figure of $120\,m^2$. For this we allowed 37 weeks, made up as follows:

(a) specification (drawing up the contract)   2 weeks
(b) tender period   10 weeks
(c) fabrication   21 weeks
(d) installation   4 weeks

This means, adding four weeks for the Drawing Office, that on average the interval from handover

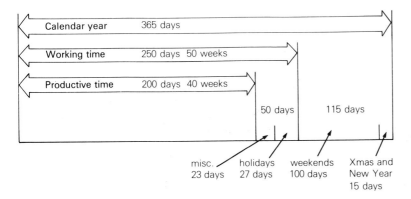

Calendar year   365 days

Working time   250 days 50 weeks

Productive time   200 days 40 weeks

50 days   115 days

misc.   holidays   weekends   Xmas and
23 days   27 days   100 days   New Year
                                                      15 days

Figure 13.2 How the year is subdivided.

to the beginning of dressing the exhibits is a minimum of 41 weeks (Fig. 13.3).

The same period is available for coping with the models. It is much more than is needed for almost any individual model, so the dominant characteristic of modelmaking and taxidermy from the scheduling standpoint is that it is a resource-limited process. Models differ greatly in size and complexity. It is, for instance, hardly meaningful to use a single average time for mounting an elephant and a sparrow. The best way of scheduling the work is therefore to deal with each item separately, deciding whether there is sufficient capacity for in-house production or whether it would be more appropriate to contract the work out.

Much the same applies to the manufacture of audio-visuals and machines. Most of the former are made outside the Museum, but some, along with all of the latter, are made in cooperation with another department of the Museum, Central Services, which also includes the Publications Section, Photography and various workshops.

The above description illustrates a point made in the description of critical path analysis in Chapter 4; much of the value of this technique as a management tool resides elsewhere than in its routine use. The project that gave rise to PERT was not resource-limited, the sole aim being to complete it as fast as possible. Outside the military field things are very different. The mounting of an exhibition certainly involves a network of activities, but for practical purposes it is much more fruitful to reduce the operation of producing exhibitions to the repetition of a chain of activities, as summarised in the stages:

development – elaboration – procurement – fabrication – dressing.

Three different time scales

In organising work on exhibitions it is useful to distinguish two operations of different timescale, conveniently named planning and scheduling. In the long term, planning time is measured in years and the object is to attain objectives that cannot be reached in less than a minimum of, say, 5 to 10 years. In the case of some museums, a long-term plan may need to look ahead as far as 30 or 40 years. It is clearly pointless to attempt to forecast the exact opening dates of particular exhibitions so far ahead, so it is best to avoid giving the plan the form of a calendar and give it instead that of a prescription for action. That is to say, instead of saying what will open when, it should describe the rate at which exhibitions are expected to be produced and the resources expected to be available. This description should be coupled with an expression of the relationship between the rate of progress and the volume of the necessary resources, and perhaps an indication of the current priorities for the various sections. The plan may be revised from time to time, but only as and when necessary. It is a waste of effort to revise it every year to take account of changes in the political and economic situation. Such changes

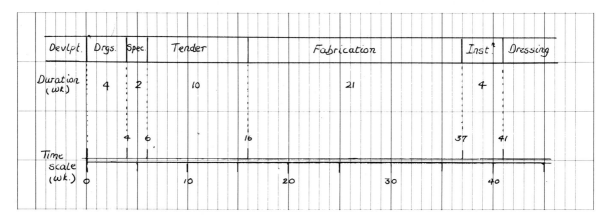

Figure 13.3 The critical activity chain.

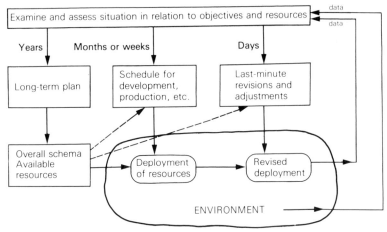

Figure 13.4 The three timescales.

always happen and there is no point in pretending that they do not. The sensible thing to do is to accept that change is inevitable and formulate a plan in such a way that it can absorb such changes.

The timescale of scheduling is an order of magnitude finer than that of planning. Time is measured in weeks or months and the objectives are much more detailed. Generally speaking, the main objective is to produce a specified output in a specified time. We have dealt at some length with specifications of outputs because if they are abstract or woolly there will be little hope of properly controlled and well managed, purposeful activity. This is a matter that can be handled objectively, but deciding the deadlines is different altogether. The output is produced by people, and the system will not work properly if deadlines are imposed from above. They must on the whole be self-imposed; that is to say, the people who have to meet them must agree them at the outset. When the attempt is first made to get people who are not accustomed to working to tight deadlines to change their ways, there is bound to be considerable reaction against the new ideas. Deadlines should be presented not as a management requirement, but as a necessity for achieving a common purpose. All sorts of people with all sorts of different skills are involved in mounting an exhibition. The purpose of the schedules is to provide the discipline necessary for them to work together as an efficient team and to help them make life easier for one another. Time spent on initial consultation saves delay and trauma later.

The third timescale (Fig. 13.4) is an order of magnitude finer still. It is measured in days, and the associated activity is essentially a corrective one. Things very rarely go exactly according to schedule, but the situation can always be rectified. What matters is that the system should provide an early warning of any deviation and should be capable of absorbing the disturbance with no more than a hiccup.

The smaller team

What we have said above has been said in the context of a substantial exhibition team, but the same activities are involved in the smallest exhibition. The way in which time is to be used needs careful planning, even for a one-man band, because there are so many items to be taken into account. Without proper scheduling, things are liable to get out of hand, especially as there are often several projects on the go at the same time. It is therefore well worth while drawing a bar chart similar to Figure 13.3 for each project. When several are in train simultaneously, a chart should be drawn with a bar for each project, and examined carefully to ensure that there will at all times be sufficient man-hours available to do everything that needs to be done. If the demand is overwhelming, something has to give – some slack must be introduced into the system somewhere by introducing delays. Forewarned is forearmed, and it is better to be realistic from the outset than to invite criticism by setting a target that is impossible to attain.

14 Improving the performance

Almost all of what has been said so far relates exclusively to exhibitions in galleries. However, the exhibition itself is only one of the media through which the exhibition team and the visitor communicate, the others being materials that the visitor can take away and supporting activities in which he can participate. All three use the primary media of print and the spoken word, including in the latter case recorded as well as face-to-face communication. All three are salient features of the approach we advocate.

The relevance of take-away materials and supporting activities has long been acknowledged through publications and lectures, but less effort has been allocated to enhancing the quality and effectiveness of these than to that of the exhibits. The flow chart (Fig. 14.1) is intended to draw attention to the way in which all aspects of communication with the visitor may be enhanced; and at the same time it distinguishes two quite different sorts of activity in which the exhibition team needs to engage if resources are to be fully exploited. It also summarises the essential features of the process of generating the three types of product that the approach requires. The boxes symbolise activities which are described briefly by their legends; annotated arrows symbolise information flows that are of particular interest in the present context; dotted arrows signify unspecified output/input relationships between the chains of activities. The column of activities down the left-hand side of the diagram summarises the way in which an exhibition department might operate. Implementation involves four chains of activities, not just the three that would be expected from the three components identified above. This is to distinguish between two types of take-away material – those directly related to the exhibits and those that are relevant but have different origins.

The two sorts of activity necessary for maximum exploitation of resources for the benefit of the visitor are:

(a) The generation and provision of take-away materials (leaflets, booklets, and so on) and the organisation of support activities. This is represented in the diagram by chains of implementation activities.

(b) The enhancement of the quality and effectiveness of all products, of the three types already identified. This is represented by the outer parts of the diagram, i.e. those surrounding the chains of implementation activities. It involves the collection and collation of information from a variety of disparate sources, separating the wheat from the chaff, and applying the new knowledge in a systematic way to future activities. Melton (1935) has given the name Museum Technology to such a body of practical knowledge.

Publications

The two uppermost implementation chains refer to two types of publications. Given a bookstall or other sales area, it is relatively easy to make available a range of carefully selected books that complement the exhibits, concentrating in the main on the less expensive paperbacks. The role of the bookstall in relation to the process of communication merits careful consideration. There are bound to be purely commercial pressures at work because of the potential income, but ideally the exhibition team should select the commercially published material to be stocked. The broad aim should be to have on sale a catholic selection of books which can be recommended to those who wish to extend their understanding beyond the confines of the exhibition.

Museum publications call for a greater effort than do external ones. A handbook that puts an exhibition into take-away form can play a valuable part in the learning process. As a general rule, one should be published as part of each phase of work, to be available by opening day. Apart from this, museum publications should aim to supplement commercial literature rather than to replace it, so that the best use can be made

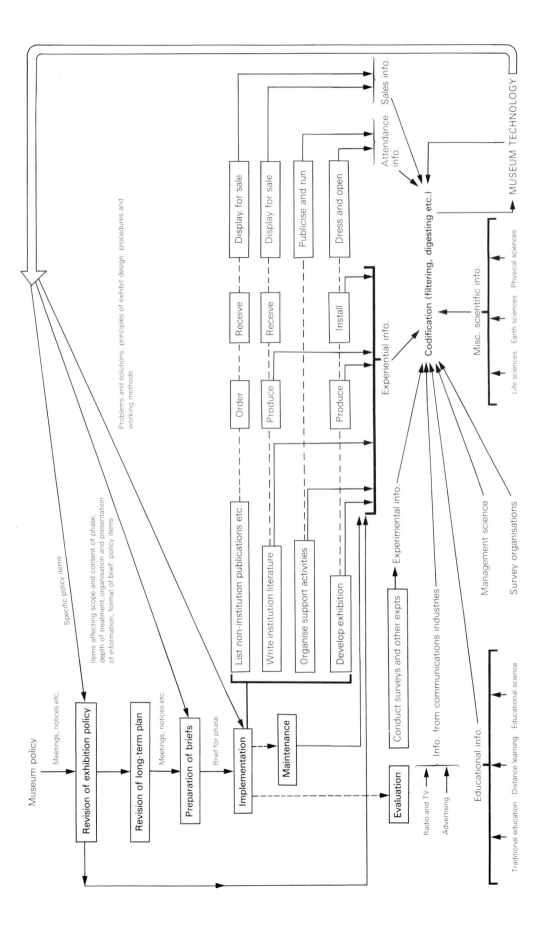

Fig. 14.1 Flow chart showing the ways in which communication with the visitor can be enhanced. This distinguishes the two sorts of activity that the exhibition teams need to engage in if resources are to be fully exploited, and summarises the process of generating the three types of product involved. Although the chart relates to science exhibitions, it is easily modified for other purposes.

of limited writing and editing capacity. Each handbook should include a comment on, or brief critical review of, the commercial literature, intended as a guide to further reading.

Apart from items on sale, supplementary literature can be provided in the form of printed or duplicated sheets. Because they are quicker and cheaper to produce than bound handbooks, they lend themselves more readily to improvement in the light of experience. Their role as a medium of communication, like that of the book-stall, merits careful consideration.

Countless books have been written on the subject of how to write, which is really beyond the scope of this work. Unfortunately, many of these books are poorly written, and only a few are of any real practical value. Some of the most useful are by Flesch (1960), Evans (1972), Kapp (1973) and Barrass (1978). In general, the rules for exhibition text (Ch. 9) apply equally to books and printed sheets. The illustrations are frequently so much a part of the whole that they cannot be conceived and developed in isolation. The aim should be to integrate text with design (Figs 14.2 & 3).

Support activities

The provision of supporting activities gives one of the best opportunities for advancing the museum technology. School visits, lectures, and so on are traditional activities, but in the past there has been a tendency for educational staff to indulge their own idiosyncrasies when taking school or other parties round the museum. This is understandable if the museum display is nothing but a haphazard collection of objects. But when a great deal of time and effort has gone into the careful and systematic development of exhibits, specifically to communicate concepts to the visitor, the aims of the exhibition (as detailed in the brief and the specification) should clearly be the starting point for all concerned.

Support activities of the type under discussion provide the opportunity for face-to-face communication between visitor and staff, but organising them for anything more than a tiny fraction of the visitors might well require an impossibly large staff. For instance, in a large museum with, say, 3 million visitors a year and a staff working 300 days per year, the average flow of visitors is 10 000 per working day – equivalent to 500 parties of 20 people. Admittedly, very few museums have 3 million visitors a year, but in proportion the smaller museum has the same problem. Try the calculation with your own figures and see what conclusion you come to!

Therefore, using educational staff of a museum

Food chains

When a herbivore eats a plant . . . . . and
then a carnivore eats the herbivore
. . . . . the sequence of events is called a
food chain.

We can think of each plant or animal as a link in the chain, so this is a three-link food chain.

In the world around us there are millions of these simple three-link food chains involving a plant, a herbivore and a carnivore.

Four-link food chains are also very common. In a four-link food chain, the first carnivore is eaten by a second carnivore which is usually larger and more aggressive.

Figure 14.2 The integration of text and design. A page from *Nature at work,* British Museum (Natural History), 1978.

What is sickle-cell anaemia?
Sickle-cell anaemia affects the **red blood cells** that carry oxygen round our bodies.

How is it inherited?
The characteristics that lead to sickle-cell anaemia are inherited through a single pair of genes. These genes control the production of **haemoglobin**, the oxygen-carrying substance in red blood cells. The normal form of haemoglobin is called **A**. There is also a slightly altered **S** haemoglobin that is caused by an abnormal gene.

Most people have normal red blood cells that look like this ...

Most people inherit a normal **A** gene from both parents, and we call these people **AA**. Their haemoglobin is normal.

People who suffer from sickle-cell anaemia have red blood cells that look like this ...

The cells have collapsed and become sickle-shaped, and cannot carry enough oxygen.

People who suffer from sickle-cell anaemia inherit an abnormal **S** gene from both parents. We call these people **SS**. All their haemoglobin is abnormal, and this is why their red blood cells become sickle-shaped.

Some people have red blood cells that look like this ...

Most of the cells look normal, but sometimes a few become sickle-shaped.

Some people inherit an **A** gene from one parent and an **S** gene from the other. We call these people **AS**. Most of their haemoglobin is normal, but some of it is abnormal.

Figure 14.3 The integration of text and design. A page from *Origin of species*, British Museum (Natural History), 1981.

as guides for conducted tours is not necessarily the best way of exploiting their specialised skills and experience. As far as school parties are concerned, there is a fairly obvious solution to the problem – to concentrate the efforts of museum staff on preparing the teachers for their visits and insist that the school teacher acts as guide. The best way of doing this is yet another matter that merits careful consideration. One suggestion is for the museum to take the initiative by organising an enquiry service, which may also help people outside the formal educational system who would like guidance in visiting the exhibition. These two possibilities are by no means mutually exclusive, and it may be possible to allocate some of the resources to each of them.

The most productive use of educational staff is when they contribute to the development work. This raises the question of how to apportion the writing activity between education, editorial and development staff. The most equitable solution is probably to give the development partnerships full responsibility for the exhibits, the editorial staff that for the handbooks, and the educational staff that for other supplementary materials. Each group also acts as specialist consultants and advisors to the other two in respect of its particular speciality, any points of disagreement

that cannot be resolved in discussion being referred up the management chain, if necessary to the overall head of the exhibition team.

Learning from experience

The main activity in advancing the technology, as opposed to implementing production, is that of codification. The raw material of this activity is a somewhat diverse set of information inputs, some of which are better defined than others. *Experimental information* is defined in the process of designing the experiment (Ch. 2) and it arises from evaluation, which is the subject of Chapters 15 and 16. *Experiential information* consists essentially of solutions to problems. Its collection is facilitated by listing, at the end of each phase of work, the problems encountered during the phase, the solutions adopted, and the outcome (though the outcome may not be known until later). *Attendance information* and *sales information* can provide some measure of the success in attracting the visitor, i.e. of the attainment of the principal affective objectives, whereas success in attaining cognitive objectives can only be measured by survey techniques.

The other types of information identified in the

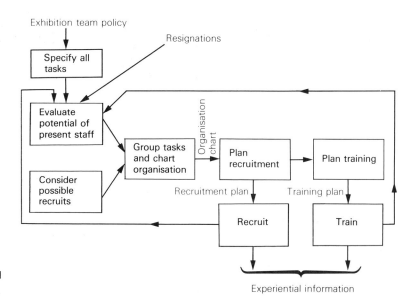

Figure 14.4 The organisational process.

diagram can only be collected by maintaining a constant awareness of activity in the various fields and repeatedly asking the question, 'What can we learn from this that might be useful to us in the future?' There is little systematic action that can be taken, beyond perhaps allocating particular fields to particular people and charging them with preparing progress reports at regular intervals.

Planning and organisation

We mentioned above the activities in the chain down the left-hand side of the diagram (Fig. 14.1), those concerned with planning and the way the exhibition department organises itself. These activities are all influenced to a greater or lesser extent by the museum technology, a body of knowledge that is continually growing through the collection and codification of information. The chain begins at the top with the revision (which includes formulation in the first place) of the policy of the exhibition team. This is, of course, greatly influenced by external factors which are summarised in the diagram as 'museum policy'. Within this last constraint the internal organisation of the team is principally determined by its own policy. And the effective solution of the organisational problems, several of which have been mentioned in the preceding paragraphs, requires the production of three out-

puts identified in Figure 14.4 – an organisation chart, a recruitment plan and a training plan. These in turn generate experiential information, which feeds into the codification activity, as indicated by the arrow on the extreme left of Figure 14.1.

The principal physical manifestation, and the only direct one, of the exhibition policy is the long-term plan for producing exhibits. Though this originates within the exhibition department, it must of necessity conform to the constraints imposed by museum policy, which is a matter for higher authority and covers more than just exhibition policy. Once it has been formulated in detail and approved from above, tacitly or explicitly, it becomes in effect a part of the museum policy. That is not to say that it is immutable or even removed from the influence of the exhibition department. This influence is exercised in the way shown in Figure 14.1, through the collection and codification of various sorts of information which can on occasion bring about a policy change.

As has already been mentioned, the long-term plan is an important factor in writing briefs, and this last activity is the place where lessons from earlier work can be applied most forcibly. Experience will have its effect in the implementation stages, of course, but more through the brief than directly because the brief controls implementation activities.

15 Evaluation: its nature, limitations and dangers

Evaluation is an activity that seeks to assess the worth or merit of things. At the risk of sounding a trifle abstract, it is worth saying at once that the 'things' in question could be almost anything whatever. If we so desire, we can evaluate ideas, plans, processes, physical objects, products, parts of products, and so on. In every case, the purpose of evaluation would be to enquire into the worth or merit of these things.

The next point to be made about evaluation is that, to professional social scientists, the word 'evaluation' has a particular *scientific* significance. When a social scientist talks about evaluation, he is talking about the business of trying to assess worth or merit in ways that would satisfy certain scientific criteria of objectivity and rigour.

There is, after all, a commonsensical way in which all of us, in all walks of life, regularly engage in what might be described as 'informal evaluation'. We write a letter, we read it through, and we say to ourselves, 'That looks OK.' In much the same way, a businessman or politician will make some decision, check it out in some informal rough-and-ready manner, and again say something like, 'That looks OK.' The question that the *professional* evaluator asks is whether activities of this kind are really and truly 'OK', or whether they have hidden defects that have gone unnoticed.

It might be said then, that evaluation – construed in the scientific sense – tries to go beyond subjective opinionation. The goal of scientific evaluation is to eschew opinionation and to probe more deeply and more systematically into the matter of 'how good' things are. The aim is to subject the things to be evaluated to much more careful scrutiny, with a view to discovering the reality behind the appearance.

If we ask why such an activity is necessary, the short answer is that things are not always what they seem (even to highly intelligent people) to be. It is very easy for people to pontificate on the worth or merit of something that somebody else has already done, or is proposing to do, but a more exacting enquiry will often show that certain plausible-looking pontifications are actually in error. Among other things, it is not at all uncommon for the professional evaluator to discover that what has been done is significantly better in some respects, and significantly worse in other respects, than popular belief supposes. By putting certain activities or products (or whatever) under the evaluation microscope, it is often possible to detect strengths and weaknesses and errors of judgement and so on which would otherwise have gone undetected. It may even be possible to cast new and helpful light on 'what went wrong' – if, indeed, anything *has* gone wrong. It may also be possible to come up with constructive recommendations about alternative and probably superior courses of action. And it may well be possible to demonstrate that, having regard to the conditions under which the activity in question was carried out, the people responsible would have had great difficulty in doing any better.

If we now apply these ideas to the business of setting up and running an educational exhibition, we can see at once that a professional evaluator might usefully be employed at *all* stages of the overall operation. At the *pre-planning* stage, for example, there is the challenge of helping to evaluate various proposals that are put forward. At the stage of *implementation*, there is the challenge of helping to evaluate how well things are going. Among other things, the professional evaluator might be asked to arbitrate among several alternative courses of action, each of which seems to be 'the best' to some of the staff responsible. When the exhibition has finally been thrown open to the public, there is the new challenge of trying to discover how successful or effective it is. Finally, there is the challenge of formulating constructive suggestions as to how the exhibition might be improved. The point to be noticed is that the professional evaluator is a person who has special skills and sensitivities which he is able to bring to bear on this matter of 'doing evaluation'. His usefulness derives from the fact that he is able to cut through subjective opinionation and see things – good as well as bad – that other people are less able or less willing to see. At the same time, he should be able to take a more dispassionate and more impartial view of whatever it is that he is being asked to evaluate. It is this ability to evaluate more keenly, cogently and dispassionately than other people that constitutes the main reason for employing him in the first place.

In order to see the *force* of the points that have just been made, it is essential to appreciate the magnitude of the difference that can exist between the careful and dispassionate evaluations of a sensitive professional evaluator, and the much less careful and much less dispassionate evaluations of the non-professional. The brutal fact is that too many people are much too uncritical about the things that they themselves do. They do things that may well seem to them at the time to be very sensible indeed. But, if their actions turn out to be less successful than was originally expected, they either (a) deny that this is the case, or (b) invent erroneous excuses for their failures. What is more, they may be utterly convinced of the accuracy of their denials and excuses.

It is beyond the scope of this chapter to embark on a detailed discussion of why people should behave in this way. But it is fairly obvious that they do. One reason for this is that most people act in accordance with belief systems and ideologies that they never seriously challenge. If a particular decision or action seems to flow, in an entirely natural and convincing manner, from some set of beliefs that the person concerned is wholly committed to, it will be very difficult indeed for that person to 'see' that his decision or action might be fundamentally misconceived. To call in question such a decision or action is to call in question his entire intellect. It is a very threatening experience for the person concerned. Unfortunately, it is this calling-in-question-of-other-people's-decisions-and-actions that the professional evaluator is *obliged* to do, from time to time. And this can give rise to all kinds of interpersonal conflict.

One further point needs to be made. When we say that professional evaluators have an approach to evaluation that is likely to be radically different from (and much more incisive than) that of the non-professional, we are not meaning to contrast the professional evaluator solely with the unqualified 'man in the street'. It is important to recognise that we are also calling in question the evaluative competence of people who are professionally qualified in *other* areas. This is a challenge that some professional people find hard to accept. For example, politicians and journalists may happily admit that they know very little about medicine. But they may be extremely reluctant to admit that they are incapable of satisfactorily evaluating their own decisions and actions.

If a professional evaluator is called upon to say why he is likely to do a better job of evaluation than other 'intelligent professional people', he may well find himself making statements that are strongly resented. For example, he might begin by saying that professional people are not sufficiently sensitive to the deeper (e.g. less obvious or longer term) implications and consequences of the things that they do. He might also suggest that professional people are frequently much more 'blinkered' in their thinking than they believe themselves to be. He might even suggest that some people are almost incapable of standing back and taking a hard self-critical look at the ways in which they conduct their affairs. The trouble is that too many people – including highly respected and very well meaning professional people – tend to see the world through a set of beliefs and presuppositions that have been with them (in taken-for-granted form) for so long – perhaps since early childhood – that it simply does not occur to them (e.g. in middle age) to start questioning themselves.

When a professional evaluator says these kinds of things about other professional people, he is *not* wanting to be offensive. And he is *not* wanting to impugn the sincerity and 'good intentions' of other people. He is simply trying to be factual. In effect, he is saying something like, 'Look, you may well be entirely well meaning and highly competent in certain areas. But, when it comes to *evaluating* the things that you do, you still have something to learn'.

Evaluation and conflict

Evaluation is often represented by its advocates as being an entirely well intentioned and constructive human activity. In the context of setting up, running and updating or revising an educational exhibition, it may seem very reasonable indeed to employ a professional evaluator to help evaluate future plans, present processes, and past achievements. There are, however, some notable snags and pitfalls.

First and foremost, we must note that there is a big difference between evaluating our own activities, and evaluating the activities of other people. It is one thing to evaluate the things that we ourselves do. (Among other things, we can of course keep quiet if we reach the unhappy conclusion that we have made several serious errors of judgement.) But it is quite another thing to evaluate the things that other people do. To evaluate the activities of other people is to put those people *at risk* – at least in their own eyes. The reason for this is that evaluation always has a dual focus. First of all, it will be seeking to reach worthwhile conclusions about, say, the merits or otherwise of an educational exhibition. But, at the same time – and this is where the shoe begins to pinch – it will *also* be saying something about the merits or otherwise of the people who were responsible for setting the exhibition up.

One consequence of this is that many people seem to have a sort of love-hate relationship with the activity of evaluation. On the one hand, they acknowledge the desirability of checking, in systematic ways, on the effectiveness of what people do. On the other hand, they know very well that if a careful evaluation study judges certain kinds of activities or products to have been *not* effective, all kinds of troubles are likely to break out. Thus, if an educational exhibition is judged to have been poorly conceived and generally 'unsuccessful', sponsors and paymasters and other critics are likely to start demanding to know what went wrong, and why. Whether they like it or not, almost everyone involved in setting up the exhibition will be thrown on to the defensive. And, even if they are able to mount a vigorous and completely valid defence, they will be aware that, if their critics are looking for blood, their defence is unlikely to be believed.

A major problem here is that we humans are not blessed with excessive amounts of foresight and prescience. There are many courses of action that look highly plausible to intelligent and well meaning people at the time when they are taken, but which turn out after the event to have been

either (a) sadly misconceived, or (b) much less effective than was originally imagined. It can therefore be crassly imperceptive and insensitive for evaluators (or, for that matter, outside critics in general) to point to things that have gone wrong and to suggest that the people responsible 'ought to have known better'. Evaluation, conceived in this way, would be little short of witch-hunting or scapegoating. The starting point for the professional evaluator *must* be more humanitarian than this.

It is sometimes said that the only people who never make mistakes are those who never do anything. The saying is not quite right because doing nothing can, on occasions, be the biggest mistake of all. A more accurate saying is, 'nothing ventured, nothing *learned*.' A willingness to try out new ideas, to plunge into the unknown (and, in consequence, to risk making mistakes) is a necessary price that has to be paid for worthwhile learning. When people *do* take such risks, and when they duly *do* make mistakes, the humanitarian evaluator or critic should pause to recognise (a) that mistakes of one kind or another are almost bound to happen, and (b) that he, the evaluator, would almost certainly have made mistakes, probably different ones but of no lesser magnitude, if he (rather than the people he is evaluating) had been 'in the driving seat'.

A recurring problem that arises in connection with any activity of an unusual or pioneering kind (and this applies, of course, to the setting up of educational exhibitions) is that too many people tend to have expectations that are unrealistically high. It is as if such activities are expected to proceed with a built-in guarantee of success. What is more, the people concerned may well be partly to blame for this state of affairs. In order to secure the funds and approval even to launch some out-of-the-ordinary venture, all sorts of people have to be convinced of its feasibility. If the venture then turns out to be significantly less successful than certain people were originally led to expect, some kind of inquest or post-mortem will almost certainly be demanded. This can easily lead to a situation in which everyone starts pointing accusatory fingers at everyone else.

When things go wrong, most people automatically assume that someone or something must be 'to blame'. Actually, a strong case can be made for asserting that this assumption is neither desirable nor correct. There are many situations in which it would seem to be more civilised and accurate to say, 'Things have gone wrong, and *nobody* is to blame.' Such a conclusion will seldom appeal to the legalistic or witch-hunting mentality. But if we take seriously the fact that humans are not blessed with infallible foresight (and are in consequence bound to make mistakes of one kind or another), and if we are also prepared to believe that people generally do try to do their best, as they see it (i.e. they are not deliberately perverse or malign), we can start to see that accusations of culpability may often be out of place. Given *this* recognition, evaluation can proceed in a completely different non-recriminatory spirit – a spirit of wanting to know what went wrong, *not* in order to dispense blame, but simply in order to discover how to prevent the same things from going wrong on future occasions.

If the affairs of man always ran smoothly, there would be very little point in evaluating anything at all. Under conditions of continuous smooth-running, evaluation could hardly be more than a self-congratulatory exercise – an opportunity to pat ourselves and others on the back for having done yet another good job. The fact that evaluation so often *does* seem to be necessary is due to the further fact that the affairs of man so often *fail* to run smoothly. Things go wrong, and evaluation studies are called for to try to discover why. This presents the evaluator with several different challenges. First, there is the challenge of discovering, as accurately as possible, what went wrong and why. Secondly, there is the challenge of making constructive suggestions about how to ensure that similar mistakes are not made in the future. Thirdly, there is the humanitarian challenge of doing all this in a way that is minimally damaging to the reputations of the persons concerned.

Unfortunately, it is not always possible, even in principle, for a professional evaluator to meet or 'rise to' this third challenge. If people are willing to take a relaxed attitude towards their mistakes – if, for example, they work in a caring and under-standing environment (the sort of environment in which everyone recognises that mistakes are likely to be made) – there may be no problems at all. However, large numbers of people seem to be terrified of having their mistakes 'publicly exposed'. This being so, they will sometimes strenuously resist any suggestion that things have gone wrong. At the very least, they will try to rebut any imputed criticism of *their* conduct.

Under such conditions, the professional evaluator is in a 'can't win' situation. Attempts will be made to undermine the validity of even his most innocuous criticisms.

This, then, is the social reality of the evaluator's predicament. At a purely intellectual level, it can hardly be denied that complex out-of-the-ordinary projects (such as the setting up and running of an educational exhibition) do need to be 'properly evaluated'. There is also no doubt that the person who is best qualified to conduct such an evaluation is a good professional evaluator who (because of the requirement of impartiality) has not himself been too intimately involved in setting up and running the project. At the same time, it is obvious that if a professional evaluator is employed, and if he starts uncovering what he takes to be errors of judgement, mis-management, and the like, he is immediately putting other people's reputations (and even, perhaps, their promotion prospects) at risk. People being what they are, this is very likely to initiate a furore of defensive and mutually recriminatory activity.

Walking the tightrope

It would take a full-length book to discuss, in adequate detail, what professional evaluators have come to describe, in recent years, as the politics and 'psycho-dynamics' of evaluation. Enough has been said, perhaps, to alert the reader to the fact that evaluation can be an extremely threatening activity – threatening, that is, to people whose activities come under the professional evaluator's discerning eye. It is a painful fact of life that most people make more mistakes than they care to admit, even to themselves. And people often promise, for a variety of different reasons, much more than they can ever hope to achieve. All this inevitably leaves them feeling vulnerable, so the presence of a professional evaluator is bound to make them nervous.

The professional evaluator, in his turn, also has problems. If he is invited to evaluate a project on which feelings run high (in the sense that some people are in favour of it, and other people are opposed to it), his findings are bound to give offence to *someone*. Even if he tries to minimise conflict – e.g. by gently calling attention to certain errors of judgement, but saying, almost in the same breath, that they were all entirely understandable or 'couldn't be helped at the time' – some critic is bound to accuse him of doing a whitewash job. Finally, if he takes care not to make any serious criticisms at all, someone is likely either (a) to accuse him of imperceptiveness, or (b) to remark that his services were never really necessary. The professional evaluator does, in any event, have problems of personal integrity. Like traffic wardens, he is paid to do things that are likely to be unpopular. If he sincerely believes that substantial numbers of significant mistakes were made, it is his duty to say so, and to put up with any flak that people throw at him. He is in a 'can't win' situation in more ways than one.

A good illustration of the 'can't win' predicament is provided by the widespread belief, within the museum world, that museums are repositories for objects, and should not be used to display concepts or ideas. Once this belief is fully embraced, no exhibition that attempts to display concepts or ideas can possibly be evaluated favourably, in the eyes of the *holders* of such a belief. Typically, fixed belief-systems operate to support the status quo, and they give rise to a particular form of social determination – namely, that things are the way they are *because* they are, so any attempt to change things must be wrong by definition. It is because belief-systems are often unarticulated and because they unconsciously influence peoples' perceptions of the world that they are so resistant to change. When a thing is *evaluated* by somebody, it is usually assessed simply in the light of his belief-system, and if it fits comfortably with this system, if it conforms with the way he construes his world, it is regarded with favour; if not, with disfavour. Often we are completely unaware of this process because we tend to associate with others of a like mind, with people who share the same world-view as ourselves. Indeed, if you observe people arguing who hold different views, you will be struck by the fact that they spend most of their time defending their viewpoints instead of examining the weaknesses of their own positions and exploring the strengths of those of their opponents. The more different their own views are from those of their opponents, the more likely they are to look upon their opponents as unreasonable and even in certain circumstances to regard them as stupid, mad or subversive. Debates between politicians are depressing examples of this blinkered form of evaluation; and many of our received ideas are expressed in the various '-isms' which attract their protagonists who become more and more introverted and resistant to other interpretations. Most of these '-isms' have their points, but they are rather like the buildings that followed the Renaissance – beautiful in their way but incapable of growth.

Evaluation can thus be a very subjective activity. The question that arises, therefore, is whether there is a more dispassionate way of doing evaluation – a way that is less vulnerable to the vagaries of the kind of pro-ing and con-ing we have just discussed. We suggest there are *two* kinds of evaluation that might convincingly be regarded as improvements on the less critical methods used in everyday evaluations. The first of these involves the systematic application of special techniques (e.g. techniques of observation and enquiry and interpretation) which social researchers and 'professional evaluators' have developed, to quite high levels of sophistication, in recent years. The second, and less often discussed, kind of evaluation involves the cultivation and sustained application of a special kind of critical but impartial sensitivity – the kind of sensitivity that is constantly alert to the possibility of error, inadvertence and misjudgement, both in oneself and in others. As a further talking point, we remark that, however potentially powerful the social researchers' techniques might be, they can never be guaranteed to give worthwhile results if they are wielded by evaluators who lack the requisite sensitivity. If an evaluator lacks the kind of sensitivity described two sentences back, there is no guarantee that he will even direct his observational techniques at the things or events or processes that really matter.

An illustrative example

As an example, consider the figures produced by the Statistical Bureau of the EEC that relate per capita strike days to increases in the national product per capita and the rate of annual inflation. We can see in Table 15.1 that there are two rather impressive relationships: a negative one between per capita strike days and increase in the per capita GNP (Gross National Product); a positive relationship between per capita strike days and the rate of annual inflation. What conclusions can we draw from this?

It has been claimed that these figures

Table 15.1   Per capita strike days, GNP and the rate of inflation.

	Strike days per 100 workers 1969–74	Increase of the national product per capita in dollars 1968–73	Rate of inflation (annual average; %)
W. Germany	240	3339	5.2
France	901	2347	7.4
England	9035	1221	8.9
Italy	5083	1089	8.0

demonstrate that strikes, and by association, therefore, the Trade Union movement, are the biggest cause of decline in Great Britain. The competent professional evaluator would rightly claim that there are at least two things wrong with this conclusion. First, the figures are not comparing like with like. Strike days per 100 workers is related to the GNP of the nation *as a whole*. On the assumption that few strikes are actually called to decrease the GNP, it would be more appropriate to determine if strikes served to advance the living standard of workers. Secondly, the inference from correlation (the connection between the sets of figures in Table 15.1) to causation, that is, that strikes *caused* a decrease in the GNP and *caused* an increase in the rate of inflation, is doubtful reasoning, although as a species of argument it is common indeed. This, in fact, is a very basic warning about the misuse of statistics and it would be very familiar to competent professional evaluators who are well versed in the nature and problems of statistical inference. Circumspect arguments based upon statistical data are aspects of the techniques we referred to on the previous page. In addition, the evaluator who has cultivated the sensitivity we referred to also would attempt as many explanations as possible of the observed relationships until he comes up with one that best seems to fit *all* the available data in the most *consistent* manner. Being sensitive in this way is partly like being a good detective who searches diligently and meticulously for as many clues as possible and who does not reach a hasty conclusion. Skills of advocacy as well as those of detection are also a necessary part of this sensitivity; the competent evaluator, having arrived at a conclusion, will

subject it to the most searching cross examination until he is convinced that the judgement he has made is the best he can in the circumstances. In the present example, the evaluator may suggest that strikes are but another manifestation of the dissatisfaction and discontent that pervades a society that is not coping very well with its inefficiencies and inequalities. In this case he would search for further evidence to put this notion to the test.

A second look

What, then, *is* evaluation? To many readers of this book, it may come as quite a surprise to learn that, over the past 20 years or so, literally thousands of books and monographs and papers have been written on this very question. Evaluation has in fact become Big Business. The main reason for this is that we nowadays live in a society which, rightly or wrongly, places a very high value on such things as accountability, responsibility and cost-effectiveness. This being so, sponsors are increasingly refusing to fund projects (such as the mounting of expensive educational exhibitions) unless some hard-nosed evaluation can be done to determine, at the end of the day, whether or not their money has been wisely spent.

The businessman's approach to the funding of projects is one that compels him to ask whether he has had his 'money's-worth' – or, in the sharper vernacular of the Americans, 'the biggest bang for the buck'. Since the businessman does not want to be fobbed off with a lot of inconclusive opinionation, he is actually demanding that a competent job of evaluation be done. In other words, he is requesting that he eventually be told, fairly definitively, whether (and in what ways) the funded project was a success. Since this question is very much easier to ask than to answer, and since there are numerous difficulties that stand in the way of obtaining a *non-controversial* answer, a new type of professional person – namely, the 'professional evaluator' – has come into existence to try to meet the demands of anxious sponsors who *insist* that a definite answer be obtained. In this sense, the professional evaluator – with his professional literature, professional tools of trade, professional training programmes, professional conferences and societies, professional codes of ethics, and so on – is essentially a product of the New Age of Accountability. He owes his existence, and his increasing influence, primarily to the fact that sponsors have themselves been bitten by the Accountability Bug. If sponsors start feeling 'accountable to others' for the ways in which they dispense money, they will also start feeling anxious and defensive about their own actions. One way of coping with their own accountability problem is to look responsible, in the eyes of the rest of the world, by requiring that the projects they fund be 'properly evaluated'.

For better or worse, the professional evaluator – with his huge back-up of professional literature, and his substantial armoury of impressive-looking techniques – is here to stay. At least for the time being. With his arrival, the question 'What is evaluation?' can be seen to have no simple answer. Anyone who doubts this might care to examine a fairly typical 'survey' of evaluation theory and practice, edited by Struening and Guttentag in 1975. The work consists of two volumes of about 700 pages each. Since the date of this publication, the literature on evaluation has continued to grow both in complexity and verbosity.

At first glance, it might seem extraordinary that a seemingly straightforward activity, such as evaluation, should have been subjected to such intensive professionalisation. What can the professional evaluator possibly do that, if the literature is to be believed, the man in the street is so less capable of doing? The short answer, as already indicated, is that the professional evaluator has skills that enable him, if the social and political environment in which he is working is sufficiently favourable, to be more incisive and more objective. Less prone to error, in fact.

Actually, the man in the street and the professional evaluator have rather similar goals. But the former will typically come up with a highly impressionistic and idiosyncratic form of evaluation whereas the latter will typically come up with an evaluation based on systematic observation and enquiry and interpretation. At one level, then, the man in the street and the professional evaluator construe the process of evaluation in similar ways. In both cases, evaluation is seen, at heart, as being an activity aimed at determining the worth or merit of things. The man in the street and the professional evaluator part company, however, over their assessment of the difficulty of

the task. To the man in the street, it might seem 'obvious' that a particular facility – a training programme for the unemployed, an educational exhibition, a leisure centre for the elderly, or whatever – is a success. To the professional evaluator, it may be very far from obvious because, among other things, he will be sensitive to a whole range of ifs and buts that the man in the street will hardly have considered at all. What distinguishes the professional evaluator is his ability to penetrate the object of evaluation much more closely, and to emerge with conclusions that are likely to be far more definitive.

A further advantage of being a professional evaluator is that the skills that enable him to pass judgement on the things or processes that he evaluates can also be used to suggest relevant *improvements*. In the very act of discerning (more keenly than the man in the street) possible defects in what is being done, the professional evaluator can come up with more compelling ideas on how to do things better. Let us look therefore, at some of the ways in which the professional evaluator goes about his business.

Evaluation in action

If we want to gain real mastery over the tasks that we are called upon to do – if we want to master, for example, the task of setting up an effective educational exhibition – then it pays us to evaluate, at the earliest opportunity, almost everything that goes on. This is especially true if it is our intention to *repeat* the tasks in question. If we are expecting to be involved in the setting up of a whole series of educational exhibitions, the sooner we get on top of the job, the better it will be for everyone concerned. Lessons usefully learned in the first attempt mean mistakes saved and avoided the second time around.

At stage 1 (see Ch. 2), for example, it pays to evaluate, both during and after the event, the success or ease or both with which the necessary pledges of support were obtained, and the official 'go ahead' signal given. At stage 2, it pays to evaluate the more detailed plans – preferably *before* plunging ahead with their implementation, and discovering that they have hidden snags. The various other stage 2 tasks, such as the recruiting of appropriate staff and consultants, can also be usefully evaluated. During stage 2, it is even possible (and often highly desirable) to build in special 'evaluation opportunities'. For example, if there are doubts about the exact form that a particular exhibit should take, arrangements can be made to construct several alternative **mock-ups**. These can then be evaluated – e.g. by trying them out on volunteer members of the public – to try to decide which alternative seems to be the best (although, as indicated later, there are very real difficulties involved in doing this). At stage 4, evaluation becomes a more conspicuous activity because, with the arrival of the first visitors, everybody wants to know 'how well' they have done. It is vital to recognise, however, that this question may be very difficult to answer, unless the evaluation that actually goes on during stage 4 has already been pre-planned, during stages 1 and 2. In order to discover how well the exhibition is doing, it may be essential to have facilities for unobtrusively observing the visiting public – e.g. to see whether they are just drifting through the exhibition in a casual and somewhat disinterested way, or whether they are pausing in front of certain exhibits and talking excitedly about them. Obviously, facilities of this kind have to be pre-planned. If the pre-planning is inadequate, the exhibition may well get set up in a manner that makes definitive evaluation (at stage 4) almost impossible. Finally, we remark that even the stage 6 *updating and revision* can usefully be evaluated.

As might be expected, professional evaluators have devised special names for the different kinds of evaluation that can go on in complex team projects of the educational exhibition kind. In order of their occurrence, they are described as (1) front-end analysis, (2) formative evaluation, (3) summative evaluation and (4) meta-evaluation. As the name suggests, front-end analysis refers to the kinds of evaluative activities that can usefully go on at the very beginning of the project. Since human plans, especially complicated human plans, have a habit of going wrong, front-end analysis has been devised to provide a whole range of suggestions as to what might, or might not, be done. Front-end analysis is evaluative in the sense that it offers detailed procedures for reviewing the adequacy of proposed plans. Among other things, it calls attention to possible *defects* in proposed plans. It also calls attention to possibly serious *omissions*, i.e. plans, or facets of planning, which the planners had not considered including at all.

Whereas front-end analysis is a rather speculative kind of evaluation, since it deals with plans that nobody has, at the time, tried to implement, **formative evaluation** focuses on things that are actually happening. As soon as attempts are made to implement a set of agreed plans, steps can be taken to evaluate the success with which the implementation is proceeding. Roughly speaking, formative evaluation is an activity aimed at improving the form of the final 'product'. In the context of education exhibitions, this means that, while the exhibition is actually taking shape (i.e. during stage 3), the professional evaluator will be busy trying to ensure that the final product, i.e. the product that the visitors will see on the Opening Day, is as effective as possible. The key notion here is one of using evaluative techniques to *steer* the *implementation* stage to a successful conclusion. Naturally, this can happen only if the people who are doing the implementing are both able and willing to listen to what the professional evaluator has to say.

With the onset of stage 4, there begins what professional evaluators describe as **summative evaluation**. Having done as much as he can to help steer the implementation stage to an optimally effective conclusion, the professional evaluator now turns his attention to evaluating the finished product. His evaluation is summative in the sense that it is no longer concerned with helping to improve 'work in progress'. Instead, it aims at evaluating work that has been *completed*.

Formative evaluation and summative evaluation differ in several, not very obvious, ways. For example, there is generally no point in doing formative evaluation unless there is a genuine hope of using the evaluation 'findings' to help make the exhibition a little better than it might otherwise be. Formative evaluation is done, first and foremost, for the purpose of offering directional guidance. But summative evaluation is done, first and foremost, for the purpose of assessing how 'successful' the finished product (e.g. the exhibition, as seen by the visitors on and after the Opening Day) was. There is usually no strong demand that the evaluator should include, in his final summative report, a set of suggestions as to how the project might either (a) be improved, or (b) have been done better in the first place. There are several reasons for this state of affairs. First of all, it is possible for an evaluator to conclude that a project has been a failure, without necessarily being able to say what, if anything, could be done about it.* Next, it needs to be noticed that there is little point in making suggestions about possible improvements if there is no intention, on the part of the sponsors, either to change or repeat the project. Finally, it may be obvious that suggestions about possible improvements would invariably prove *threatening* to some of the parties involved. If improvements are suggested, some critic is bound to ask why the people responsible for the project did not think of them in the first place. And the people who are criticised in this way are likely to turn on the professional evaluator and condemn him for coming up with suggestions that are too late to be implemented. We have already remarked that professional evaluators regularly find themselves in this sort of 'can't win' situation. If their evaluation data show that the project was 'a success', everybody says, 'Well, we knew that already!' And if their evaluation data show that the project was not an unmitigated success, everybody says, 'Where were you when we were planning it?' It is partly for this reason that professional evaluators are increasingly adding front-end evaluative techniques to their armoury of practical tools.

The situation is rather different, however, if explicit provision has been made for a periodic revision and updating of the project. In this case, the professional evaluator *is* usually expected to do his first summative evaluation in a way that enables him to offer directional guidance on the matter of revision. As already indicated, the expectation is not entirely reasonable, because the discovery of error and ineptitude does not necessarily enable the professional evaluator to say what needs to be done to put things right. When this state of affairs occurs, imperceptive critics may well accuse the professional evaluator of being excessively destructive, and insufficiently 'creative'. The sort of thing that gets said is that the evaluator has a good destructive intellect, but he is 'pretty hopeless' when it comes to saying what *ought* to be done. To forestall sniping of this kind, the experienced evaluator can do two things. He will first of all take care to control the expectations of relevant parties, so that they do not expect more than is reasonable.

* For example, attempts to control inflation regularly fail, but it does not follow that anybody knows, at all accurately, what to do about the matter. Recognition of error does not entail an ability to perceive the truth – and that is what gives both poignancy and point to much that goes on in the name of evaluation.

And he will also try to 'jack-up' the whole summative evaluation operation, especially at the *pre-planning* stage, to ensure that his evaluation data do succeed in providing at least *some* directional guidance. Of course, neither of these steps will be effective if the relevant parties do not listen, and if he is unduly constrained with respect to the kind of evaluation data that he can obtain.

What does the professional evaluator do when his summative report is completed? Well, if he has not departed for fresh pastures, it would be appropriate and timely for him to try to evaluate his own evaluation. One intriguing feature of the more sophisticated techniques of the professional evaluator is that they are (as, indeed, they should be) *self-applicable*. The evaluation of evaluation can be more briefly described as meta-evaluation. It is an activity that evaluators inevitably engage in, whenever they ponder the adequacy of their own techniques. If the project *is* being revised, and if the evaluator's summative report is being used to guide part of the revision process, an evaluation of the effectiveness of the revised project automatically involves an evaluation of the evaluation data on which the revision is partly based. If the evaluation data have pointed to a certain course of action, and if the course of action turns out to be no more successful, the evaluator has some fast explaining to do. Unless he can think of some face-saving excuses, his evaluation data will receive very negative evaluations from those people who have trustingly followed it. Perhaps there is some cosmic justice in this. It is never a very pleasant experience to be at the receiving end of a professional evaluator's negative evaluations. So it is appropriate and salutary that the evaluator should himself undergo the experience from time to time.

So far, we have painted two contrasting pictures of evaluation. There is the everyday, impressionistic kind undertaken by all and sundry and the systematic variety practised by professional evaluators: clearly, if the arguments have been accepted then we ought to be aiming for the latter sort. Nevertheless, there are distinct limitations to the kinds of information and conclusions that even professional evaluators can provide and these need to be thought about and discussed before embarking on any evaluation exercise. Broadly speaking there are *methodological* limitations and there are – for want of a better word – *political* limitations associated with practically all attempts at evaluation. Methodological limitations refer to the kinds of problems that are tractable and those that are intractable given the current methods available for evaluation; and political limitations are ones that impinge on the evaluator as a consequence of the environment in which he is working as different groups jockey for influence.

Methodological limitations

Evaluations are usually undertaken to answer questions, and action is then taken on the basis of the answers to the questions. Obviously, if as a result of certain answers we envisage taking significant action, we want to be pretty sure that the answers are correct and not artefacts of the methods we used to collect data. The faith we can place in the veracity of the answers we obtain depends in part on how well the investigation was designed and performed. Throughout this chapter, frequent reference has been made to the professional evaluator's techniques, or 'tools of trade'. These tools are of course partly conceptual and partly practical. The conceptual tools provide 'helpful ways of looking' at evaluation problems. The practical tools are the procedures (of observation and interpretation, etc.) that *actually* enable professional evaluators to evaluate in ways that seem to them to be most helpful, and we shall be looking at some of these in Chapter 16.

It is well beyond the scope of this chapter to survey the totality of conceptual tools that have been developed by professional evaluators, and by other social researchers as well, over the past 20 or so years. But there are just a few conceptual issues, and conceptual distinctions, that *do* need to be mentioned.

How successful is successful?

First of all, let us look at this slippery word 'success'. What does it mean? And how does a professional evaluator (or, for that matter, the man in the street) know what to look for, if he is 'simply' asked to determine whether or not an educational exhibition *is* a success? The remit to the evaluator is manifestly unclear. Does the evaluator dream up his own criteria of success, and evaluate the exhibition with respect to *these*? Or does he try to extract from the exhibition team (or sponsor) what its idea of success is – so that he

can then evaluate the exhibition in this light? As might be expected, professional evaluators have agonised endlessly about dilemmas of this kind. And all of the seemingly obvious solutions have tantalisingly awkward drawbacks. The trouble is that nothing in this world can convincingly be described as good in any absolute sense. What is 'good' for one purpose can be less good for another purpose, and no good at all for a third purpose. What this means is that, in order to evaluate anything at all as 'good' or 'successful', one must introduce relativistic notions of purpose and intentionality. One must move in the direction of saying that, if such-and-such was the intention, then the exhibition (or whatever) appears to have achieved *some* measure of success with *some* sections of the original **target audience**. But this kind of 'iffy-ness' can bring a great deal of trouble in its wake. First of all, there is no shortage of people, some of them quite influential, who tend to regard all conditional statements as evasions ('Quit stalling, and just tell me whether the exhibition was or was not a success.') With people who are as imperceptive as this, the professional evaluator can find himself in real difficulties, because the situation may well *demand* that, in the interests of honesty, his conclusions be hedged around with a whole cluster of conditional reservations. What the professional evaluator may well *want* to say is something like the following. 'I have examined some of the more obvious goals that you seem to have been trying to achieve in this project. For the reasons that I give, some of these goals seem to have been misconceived, others seem to me to have been not worth pursuing, and just a few seem to be mutually incompatible (in the sense that the effective pursuit of one tends to rule out the possibility of effectively pursuing others at the same time). However, if we start with the assumption (your assumption, in fact) that these goals were, in the main, *worth* pursuing, my report indicates the extent to which each of the goals in question tended to be achieved, with respect to each of the main segments of the intended target audience . . . ' It does not need much imagination to predict that very few of the relevant parties (especially sponsors) will want to read *that* kind of message.

One way of trying to sugar-coat an irredeemably bitter pill is to partition the evaluation study into separate sections. With regard to educational exhibitions, for example, it is possible to duck the issue of overall 'success' and focus, instead, on two sub-problems. These are (a) the problem of whether the target audience actually *liked* the exhibition, and (b) the problem of whether the target audience actually *learned* anything while they were there. Roughly speaking, the (a)-problem asks whether everyone is happy, and the (b)-problem asks whether any worthwhile learning is going on. It would be surprising to discover that people learn if they are not happy, but experience of Bingo Halls suggests that people are entirely capable of being happy without learning. The answer to the question posed by (a)-problems is given most readily by surveys of visitors and there have now been a vast number conducted in museums throughout the world. (b)-Problems are much less tractable than (a)-problems to the kinds of methods the professional evaluator has at his disposal and one of the main reasons for this state of affairs is that it is much more difficult to measure whether a visitor has learned something from an exhibition than it is to discover whether he liked an exhibition.

One approach to this problem has been to set down performance standards *in advance* and then design a test that, when administered to a sample of visitors, yields results that tell us whether the visitors have reached certain expected and acceptable standards. The question of how to set realistic and meaningful performance standards is not one that can be solved by resort to logic or reason; it is clearly a question of experience. It is only possible to guess realistically at how well you expect a particular exhibit to communicate its intended message by comparing it with other exhibits about which you already have information. In other words, performance standards should be set against *norms* that themselves are established as a result of the accumulation of empirical data. Accordingly, in the field of exhibition evaluation (where, to our knowledge, no such norms exist), the setting of meaningful performance standards is not yet possible. One method of proceeding is simply to set a standard against which you can begin to calibrate exhibits as you carry out evaluations. One reasonable standard would be to state that for an exhibit to be at least 'marginally successful', a representative sample of visitors seeing the exhibit should perform at least 10 per cent better than a similar sample of visitors who had not seen the exhibit. By the same token, a 'marginal failure' would be one where no demonstrable difference could be shown between samples of visitors seeing and not seeing the exhibit. As data are accumulated, these simple notions of success and failure could be elaborated and enriched to include standards of 'dramatic' success and, conversely, those of 'dramatic' failure.

The problem is made altogether more complicated by the fact that the nature of the test that is used to measure performance does itself affect the level of performance an individual will be seen to achieve. For example, tests of recognition (for instance, multiple-choice questions) furnish higher levels of performance than tests of recall (for instance, open-ended questions). Thus, in stating the performance standards it is also necessary to state the sorts of tests to which these standards apply. This then introduces yet another problem – the problem of 'generalisability', i.e. the extent to which results from one test apply to another sample of visitors taking another different, though related test designed to measure the same sort of thing.

Setting standards for qualities such as an exhibit's ability 'to change attitudes' or 'to promote interest in the subject' are, in principle, no different from setting standards in the know-ledge field. They can be established on the basis of differences between samples of visitors seeing the exhibit and samples that have not seen it.

Certainly, the need for a careful consideration of performance standards is one that should preoccupy all evaluators at the start of a study. Even if the evaluator is unable to answer the question, 'How attractive is an attractive exhibit?', he should at least appreciate that it is an extremely pertinent question.

The limitation of statistics

Written over the door to Plato's Academy were the words: 'Let no one enter here who is ignorant of geometry.' If we were to think of a cognate inscription for the putative evaluator about to enter the world of evaluation it might be: 'Let no one enter here who is ignorant of statistics.' Statistical methods are at the root of systematic evaluation, and notwithstanding Disraeli's famous aphorism concerning their mendacity, it is difficult to conceive of a professional evaluator who is not familiar with at least some of the techniques that have arisen from mathematical statistics.

However, the instances in which we can rely

solely on statistical inferences in evaluation are extremely rare and we should not be blinded or impressed by high-faluting mathematics.

Consider the following:

The head of a museum is concerned about attendance figures. In an attempt to increase the numbers visiting his museum he advertises its attractions in the local press. To ascertain the effectiveness of this small advertising campaign, he organises a count of visitors to the museum. for the month preceding and the month following the appearance of the newspaper advertisements, and he sets out to calculate whether the campaign has been successful. He reports that attendance has increased from 6300 to 7600 which is, he claims, an increase larger than one would expect due to chance fluctuations and, therefore, attributable to his wise investment in advertising expenditure. Specifically, if every visit is independent of every other visit, then visits to the museum are examples of a *Poisson* process. The square root of the number of visits in a given month is a random variable distributed normally with variance $0.25 + 0.25$. On this basis, the z value (Ch. 16) of the observed difference is given by:

$$z = \frac{7600 - 6300}{0.25 + 0.25} = 11.03$$

When this value is referred to the normal distribution it is found to lie very far out in the tail and would occur by chance very infrequently. There is thus sound statistical evidence that the campaign was a success.

Frequently people are very impressed by calculations of this sort and at first glance it is pretty impressive. Suppose, however, somebody informs us that there is always, every year, an increase of this order over the period in question, which coincides with school holidays! Viewed against this new information, we are less sure that the money spent on advertising was money well spent. In fact, viewed in the new light we might be inclined to say that it was a waste of money. This apocryphal tale points out the dangers of wrongly interpreting correctly applied statistics. There was a significant difference in

attendance but it would be incorrct to attribute the increase to the effects of advertising; it was more likely to be attributable to the effects of school holidays. The simple moral from this tale is that it is necessary to take care when drawing conclusions from seemingly impeccable statistical data.

The important thing to understand is that the results of statistical analysis apply *only* to the conditions and considerations that prevailed at the time of analysis. Judgements about their relevance to the real world can only be made sensibly by experts in the field who have a good grasp of the total situation. Thus their applicability depends on sound judgement and not upon statistical theory; they depend upon the sensitivity of the evaluator. It is worth spelling out the limitations of statistical inference in a little more detail as they are most frequently overlooked.

First, as we have seen, they refer only to the material that was studied. This means, for example, that inferences from a study on one exhibition cannot apply, on logical grounds, to another exhibition. It also means that inferences refer only to the population of visitors studied. And, as our example on attendance patterns has shown, it applies only to the variables studied which may not be the most relevant ones. Secondly, inferences refer only to the instrument of the test and the method of using it. Inferences from the results of a particular survey using a questionnaire administered using a person-to-person interview technique do not refer to a different but closely related questionnaire filled out on a self-completion basis. Thirdly, the results apply only to physical and environmental conditions that prevailed at the time of the study. For example, information about visitors to a museum obtained from a survey on a rainy day might be quite different from information collected on sunny days.

In many instances, these limitations may not have serious practical consequences and broadly similar results have been obtained in somewhat different conditions and circumstances. Decisions can be made more wisely on the basis of evaluation, warts and all. Generally speaking, however, the further from the real world an evaluation study is, the more difficult it becomes to apply the results. An analogy may make this clearer. In pharmacological research on the efficacy of new drugs, it is customary (and, indeed, a statutory requirement) to test drugs on animals. No matter how thoroughly the tests are done, and no matter how close genetically the experimental animal is to man, generalisations to people are a perennial problem. Unfortunately, sometimes, for unforeseeable reasons, mistakes are made because humans react differently to the drugs from the experimental animals chosen. However, the closer one is to the real situation, the more reliable (i.e. generalisable) the results are. Considerations related to the artificiality of laboratory studies of narrow populations of subjects in academic psychology have led an increasing number of psychologists to eschew the laboratory approach altogether in favour of naturalistic studies of people. Whereas the pharmacologist cannot study real people, the psychologist can! These considerations have an echo in the pros and cons of formative and summative evaluations of museum exhibitions which we shall now consider, by reference to a realistic but fictitious example.

Let us suppose that an exhibition team is faced with the problem of developing an exhibit to explain the biological concept of homeostasis. It is not clear whether to attempt this explanation by way of analogy, using a domestic central heating system (A) which is familiar to most people, or whether to present a few obvious examples of homeostasis from the field of human biology (B). The team has no basis for making a wise decision but it has to make a choice. There are three possible difficulties that it can get into at this stage:

(a) the team may develop an exhibit based on B in preference to A, only to regret it later when the exhibit has been built;
(b) it may fail to develop an exhibit round B, develop one round A, only to regret later the failure to develop one round B;
(c) irrespective of whether it develops an exhibit round A or round B, it is unhappy with the final exhibit.

The team realises that nothing can be done about (c), since it cannot think of any better alternatives to A and B, but it is unhappy about

making a decision between A and B on the toss of a coin. It decides, therefore, to build two mock-up exhibits, one based on A and the other based on B, and test them. It specifies in advance the teaching points the exhibits are to make and lists the performance standards visitors are required to achieve.

A satisfactory experimental design is worked out to permit comparisons between A and B, and a test is constructed to measure the standard of performance visitors achieve when viewing A and B. The formative evaluation is then carried out. The results show that both A and B are *marginally* successful but that A is significantly better than B even though the difference between them is not great. Has the evaluation as described, put the team in any better position to make a decision by reducing its chances of making mistake (a) or mistake (b)? Logically, the answer is no!

We can show schematically the differences between a visitor's experience of a 'real' museum exhibit and an evaluator's interpretation of a visitor's experience of a mock-up exhibit gained through formative evaluation.

$$E_1 \longrightarrow V_1 \longrightarrow R_1$$

$$E_2 \longrightarrow V_2 \longrightarrow R_2 \longrightarrow \text{INT.} \longrightarrow \text{EVAL.} \longrightarrow R_3$$

V_1 represents a visitor exposed to a real exhibit, E_1, and R_1 is his reaction to it. V_2 represents a visitor exposed to a mock-up exhibit, E_2, and R_2 is the reaction of V_2 to E_2 obtained by an interviewer, INT. Then the interviewer and the evaluator, EVAL., interpret R_2 and arrive at R_3 which they suppose is an estimate of R_1. As can be seen, it is not very sensible to regard R_3 as an estimator of R_1. Generalisability to 'real' exhibits from mock-ups tested in isolation in contrived conditions is a recurrent problem.

Formative evaluation can only tell us about mock-ups tested in unusual conditions. Attempts to make the whole process more realistic can involve testing mock-ups in the context of a real exhibition rather than in a small experimental room; and attempts can also be made to present the mock-up in as finalised a form as possible. As can be seen above, such attempts are merely nibbling at the edges of the problem and we must conclude that it is very unlikely that formative evaluation will show *how* successful the final exhibit will prove. The most we can demand from formative evaluation is direction on very particular types of question concerned with the way information is organised, once the medium for presenting it has been chosen. The value of formative evaluation probably lies mainly in providing the exhibition team with indications of the advantages and disadvantages with the approach it has chosen to a particular problem; generalisability to other problems and situations is probably very low. Nevertheless, many find it useful to put a mock-up in front of visitors and analyse their reactions in order to assess the viability of the approach that has been chosen. In one sense, this type of data is no different from any other in that it has to be interpreted to find out what it all means.

It is fairly clear that formative evaluation of a mock-up will not indicate much about the emotional appeal of the exhibit as it appears in a real exhibition. Therefore, formative evaluation is restricted to assessing the impact of the *content* of the exhibit. The point here is that the strength of an effective *rational* argument is more likely to be apparent despite crude representation, since it depends on logic. A further point to be made is that valuable negative information is more likely to emerge from formative evaluation than any meaningful indication of the degree to which an idea may be a good one. That is to say, formative evaluation is allowed the credit for pointing out what probably will not work, and saying why; but sorting out the good from the mediocre is an altogether different matter.

Let us now return to the problem we posed for our imaginary team; despite all our reservations about the limitations of formative evaluation, suppose that nevertheless, after a good deal of discussion, it is decided to design an exhibit on the basis of *A*. A number of objectives are set which include the following:

(a) the exhibit will attract 30 per cent of all visitors to the museum;
(b) the exhibit will communicate 50 per cent of its main teaching points (each one is listed) to 15 per cent of all visitors to the museum to be considered a marginal success;
(c) the exhibit will be judged as extremely enjoyable by at least 15 per cent of all visitors to the museum to be considered a marginal success.

Once the exhibit has been installed, a programme of summative evaluation is carried out and the exhibit is assessed in the light of the objectives.

Let us assume that, overall, the exhibit is judged a *marginal* failure, and as a result it is decided that further modifications will be made to the exhibit. Accepting that the summative evaluation was carried out with sufficient scientific rigour, how confident can we be that the results do not over-estimate or underestimate the effectiveness of the exhibit? The answer is, that in summative evaluation the risk of being wrong can be calculated mathematically as the consequence of the theory of sampling, *if* our measurement techniques do *not* affect the visitor's *actual* experience of the exhibits being evaluated. Many museum evaluations are concerned with unobtrusive observations of visitors as they wander through exhibitions to discover the exhibits that draw people more than others; and to discover those in front of which visitors tend to stand for longer than others. Attainment of objective (a), for example, can be assessed as accurately as the sample of visitors upon which the unobtrusive observations were made will allow. Furthermore, **psychometric theory** also enables us to establish the extent to which objectives such as (b) and (c) are achieved within estimated degrees of *reliability* and *validity* associated with the tests we use, and on these occasions we approximate far more closely the 'real' experience of casual visitors at 'real' exhibits. This makes summative evaluation a powerful aid to decision-making.

Having said all this, and having made the distinctions between the limitations of formative and summative evaluation, it now needs to be said that formative and summative evaluation should be seen as complementary activities. For example, the decision to use an interactive exhibit or a graphic panel *cannot* be made on the basis of formative evaluation. This is a decision that can only be informed on the basis of experience, that is, on the basis of knowledge of what has been successful in comparable situations in the past. This kind of knowledge, while not infallible, can best be accumulated from summative evaluations of exhibitions containing interactive devices and graphic panels. Nevertheless, formative evaluation may help in deciding the form of an interactive device or a graphic panel, once the decision to use one or the other has been made. It can thus be seen that summative evaluation has a *primary* value and formative evaluation runs the risk of providing irrelevant information about acceptable forms of exhibits if the *type* of exhibits used are not themselves evaluated utilising the substantive data provided by summative evaluation.

In an ideal world, it would be possible to test alternative types of exhibits in their final forms in an exhibition before they became installed as *permanent* exhibits. In this way, comparisons could be as realistic as possible. Whichever approach to evaluation is adopted, however, it is well worth remembering the following maxim:

Opinions based on experience and reason will, in general, prove more reliable than those based on poorly designed evaluations.

The psycho-dynamics and politics of evaluation

As indicated earlier in this chapter, everyday evaluations are highly subjective, frequently uncritical reflections of the likes and dislikes, and of the personal tastes and attitudes, of the persons making the evaluations. We have also attempted to characterise a different sort of critical evaluation, that of systematic evaluation carried out by a professional who brings particular kinds of skills to the (difficult) task of discovering whether an exhibition has been successful. Here, of course, is the rub. What might be considered successful to one person will be unsuccessful to a second and downright irrelevant to others. In this situation, the findings of the professional evaluator will be music to some, discord to others, and largely irrelevant to yet others. The everyday working environment in which the professional evaluator will find himself is always going to be occupied by people with different views; such is life. Thus the professional evaluator is likely to be praised, reviled and ignored simultaneously by different people.

It is interesting to attempt an analysis of the possible ways in which the professional evaluator's work might be received. Here is a list of some of the possible ways in which an evaluation may be seen, any number of which may be operative when an evaluation project has been carried out and the conclusions reported.

(a) Evaluation data seen as information about the ways in which the exhibit(s) performed against expected standards of success. Evaluation data seen as providing information about possible improvements to exhibits, or about the process of exhibition design in general.

(b) Evaluation data seen as vindication of certain people's predictions or judgement.

(c) Evaluation data seen as an act of conformity (e.g. as being provided because some influential person insisted that it be provided).

(d) Evaluation data seen as a move in some political game – e.g. to settle an argument or an old score with some party, or to use as a weapon for or against a particular faction or institution.

Most idealised accounts of the use of systematic evaluation suppose that (a) is the only one that exists. In practice, all the others tend to exist side by side with the well intentioned motives behind (a). In these circumstances, whenever evaluations are made public, many findings are suppressed if they disagree with the opinions of the decision-makers. And they are often suppressed because certain people are worried about their reputations, or about the damage that such disclosures might do to the team under their care. People will seldom go so far as to admit that they are actually scared, because this is not the sort of thing that 'strong' people do. Anyway, to admit to feeling scared would be to make them, in their own eyes, even more vulnerable. Very often, these people do not even admit to *themselves* that they are scared – scared (for example) about their public reputation; or their promotion prospects; or even, perhaps, their jobs. Instead of privately admitting to themselves that they are scared, they will tend to say, instead, that they feel concerned about the welfare of the organisation, concerned about the poor quality of other people's work, concerned about lack of co-operation, concerned about what influential critics might say, and so on. Seemingly, it is much more responsible to wear the mask of 'concern' than to admit to being scared.

One consequence of this is that people in this state of fear-masquerading-as-concern can rarely be open with one another. Communication within an organisation afflicted in this way therefore becomes increasingly cryptic. Executives, in particular, focus on doing things that can be defended against subsequent attack. At the same time, the desire for friends gives way to a felt need for allies and supporters. Frequently, the phenomenon of self-frightening goes on. People who are privately worried (perhaps with good reason) about their own position, or their own ability to cope, start imagining all sorts of horrors that could befall them or their organisation, if certain things are not done (if, for example, nobody is willing to 'make a firm stand'). Intrigue develops. And this reinforces the feeling that allies or henchmen are urgently needed. What began as an essentially *baseless* fear ends up, by a series of ineptitudes, being a very realistic fear. This is so because fear is, in the long run, always *iatrogenic*. It always makes difficult situations worse and, if there is a taboo on even admitting its very existence, little can be done to improve things.

This, then, is the milieu – the everyday working environment – in which the professional evaluator lives, moves and breathes. On his right hand sit the sponsors of the project – anxious people who are hoping either (a) that the project will be a success, or (b) that nobody will make a fuss (or, better still, even get to hear about it) if it is not. On his left hand is the project leader whose sentiments may be almost identical. And then there are the rest of the staff, all of whom may have different hidden agendas concerning what they hope to get out of the project.

In this sort of situation, it is almost inevitable that something like a love-hate relationship will develop between the professional evaluator and nearly everyone else. The reason for this is that, in his capacity as 'the official evaluator', he is inevitably seen by nervous people as a possible threat. It is he, above all others, who can 'blow the whistle' if the project starts going seriously and demonstrably wrong. At the same time, everyone is likely to feel that they should be as friendly as possible towards him, since he is not the sort of person that one wants to have on the other side. If there are already divisions of opinion within the team, as to how certain aspects of the project should be handled, attempts to win the evaluator over to a particular point of view will commence almost as soon as he arrives on the scene. And if the evaluator is himself a man of firm convictions, disagreements will soon begin to simmer. The resolution of such disagreements tends to be an all-or-nothing business. Because the stakes are believed to be high, the evaluator will be perceived, in fairly black and white terms, as being either 'for us' or 'against us'. As indicated

above, some members of the team may hold one view, and others might hold the opposite view.

Whatever the professional evaluator does, he is likely to be on a hiding to nothing. When anxiety and fear get a grip on people, nothing that he does will seem right in the eyes of some people. Since he is perceived as being a potentially dangerous person, they will not leave him alone, either. Bickering and confrontation will escalate, and the only surprise in the situation is the surprise of discovering that some people are surprised by it all.

The whole situation is rendered an order of magnitude more confusing if there are additional outside parties chipping in with their opinions and complaints. In our own experience, for example, the activities of the evaluator have sometimes been paralleled by somewhat noisier evaluations from outsiders who felt that certain aspects of the exhibition were misconceived. Since many of these critics hold quite prestigious positions in the professional world, and since they aired their grievances rather persistently in the media, they were not easily ignorable, in spite of the fact that many of their specific complaints got convincingly repudiated in the arguments that followed.

Incidents of this kind show that evaluation can rapidly turn, or degenerate, into something of a power struggle between different vested interests. If pressure groups dislike what is going on, they may well try to bring the activity to an end, *whatever* the professional evaluator (or, for that matter, the team responsible) might have to say in its favour. What is more, they might use quite questionable tactics to achieve their ends, e.g. by making unjustified insinuations about the motives behind activities that they regard as threatening. Since pressure groups can (and do) exist both inside and outside of large organisations, the professional evaluator may find himself embroiled in battle on all sides, if he genuinely believes, on the basis of the evidence that he has collected, that he is right (or more right) than the various pressure groups aligned against him. In recognition of this difficulty, yet another new professional has sprung up in the United States – namely, the profession of 'Change Agent'. Briefly, a Change Agent is a person who has special skills (skills of negotiation and persuasion, etc.) that enable him to shift organisations in the direction in which they seemingly most need to go. In view of the resistances that professional evaluators so often encounter, when they try to convince others of the rightness of their conclusions, there is much to be said for adding the skills of a Change Agent to the already substantial skills of professional evaluation.

Readers who have a background knowledge of social science will be aware that the profession of evaluator is a comparatively recent one. It has been around, in the field of education, for only 25 years or so. In the early days, the professional literature that accompanied and fostered the development of the profession had comparatively little to say about the so-called 'politics of evaluation'. Over the years, however, the phenomenon of politicking – of picking holes in the professional evaluator's findings, and of launching pro and con arguments about the validity of the evaluator's entire *modus operandi* – has gradually come to be seen as one of the most central problems of the profession. To deny that such politicking exists would be to make a straight denial of reality. The challenge to the sensitive professional evaluator is therefore two-fold. The first challenge is to grasp the essential nature and inevitability of the kind of politicking that can arise when he announces his findings. The second challenge is to try to treat the politicking in an understanding (i.e. non-confronting and non-personalised) manner. This is of course much easier said than done. But it will be almost impossible to do if the would-be evaluator is not even aware of the politicking phenomena.

What, then, can be said about the 'politics' of evaluation? One comment that deserves to be made is that, although there is no harm in speaking of political obstacles to the acceptance of the professional evaluator's findings, there is actually a deeper sense in which the resistance is due to *fear*. More often than not politics is itself both fear-based and fear-exacerbating. It is also divisive, because it encourages people to band together in groups, to enhance their protection against others who they fear may be their enemies. The point is not an unimportant one because professional evaluators often claim that it is 'politics' that obstructs the acceptance of their findings. In a sense, this is true. But it can lead beginners (would-be evaluators) up a blind alley. If an evaluator really wants to find out why his findings are encountering resistance, he would be much better advised simply to ask what the resisters are frightened about. If fear is the driving force, then fear, not politics, is what needs to be made the main focus of concern.

16   Designing and carrying out the evaluation study

On a number of occasions in the previous chapter we referred to the 'tools of the trade' that professional evaluators use when carrying out their work. Much has been written elsewhere about these tools; and new tools and methods of using them are invented as quickly as old ones become worn out and thrown away. Clearly, there is no chance (or necessity) of us covering the field in detail, and even a superficial canter through would take up more space than is available here. In this chapter we shall attempt a classification of the common types of investigation carried out in exhibition evaluations, indicate the considerations to bear in mind when designing them, and describe some of the basic tools necessary for actually doing the work. We shall concentrate on some of the techniques of **formative** and **summative evaluation**.

Classification of evaluation techniques

Initially, it is useful to think of evaluation in terms of the questions we might tackle. They tend to incline to one or other end of this spectrum:

holistic —————— atomistic

(Alternatively, we may think in similar terms of macro versus micro evaluation.) The more 'holistic' the questions, the more likely it is that our evaluation studies will be:

(a) ones that aim to discover what happened when the public was let loose on an exhibition;
(b) concerned with the entire exhibition policy, that is, with whether the public thinks it is getting or is going to get what it wants from the exhibitions presented.

The more 'atomistic' they are, the more often they will:

(a) test individual exhibits, as individual queries arise using material in any state of finish;
(b) test main legends, illustrations, text and other details.

It can be seen that there is a close correspondence between the holistic versus atomistic classification and summative and formative evaluations.

Another way of looking at evaluation is in terms of the techniques and approaches that are used to answer the questions that have been posed. Broadly speaking, we can make a split between *qualitative* approaches and *quantitative* ones. In qualitative studies, a relatively small number of individuals are intensively interviewed. No formal questionnaire and sampling method are involved and informants are given a certain amount of freedom to explore and develop areas introduced by the interviewer. These are known as open-ended interviews and typically last between one and two hours. They can involve groups of individuals (group discussions) where members prompt one another to discuss differences of opinion, or they may take the form of individual face-to-face interviews between interviewer and informant. Often such methods are used in exploratory studies as preludes to quantitative investigations. Quantitative studies are more formal, more structured and are carried out among representative samples of visitors. Both approaches are commonplace in pure and applied research.

In this chapter we shall consider quantitative methods only, and the reasons for this are both practical and theoretical. The idea behind qualitative research is that you have to dig deeply if you want to find anything of value. It is difficult, if not impossible, to imagine a situation in which visitors would be prepared to devote upwards of an hour of their time to discussion with an interviewer when they had intended to look at exhibits. Our experience has shown that 20 minutes is the absolute maximum amount of time you can expect a visitor to give over to an interview, and that, ideally, interviews should last around 10 to 12 minutes. Qualitative methods rely heavily on the interpersonal skill of the interviewer in 'drawing out' the informants during discussion. The more intensive the interview, the smaller the chances are that it will be administered in a standard way. This makes any interpretation of the results a particularly tricky matter, especially if working in a field where people feel threatened and need to defend their position. A common defence against evaluation findings is to attack the professional competence of the study by claiming it is biased and unrepresentative. Clearly, qualitative studies run a very real risk of being discredited in this way and the aim of this section of the book is to explain how to get hold of comparatively 'hard' (i.e. difficult-to-argue-against) data.

Sometimes, however, there are problems to which rough and ready answers may be acceptable. In these instances, it may not be necessary to carry out rigorous quantitative evaluations if all parties agree *beforehand* to accept the limitations of less rigorous studies and those responsible are prepared to abide by the outcomes and take the necessary decisions. Indeed, it is a good idea to draw a number of possible scenarios as to the outcome of any evaluation study (this applies equally to rigorous and non-rigorous, quantitative and qualitative studies) which include conditional courses of action, and then try to get agreement on the course of action *before* carrying out the study. In this way people will find it more difficult to hedge their bets.

Now let us consider some typical investigations in summative and formative evaluations.

Types of investigations in summative evaluation

Many summative evaluations are essentially fact-finding or descriptive in nature. Visitor surveys and most observational studies undertaken to discover the **attracting power** and **holding power** of exhibits fall squarely into this category. For example, at the British Museum (Natural History), we have been concerned to describe the sorts of visitors we attract, the exhibits they see, the ones they find interesting, and so on.

These relatively straightforward descriptive studies involve a minimum of statistical methodology. Of course, we need to draw a representative sample of visitors if we are to be confident that our results apply to all our visitors but beyond this we do not need to be concerned with complicated experimental designs. The major considerations of fact-finding surveys are the design of the questionnaire, adequate interviewing skills and the preparation of data for, and analysis by, a computer.

Testing hypotheses in summative evaluation

In contrast to the straightforward descriptive studies just mentioned, sometimes we may wish to test a particular hypothesis. For example, it has been claimed that the new exhibitions at the British Museum (Natural History) cater only for the lay person who has no qualifications in biology or natural history. One testable hypothesis that stems from this assertion is that persons with above some minimum standard of achievement in biology would like the new exhibitions less than those persons without qualifications in biology. For the sake of argument, let us set this minimum level at 'Advanced' ('A') in a biological subject. We note from the annual surveys at the Museum that less than 10 per cent of all visitors are likely to have achieved this minimum standard. The main problem, therefore, in testing the hypothesis is finding in the population of visitors, samples on which the hypothesis can be tested with an acceptable degree of exactitude. What is required on the one hand is a sample of visitors with an educational attainment in biology at or above 'A' level and, on the other, a *comparable* sample of visitors (known as a *control* group) whose educational attainment is below the prescribed level. Since educational attainment is known to be correlated with age and socio-economic status (among other variables), matching visitors in our two groups is not an easy task.

Frequently, of course, groups that we might wish to compare with respect to some response to an exhibition are readily obtained among a cross section of visitors. Males and females, solitary and accompanied visitors, first-time and repeat visitors, are three obvious examples. Useful information can be obtained when groups such as these are compared, provided strenuous efforts are made to match members of the groups on variables that might otherwise bias the comparison.

The generalisability of the results will depend on how representative the samples in the comparison are of the groups of individuals being compared. Experience has shown that in practice it is very difficult to obtain two groups that are alike in all respects *except* in terms of the factors against which they are to be compared. Often, however, in exhibition evaluations, the difference between groups would have to be really quite large if any action was planned on the basis of the differences. In these instances the need for perfect matching decreases as we would be looking for large differences for our rule of thumb. Sometimes, in an attempt to match groups too closely, there is a very real danger of achieving a match on the very factors we wish to compare. Suppose, for example, we wished to compare the knowledge of boys and girls of similar ages after looking at a particular exhibit on the assumption that any differences between them are attributable to the effects of the exhibit. It would be misleading to match them on educational attainment since the level of knowledge in a particular subject and educational attainment are more than likely to be highly correlated, and therefore any differences between the sexes would be obscured. In this instance it would be better to base the comparisons on large samples of boys and girls drawn randomly from the population of visitors.

Retrospective and prospective studies in summative evaluation

A retrospective study is one in which, starting with a plausible cause-and-effect hypothesis, an investigation is carried out backwards in time to see if the hypothesised cause is associated with the observed effect. For example, suppose from a survey of visitors we notice that some visitors prefer new exhibits whereas others prefer the older ones. We might hypothesise that those who prefer the new exhibits are less qualified in biology than those preferring the older ones. To test the hypothesis we would look at visitors preferring new exhibits and those preferring old and then compare the proportion of visitors with 'A' levels in biology in each group. This type of study has the advantage that visitors known to have achieved a standard of attainment in biological education ('A' levels) can easily be identified. We should note in passing that this example attempts to answer the same hypothetical question posed at the beginning of the previous section but in this case we have proceeded from 'back to front' as it were to find the answer.

In contrast, studies that proceed forward in time are known as *prospective*. In these cases the occurrence of a characteristic of visitors is noted that is thought to have certain consequences in terms of how visitors behave or react in an exhibition; and the visitors are then observed to see if these consequences materialise. For example, it has been suggested that adults in family groups with young children behave differently from those in groups without young children in respect of the exhibits they look at and their behaviour at exhibits. One way of examining this proposition is to ask 'matched' adults in groups with and without children which exhibits they looked at and what they did while looking at them, at the end of their visits to the exhibition. This method is likely to prove unsatisfactory for a number of reasons. Visitors might be inclined to forget exhibits they looked at for short periods of time. And, quite apart from its reliance on memory, information about exhibits that were found difficult to comprehend might be withheld. To obtain reliable information it would be necessary to carry out prospective studies by following unobtrusively adults in groups with and without children and noting their behaviour at certain exhibits.

Prospective studies have obvious advantages over retrospective studies in that there is less opportunity for bias in the response of individuals taking part but they are much more difficult and time consuming to carry out.

Types of investigations in formative evaluation

Formative evaluations are prospective investigations in which we are concerned to discover whether exhibits in some rudimentary or mock-up form are capable of communicating what is intended, and if not how they might be improved to achieve the desired ends. This general notion can be extended to include comparisons of several exhibits and several different groups of visitors to determine which types of exhibits are successful among all or some groups of visitors. The major consideration in designing satisfactory formative evaluations is to design studies that as far as possible eliminate ambiguity in the interpretation of the results. Central to the aim of reducing ambiguity is the idea of experimental control. This is possible in most cases of deliberate experimentation where visitors are exposed to mock-up exhibits in a manner determined by the investigator. Successful experimental designs are ones in which meaningful comparisons can be made between the experimental groups and ones in which the results are generalisable to visitors other than those specifically incorporated in study.

Sampling visitors for museum evaluations: preliminary considerations

If we know about every visitor who had ever been to our exhibition and about every visitor who would visit in the future, then we could describe their characteristics perfectly. That we could never have this knowledge is obvious enough, and yet we still talk happily about the characteristics of our audience as countless visitor surveys will attest. Research workers are concerned with many *populations*, some hypothetical (as in the case of exhibition visitors) and others so large that an investigation has to be carried out on a sample only. Clearly, the amount of credence that we can place on the results of a study among a sample of visitors will depend in part on how representative the sample is of the populations being studied. The representativeness of a sample will depend on its size and how it was drawn. We shall consider these points separately but first we need some elementary statistical concepts.

The arithmetic mean ($\bar{x}$) and standard deviation (s) of a sample variable

Suppose we interview a random sample ('randomness' will be discussed later) of 100 visitors (the sample size is usually represented by n) as they are leaving a museum and we ask each visitor in the sample how many galleries he visited. Let us further suppose that the museum has eight galleries and we obtained the following 100 answers, which we have arranged in terms of *frequency distribution*, i.e. a count of the number

of visitors who viewed 0, 1 . . . 8 galleries (Table 16.1).

If we examine the column of frequencies in this example, we see that the number of galleries visited most frequently is 4, and that the frequency of the numbers above and below 4 tends to diminish as we move away from 4. The distribution of the number of galleries visited tends to be symmetrical around 4. This can be shown most clearly if we arrange the data in a *histogram* in which the frequency of the number of galleries visited is represented by the height of a column with the score at the centre of its base. The histogram is shown in Figure 16.1.

The average number of galleries visited (represented by $\bar{x}$, the bar above the x indicating that it is the average value of a set of values of x) is obtained by dividing the total number of visits by 100 (the number n in the sample of visitors). Thus the arithmetic mean is then the sum (represented by the symbol Σ) of the xs, divided by n. The mathematical shorthand is therefore:

$$\text{arithmetic mean} = \frac{\Sigma x}{n}.$$

Table 16.1   Frequency distribution of galleries visited by visitors to a museum.

Number of galleries (x)	Frequency (f)
0	3
1	9
2	12
3	15
4	20
5	16
6	11
7	10
8	4
	$n = 100$

The calculation of $\bar{x}$ when a frequency distribution has been formed is only a little more difficult. Remembering that the frequency (f) column simply tells us how many visitors there were visiting the corresponding number of galleries, it would be possible to write down 0 three times, 1 nine times, 2 twelve times, and so on. This would require the summation of the number of visits by 100 visitors and division by 100. However, it is much quicker to multiply the number of galleries

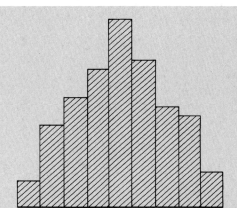

Figure 16.1 Histogram of number of galleries visited.

visited by the number of visits, giving fx (Table 16.2). The sum of these products is the same as the sum of the original 100 individual answers.

The arithmetic mean is therefore given by

$$\frac{406}{100} = 4.06 \text{ visits.}$$

In a general form this is

$$\bar{x} = \frac{\Sigma fx}{\Sigma f}.$$

although in many cases Σf will be shown by n. In our example, it can be seen that $\bar{x}$ is very close to 4, the number of galleries visited that appears with the largest frequency in Figure 16.1. The most

frequently occurring number in a distribution of numbers is known as the *mode*, and both the mode and the mean give good indications of the central value of a series of numbers when the distribution of the numbers is symmetrical.

Figure 16.2 shows four symmetrical distributions of variables x_1, x_2, x_3 and x_4 where $\bar{x}_1 = \bar{x}_2 = \bar{x}_3 = \bar{x}_4$.

Clearly, from Figure 16.2, we can see that the mean values of each distribution tell us nothing about the *scatter* or *dispersion* of the different values of x_1, x_2, x_3 or x_4. We need a statistic that indicates the dispersion of the different x values about their respective means.

One way of measuring dispersion about a mean would be to compare each observed value in the series with the arithmetic mean of the series. This has been done in Table 16.3 (Remember $\bar{x} = 4.06$ visits.)

It seems that our efforts have been in vain, for we find that the total amount of dispersion as given by summing the $f(x - \bar{x})$ column is zero. In fact, this should be no surprise, for if the arithmetic mean is to be numerically representative then the sum of the positive and negative deviations of the individual values round it must by definition equate to produce a zero answer.

The generally accepted and most used method of overcoming the zero sum, in our case $\Sigma f(x - \bar{x})$, is one that makes use of the fact that the square of both positive and negative numbers is positive. This is done by squaring each deviation from the mean (Table 16.4).

Table 16.2 Frequency distribution as in Table 16.1, showing the calculation of fx.

Number of galleries (x)	Number of visitors (f)	fx
0	3	0
1	9	9
2	12	24
3	15	45
4	20	80
5	16	80
6	11	66
7	10	70
8	4	32
	total 100	406

Table 16.3 The data from Table 16.1, showing dispersion about the mean.

Number of galleries (x)	Number of visitors (f)	f(each value − arithmetic mean) $f(x - \bar{x})$
0	3	3(−4.06) = −12.18
1	9	9(−3.06) = −27.54
2	12	12(−2.06) = −24.72
3	15	15(−1.06) = −15.90
4	20	20(−0.06) = −1.20
5	16	16 (0.94) = +15.04
6	11	11 (1.94) = +21.34
7	10	10 (2.94) = +29.40
8	4	4 (3.94) = +15.76
	total 100	0

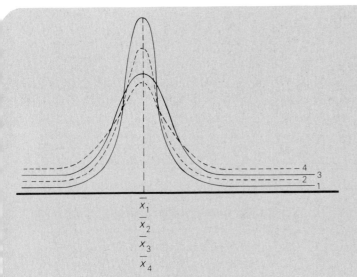

$\overline{x}_1$
$\overline{x}_2$
$\overline{x}_3$
$\overline{x}_4$

Figure 16.2 Four normal distributions with the same mean but different dispersions.

Table 16.4   The data from Table 16.1, squaring each deviation from the mean.

Number of galleries (x)	Number of visitors (f)	$f(x-\overline{x})^2$
0	3	3(16.48) = 49.44
1	9	9 (9.36) = 84.24
2	12	12 (4.24) = 50.88
3	15	15 (1.12) = 16.80
4	20	20 (0.0036) = 0.07
5	16	16 (0.88) = 14.08
6	11	11 (3.76) = 41.36
7	10	10 (8.64) = 86.40
8	4	4 (15.52) = 62.08
	total 100	408.95

Rather than use the total, we prefer to average once again so that our measure of dispersion (the *variance*) is given by

$$\frac{\Sigma f(x-\overline{x})^2}{n} = \frac{408.95}{100} = 4.09.$$

The variance is frequently employed in statistical methods, but it should be noted that the figure achieved is in 'squared' units of measurement. Our variance is 4.09 'squared galleries visited', which is obviously ridiculous. We can reduce the variance to the original unit of measurement by taking the (positive) square root. The result is described as the standard deviation, symbolised by s, so that the standard deviation number of galleries visited is $\sqrt{4.09} = 2.02$. The number of galleries visited by our 100 visitors can now be described by the following summary statistics:

sample size, n $\quad\quad$ = 100,
mean, $\overline{x}$ $\quad\quad\quad\quad$ = 4.06,
standard deviation, s = 2.02.

An obvious question concerns the adequacy of these statistics as complete descriptions of the data. To answer this question, it is necessary to describe a distribution very widely used in statistical work, known as the *normal distribution*. The major characteristics of normal curves are unimodality (one peak), symmetry (one side the same as the other) and certain mathematical properties such that if the mean and standard deviation of a normal distribution are known, it is possible to draw with deadly accuracy the shape of the curve. In fact, the symmetrical distributions shown in Figure 16.2 are all examples of normal distributions.

Some of the important mathematical properties of the normal distribution are shown in Figure 16.3. Here we can see that approximately 68 per cent of all values of the variable x lie between $\pm$ 1 standard deviation from the mean, $\overline{x}$; approximately 95 per cent of all values of the variable x lie between $\pm$ 2 standard deviations from $\overline{x}$ and over 99 per cent lie between $\pm$ 3 standard deviations from the mean. If we imagine a normal distribution in which $\overline{x} = 0$ and $s = 1$,

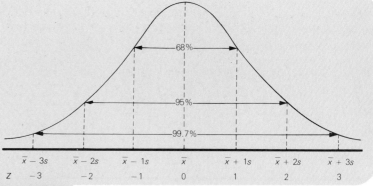

Figure 16.3   Mathematical properties of the normal distribution.

then the distribution is said to be *standard* and the scores are known as *standard scores* or *z* scores. It is possible to *transform* the value of any variable that is normally distributed into its corresponding *z* score using the formula

$$z = \frac{x - \bar{x}}{s}.$$

The distribution in Figure 16.1 is approximately normal and this is clearly shown if we convert the number of galleries visited into *z* scores (Table 16.5). This we have done using the values of $\bar{x}$ and

Table 16.5   The data from Table 16.1 with the *z* scores.

Number of galleries (x)	Number of visitors (f)	z score $\left(\frac{x - \bar{x}}{s}\right)$
0	3	−2.01
1	9	−1.51
2	12	−1.02
3	15	−0.52
4	20	0.03
5	16	0.47
6	11	0.96
7	10	1.46
8	4	1.95

s calculated earlier. The distribution in Figure 16.1 does not have the 'tails' that are found in a normal distribution and this is reflected by the fact that the *z* scores range from −2*s* to 2*s* and not from −3*s* to 3*s* as they would if the distribution was truly normal. Nevertheless, it is an acceptable approximation.

Standard error of the mean and sample size

After the brief discourse on the nature of *means*, *standard deviations* and *normal distributions*, we can now return to our original concern about the sample size, in particular to how the representativeness of a sample is affected by the size of the sample.

In our example, $n = 100$, $\bar{x} = 4.06$, $s = 2.02$ and the distribution is approximately normal. Our interest is in the reliability of the mean; how much can we depend on this statistic? Let us suppose that many more random samples of size 100 are drawn from our population of visitors and the mean number of galleries visited is calculated from each sample. Practical experience (as well as common sense) would tell us that the values of the $\bar{x}$s would not all be 4.06; some would be larger and others smaller. How accurate then is our estimate of 4.06 from a single sample of 100? An answer to this question is given by a statistic known as the *standard error*.

Just as we plotted our histogram in Figure 16.1, we could in theory plot a histogram of the means of the many random samples of size 100. Whenever this has been done in comparable situations (e.g. tossing a coin 100 times over and over again), it has been found that the histogram tends to be symmetric about the mean of the sample means. The standard deviation of the sampling distribution of the means is known as the *standard error* of the mean. Luckily there is no need to draw a large number of different random samples to estimate the standard error. In our case, an estimate of the standard error of the mean, s_{mean} can be estimated as follows:

$$s_{mean} = \frac{s}{\sqrt{n}}.$$

In our example, each visitor in a random sample of 100 was asked how many galleries he had visited and we obtained the following results:

$$\bar{x} = 4.09 \text{ galleries,}$$
$$s = 2.02 \text{ galleries,}$$
$$n = 100.$$

Therefore,

$$\text{standard error } \bar{x} = \frac{2.02}{\sqrt{100}} = 0.2.$$

Remember that the standard error of the mean is a standard deviation and the distribution of sample means is normal. These two properties permit us to interpret the standard error as we would any standard deviation of a normal distribution. In Figure 16.3, we noted that 95 per cent of all values in a normal distribution lie between ± 2 standard deviations from the mean. If we apply this knowledge to the standard error of the mean and the sampling distribution of the means, we can say that 95 per cent of all sample means would lie between ± 2 standard errors. Thus with repeated sampling, with $n = 100$, we would expect the sample means to lie between $4.06 \pm 2 \times 0.2$ galleries, that is, between 3.66 and 4.46 galleries, 95 per cent of the time in the long run.

In many instances in visitor surveys, we are simply interested in knowing whether each individual visitor possesses or does not possess a certain characteristic – 'previously visited the museum', 'approves of the exhibition', and so on – this characteristic may be called an attribute. Quantification then lies in *counting* how many possess this attribute and how many do not, and the proportion (or percentage) with the attribute provides a useful description of the population. In these instances, it is possible to change the attribute into a variable by allocating the score '1' to all those who possess the attribute, and '0' to those who do not. Suppose 40 out of 100 visitors have visited the museum before, one could treat this as a variable, scoring 0 for those who had not visited the museum previously and 1 for those who had. The average, or mean value, of this variable for the 100 visitors is

$$\frac{(60 \times 0) + (40 \times 1)}{100} = 0.4$$

or alternatively 40 per cent.

In general, if p is the proportion of visitors possessing the attribute, and q the proportion not possessing it, then the variance is given by the product of p and q and the standard error of p is given by

$$\sqrt{\frac{pq}{n}}.$$

(N.B. $q = (1 - p)$ or $(100 - p)$ if p is expressed as a percentage.)

If a random sample of 400 visitors gives the result that 40 per cent have visited the museum on a previous occasion, then $n = 400$, $p = 40$ per cent and $q = 100 - 40 = 60$ per cent; and

$$\text{standard error } (p) = \sqrt{\frac{40 \times 60}{400}} =$$
$$\sqrt{6} = 2.45 \text{ per cent.}$$

Again, applying our knowledge of the properties of the normal distribution, we would expect the average values to lie between $40 \pm 2 \times 2.45$ per cent, that is between 35.1 and 44.9 per cent, 95 per cent of the time in the long run.

The limits or bounds of the 'true' means calculated in the above ways are called *confidence limits*. The width of the confidence limits indicates the accuracy of the mean derived from the sample. Obviously, the closer the limits, the more accurate the estimate is. One way of reducing the width is to reduce the size of the standard error, and since the size of the standard error is inversely proportional to the square root of the sample size, the confidence limits can be narrowed by increasing the sample size. Indeed, as n is increased, the standard error tends towards zero until in the limiting case it equals zero: this is when everybody in a population is sampled, and the result is called a *census*.

'How big a sample do I need?' is almost certainly the question to be asked and as a general rule it can be seen that the answer is 'the larger the better'. However, the size of the standard error is *not* directly proportional to the size of the sample; instead the relationship is rather more complicated, as indicated by Figure 16.4.

As can be seen, there is a Law of Diminishing Returns in increasing the sample size such that a point is reached where larger increases in the sample size result in a small decrease in the standard error (and hence the precision of the quantity being estimated). In deciding on the

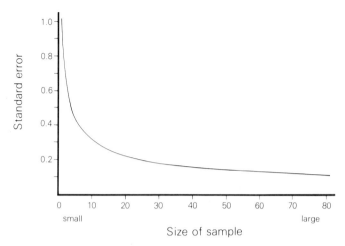

Figure 16.4 Relation of the size of sample to standard error.

sample size, the evaluator must decide on the precision he requires. This is a question that *cannot* be answered by statistics and depends on the purpose of the study. (Statistical theory can only tell you how precise your answer *is*, not how precise it *should be*.)

So far we have looked at only one side of the typical decision regarding sample size, i.e. what size of sample is required to give a given precision in estimating some quantity. In practice, the aim is either to get maximum precision at a given cost (or in the time available) or to reach a pre-determined level of precision at the lowest cost; so that a decision on sample size is as much governed by an estimate of the costs and time involved as it is by the standard error. However, in some evaluations we are not concerned only with obtaining an estimate of some quantity within acceptable limits of precision; rather, we are concerned in *comparing* differences between variables, either means or proportions. For example, let us suppose we are interested in seeing whether the proportion of young people (say, of less than 16 years of age) visiting a museum alters as a result of the opening of an exhibition that has been aimed at them specifically. Here, we might carry out a survey *before* the exhibition opens and after it has opened and see how many young people there are in each sample. Let us imagine we find p_1 per cent of young people before it opens and p_2 per cent of young people after it opens. If the aim is to measure the difference between p_1 and p_2 per cent with a desired level of precision, the same general approach as before can be applied, except that there are now two samples, a sample size of n_1

yielding p_1 per cent and one of n_2 yielding p_2 per cent young people.

In the simplest case, if two samples are drawn using simple random sampling and are independent of one another, the standard error of the percentage difference $(p_1 - p_2)$ per cent is given by:

$$S_{(p_1 - p_2)} = \sqrt{pq\left(\frac{1}{n_1} + \frac{1}{n_2}\right)},$$

where

$$p = \frac{n_1 p_1 + n_2 p_2}{n_1 + n_2} \quad \text{and} \quad q = 100 - p.$$

To simplify matters, let us suppose that $n_1 = n_2 = n$, which is often the case when we are planning surveys and can, therefore, have control of our sample sizes. In this instance, the expression for the standard error of the percentage difference becomes $\sqrt{2\,pq/n}$ and the one for p becomes $\frac{1}{2}(p_1 + p_2)$. If the percentage difference $(p_1 - p_2)$, say d, is more than twice its standard error, we may say with 95 per cent confidence that there is a difference between p_1 and p_2. Suppose, for example, that $d = 5$ per cent, $p_1 = 52.5$ per cent and $p_2 = 47.5$ per cent, then we need to discover what minimum size of n is required such that 5 per cent is greater than twice the value of $S_{(52.5 - 47.5)}$. Or put another way, we want to find the smallest value of n such that the expression $5 > \sqrt{2 \times 50 \times 50/n}$ is satisfied. (Remember, in this example, $p = \frac{1}{2}(52.5 + 47.5) = 50$, and $q = 100 - 50 = 50$.) Rearranging this expression we can see that the value of n we require is given by

$$n > \frac{8 \times 50 \times 50}{25} = 800.$$

Notice particularly, that the value of n is not simply dependent on the value of d, but also on the values of p and q. In our example, we chose values of p_1 and p_2 such that the product term pq was at its largest. In other words, in the *worst possible case*, we need a sample of 800. When $p \neq q$, smaller values of n varying in accordance with values of p and q would be sufficient.

An analogous formula is available to help us determine the necessary sample sizes if we wish to establish the difference between two arithmetic means at a predetermined level of precision.

So far, we have looked at the importance of sample size and how to go about determining the sample size for a given purpose. Shortly, we shall turn to the method of sampling itself, i.e. how to select a sample of visitors, but before we do this we shall examine the notions of *randomness* and *random* sampling that we have referred to throughout this chapter and their importance in determining the *representativeness* of the sample.

Randomness and random sampling

The notion of randomness is at the core of modern probabilistic methods which are themselves central to all scientific investigations. For example, early this century randomness became the bedrock of quantum mechanics, and is at the root of modern evolutionary theory. This crucial scientific idea has also had an influence on the random art of abstract expressionism, in the random music of such composers as John Cage and in the random word-play of a book like James Joyce's *Finnegans wake*. The idea of randomness has had a profound effect on 20th-century thought and, yet, it is extremely difficult to state what we mean by 'random'. The dictionary definition of haphazard, accidental, without aim or direction, is not very helpful either for we know that scientists are very systematic about randomness; there is nothing haphazard or accidental in the way they select random samples. Most mathematicians agree that an absolutely disordered series of numbers is a logically contradictory concept. Evidently, the best one can do is specify certain tests for types of randomness and call a series random to the degree that it passes them. The best way to get a series of random digits

(the 'numbers' 0, 1, 2, 3, 4, 5, 6, 7, 8, 9) is by using a physical process involving so many variables that the next digit can never be predicted with a probability higher than $1/n$ where n is the base of the number system being used. Tossing a coin generates a random series of binary digits ($n = 2$). A perfect die randomises six numerals ($n = 6$) and so on. Nowadays, it is customary to use random numbers generated by a computer rather than tossing a coin or throwing a die each time a series of random numbers is required. Table 16.6 shows a set of random numbers generated in this way. Strictly speaking they are known as pseudo-random numbers. This reflects the fact that philosophically it is impossible to define randomness.

The idea that a series of numbers is only random when there is no discernible pattern in it is so firmly entrenched in the psyche that it is worth digressing for a moment to squash this idea. Suppose that somewhere in the very long and apparently patternless string of digits produced by the computer we come across the sequence 0 1 2 3 4 5 6 7 8 9, our first impression is that at this point the randomiser has broken down, for these 10 digits are quite obviously fully patterned and therefore not random. This is, of course, a mistake. The sequence 0 1 2 3 4 5 6 7 8 9 is just as likely as any other combination of 10 digits and, indeed, in an 'infinite' series of numbers we would *expect* to see this pattern occur. The sequence appears ordered to us because we have assigned meaning, importance and prominence to this outcome and have bunched all the others together as having no order, as being *random*. We tend to think of randomness as meaning the absence of pattern and therefore whenever we see a pattern we give it special meaning. This concept of randomness bears meaning only in relation to the observer and if two observers habitually look for different kinds of patterns they are bound to disagree upon the series that they call random.

Remember, we call a series random if we cannot predict successive digits in the series with a probability greater than $1/n$. For example, there is no known way to win a penny-tossing game, in which the probability of any 'toss' being a 'head' or a 'tail' is $\frac{1}{2}$ ($n = 2$). However, we can predict quite well in the aggregate, i.e. we can predict the outcome of large numbers of events, e.g. if we toss a coin 10 000 times, we can predict, with considerable accuracy, the total numbers of heads and tails. This apparent contradiction gives

Table 16.6 Random numbers generated by the British Museum (Natural History) computer.

```
06035   58403   66897   68081   80549   91830   48174   50207   26776   56305
93833   04931   46319   63267   82613   94751   30350   14502   05218   70249
57661   29459   76831   83812   60662   99754   53014   84560   92692   33127
37854   39298   48918   13029   00700   70279   20739   65727   06114   82519
73737   96600   49571   82755   15097   54253   22619   89870   61134   00489

42962   59381   33891   71928   91390   87686   47050   71506   45448   00238
91680   22447   78190   65622   08022   42958   98509   12223   49130   26714
72906   83363   60069   21921   72485   11765   53306   74026   24693   56114
51410   96830   87659   11101   03893   14103   40801   45366   05806   73412
27761   26258   88199   07477   12264   11553   84827   27578   27498   72747

07787   79212   01441   32239   57604   82880   58770   67534   33475   31877
80905   79574   81872   18846   72624   16479   40336   48533   32190   13603
76235   55575   78663   38575   75208   40748   15012   95373   89802   46687
01912   83046   34619   56559   82034   65817   52534   18899   93642   84017
61013   37292   89777   01421   61607   60232   17770   22659   89367   11274

10494   30103   21764   77601   88901   15004   95721   38828   16327   67865
31584   65670   27312   56917   44163   74740   76351   31460   44884   58404
23457   63897   47369   18739   46944   04741   52536   05630   82936   76910
71114   05429   83029   82770   03694   57241   56957   86301   59550   81874
58624   23769   90534   67290   62644   64138   96573   19999   68082   54614

56714   97692   55366   07798   06367   77688   07398   68129   07665   84036
11379   02866   48844   17340   05524   19650   43484   85234   97874   56272
07531   55484   42550   86346   02571   25436   52093   57798   89250   88496
26775   20975   16577   93467   62938   62921   63684   56734   31705   99535
67407   92443   08196   33474   52654   26832   51848   24379   26988   23752

14529   53318   21417   04724   95000   95114   28485   29072   18315   65395
01869   63603   39571   65042   19245   08543   15892   19427   93697   75644
90626   65721   10958   52867   17759   29990   56949   48162   86549   05993
77559   87552   78229   09723   49708   16762   64082   41983   10273   86210
43293   48096   98525   78704   91685   79559   61868   58310   07196   12171

03440   35826   24030   13013   71020   22018   43799   37543   12040   65781
33068   73019   30581   93434   58220   66860   22422   82196   13243   42173
68541   44737   43279   17677   59145   48018   40607   89044   81045   89931
73116   65913   35441   80740   65144   52194   63259   79890   32333   02664
85242   61101   62944   26447   22063   26539   79503   10388   11459   70902

06196   29140   79682   26321   85300   48675   73752   73165   14743   33061
44735   89399   61589   72790   33815   75844   15086   12857   81273   56460
07467   04722   82342   14675   08134   11256   12635   45271   23847   38543
29738   64400   02018   41873   65340   35042   84576   49805   81950   73201
12968   73019   24845   29602   32890   09948   36147   95030   94739   06392
```

rise to what philosophers have called the *gambler's fallacy*. For example, if in tossing a coin you get three 'heads' in a row, the temptation is to predict that on the next toss you will get a 'tail'. This is, of course, faulty reasoning.

Having discussed the nature of randomness, we are now in a position to see its importance in sampling. In taking a random sample of the population under study, every member of the population has an equal chance of being selected. A sample drawn at random is *unbiased* in the sense that all possible samples of size *n* have an equal chance of being selected. If we do not draw our sample at random, some factor or factors unknown to us may lead us to select a biased sample. Random methods of selection do not allow our own biases or any other systematic selection factors to operate. Random sampling is objective in the sense that it is divorced from an individual's own predilections and biases.

Sampling museum visitors: practical considerations

There are two fundamental questions to be asked before a sample is drawn. These are:

(a) What is the definition of the population from which the sample is to be selected?
(b) Is there a suitable sampling frame (i.e. list, map, register or whatever from which a sample is selected) for that population?

The first question seems easy to answer, but there are problems with infinite populations such as visitors to exhibitions. Here, we can state that the *target population* is past, present and future visitors to the exhibition, but because of the cost and length of time involved we can *never* sample the whole population. This leads us to specify our *survey population* as all the visitors to the exhibition during a specified period during which we are carrying out the survey. Then the results from our survey refer only to the survey population and not to all the visitors, a fact that is often overlooked. In addition, we might, for example, decide to exclude young children or foreign visitors from our survey population. Whatever the decision, the *survey population* should be defined precisely.

The second question on the availability of a sampling frame is extremely important. It makes the sampling process so much simpler if there is a good list of population members. An ideal sampling frame should contain all the members of a given target population. In addition, it should exclude people who are not part of the target population, and should not list members more than once. Clearly, there is no sampling frame available for sampling exhibition visitors and, therefore, many of the methods adapted for sampling domestic populations by political pollsters and government survey workers are not appropriate.

One method of sampling visitors to exhibitions that yields a representative and unbiased sample of a defined target population is to arrange for interviewers to count people as they enter and then select the *k*th visitor to be interviewed, starting with a random number between 1 and *k*. The procedure is easy and provided sufficient numbers of interviewers are available it is very convenient. Strictly speaking, the sampling procedure is not random, since it does not give all possible samples of size *n* from the survey population of size *N* an equal chance of being selected. Once the random starting point and sampling interval, *k*, have been selected, then all the remaining interviews are automatically pre-determined. This is an example of the method of *systematic* sampling in which the selection of one sample member is dependent on the selection of the previous one, while with random sampling from a large population the selections are virtually independent of each other. However, we can regard the method as approximately equivalent to simple random sampling if we assume there is no 'order' in which people visit an exhibition.

There is, however, a further problem with this method of sampling and it is this. During very busy times, the value of *k* has to be fairly large if only a small number of interviewers are available, otherwise it would not be possible to interview every visitor selected. However, as *k* increases, the sample selected runs the risk of becoming unrepresentative. We can see this intuitively as, for example, in an extreme case with $k = 1000$, when large groups of visitors would have no chance of being selected. Generally speaking, satisfactory samples are obtained when *k* is between 25 and 50.

A compromise is to develop a method of sampling that takes the selection of visitors out of the hands of the interviewer (as this is the most obvious cause of bias) and yields a sample of visitors that is representative but that requires the same, small number of interviewers on duty at quiet and busy times. The following sampling procedure has been developed and well tried at the British Museum (Natural History).

The Museum is open every day, except Sunday, for eight hours. For administrative convenience, the day is divided into four two-hour interviewing blocks. Interviewers are instructed to station themselves at their allocated interviewing point and draw an imaginary line on the floor next to them. Two minutes after the beginning of a two-hour interviewing period, they attempt to interview the first person to cross this line, they attempt their second interview 20 minutes after this time, and so on. Thus in a two-hour period, the maximum number of interviews a single interviewer can hope to obtain is six. If the person they approach refuses to be interviewed or is ineligible for interview (i.e. not in the survey population), they wait 30 seconds only before approaching the next person to cross the imaginary line. If more than one person crosses the imaginary line simultaneously, they use a random method of selecting the person to be interviewed.

Even though this method biases the selection of individuals so that visitors at busy times have a smaller chance of being interviewed than those at quiet times, we have shown that this bias does not alter the composition of our sample to any significant extent. The method is very simple and straightforward, requires few interviewers and furnishes stable and representative samples.

Sampling and experimental designs for formative evaluation

As we have noted, many summative evaluations are designed to measure characteristics of the population of interest, whether the populations are visitors or exhibits. For example, if our population is visitors we might want to find out their age distribution, their sex and the exhibits they liked; and in the case of our population of exhibits, we might wish to know their attracting and holding powers. For such descriptive studies, the general idea is relatively simple: information is collected for a sample of the population, and from this the required descriptive measures are calculated. So far in this chapter we have been concerned in the main with sample designs for descriptive studies. Now let us turn briefly to the additional factors we need to bear in mind when designing formative evaluations.

Suppose we wish to discover whether visitors who have looked at a particular mock-up exhibit achieve a lower level of misunderstanding about the topic exhibited than visitors who have not been exposed to it. One way of proceeding would be to select two groups of visitors, ask one group to look at the mock-up exhibit, and administer some test, developed to measure misunderstandings of the topic, to both groups. The difference in performance between the two groups on the test is a measure of the effectiveness of the mock-up exhibit. If the results of this simple but typical study are to have any meaning, it is fairly obvious that the two groups must be equivalent in their understanding of the topic *before* one of them looks at the mock-up, i.e. they should be equivalent in all respects apart from the fact that one of them is exposed to the mock-up exhibit and the other is not. How are such equivalent groups to be formed?

It is useful here to distinguish between the variables we can *manipulate* in formative evaluations and those that we cannot. In our present example, we can determine which of the groups looks at the mock-up and which one does not; this is a variable we can *manipulate*. On the other hand, many variables such as age, sex, socio-economic status and educational background are God-given and cannot be manipulated. Being ready made these variables are, so to speak, already manipulated and cause us, at least at first glance, some difficulty in making the groups equivalent.

As we saw in the discussion of hypothesis testing in summative evaluation, one way is to match the two groups on the 'already manipulated' variables such as age, sex, social class, educational attainment. We also saw that this is extremely difficult and sometimes not even desirable. Another approach is to restrict the visitors taking part in the study to a well defined, homogeneous group, e.g. females of the same age, socio-economic group, educational attainment, and so on. Even supposing it were possible to describe the characteristics of the groups fairly precisely, the generalisability of the results would probably be very low. Certainly, they would not apply to the majority of visitors.

A third way of proceeding is to allocate visitors selected for the investigations to one or other group in a random fashion by the toss of a coin or by the use of a table of random numbers. This procedure is known as randomisation and it is the cornerstone of sound experimental design. The intention of randomisation is to distribute the variability associated with individual visitors randomly *between* the groups. Therefore, the two groups *must* be similar apart from the random fluctuations due to differences between individual visitors. This variation is known as *extraneous* variation as it is extraneous to the effects of the experimental manipulation and is assumed to be due to the God-given variation, as it were. The experimental manipulation is *designed* to produce variability *between* the groups on some manipulated variable. In the case of formative evaluation, being exposed or not being exposed to the mock-up exhibit is the experimental manipulation or manipulated variable designed to produce variability on the variable(s) measured by the test.

If we are interested in establishing how different sorts of visitors respond to a mock-up exhibit, then greater control of extraneous variation is achieved if randomisation is done in a stratified way. We might, for example, have good reasons for wishing to discover if males and females or visitors of different ages respond differently; in this case we would wish randomly to allocate visitors falling within the various categories to the two groups. In this example, we could first of all draw a sample of visitors *stratified* according to age and sex. Such a stratified sample is laid out in Table 16.7. We would then allocate visitors from each cell in the matrix at random to one or other group. At the analysis stage, as well as looking at the differences between the two groups overall, we could also compare differences between males and females, differences between the various age groups, and also look at the *interactions* between the two variables.

Of course, randomisation cannot ensure that

Table 16.7 Sample of visitors stratified according to age and sex.

	Age (years)				Total
	17–24	25–34	35–54	54+	
male	20	20	20	20	80
female	20	20	20	20	80
total	40	40	40	40	grand total 160

the groups are alike in all respects, but it does eliminate the possibility of bias in allocation; and moreover since the extraneous variation is distributed at random between the two groups, it permits the investigator to calculate within known limits, the probability that any observed difference between the groups could have arisen by chance.

Using the following symbolism, we can now describe a design for formative evaluation:

E is the experimental treatment (the mock-up exhibit, say) to which a group of visitors is exposed.

O is an observation or measurement made on visitors.

R is random assignment of visitors to groups.

A single row of symbols applies to a single group; the left to right order of symbols is the temporal order of the processes.

Applying this symbolism to the example cited throughout our discussion of experimental designs for formative evaluations, we obtain an acceptable design as follows:

$$R \quad E \quad O_1$$
$$R \quad \quad O_2$$

Two groups are randomly secured from the total sample. One group is exposed to the mock-up exhibit, and both groups are tested.

The outcome of the experiment is a straightforward comparison of O_1 and O_2. This simple design is very powerful and easy to set up. First, there is no pre-testing – this is a threat to most formative evaluations which are telescoped in time. Testing a group before it looks at a mock-up exhibit (as well as shortly afterwards) is almost bound to sensitise individuals to certain points as they look at the mock-up, no matter how well the test is designed. Though many illusions may be shattered, it is true to say that pre-testing is not actually necessary and it is impossible in many circumstances. People tend to 'make sure' that the groups are equivalent. This equivalence is secured a little less efficiently by randomisation; and furthermore the process of randomisation secures representativeness in each group without which it would not be possible to generalise to other visitors. Moreover, as already hinted, it is the *basis* of most statistical tests that we might wish to use to compare O_1 and O_2.

This experimental design can be extended to test more than one version of a mock-up exhibit as follows:

$$
\begin{array}{ccc}
R & E_1 & O_1 \\
R & E_2 & O_2 \\
\cdot & \cdot & \cdot \\
\cdot & \cdot & \cdot \\
R & E_{n-1} & O_{n-1} \\
R & & O_n
\end{array}
$$

The experimental design we have just described is known as a *post-test only control group design* and it is only one of numerous types of designs that statisticians and psychometricians have developed. While it would be impossible and even inappropriate to describe even a selection of them here, there are a few basic principles in the planning of experiments for formative evaluations worth stressing.

The importance and advantages of randomisation have been emphasised already. Another fundamental notion is that of *replication*. If comparisons are being sought, then we cannot place much confidence in evaluations carried out with only a few visitors because of the inherent variability between visitors and their responses in test situations. Variability in formative evaluations of, for example, museum exhibits is great and precision can only be obtained by using fairly large samples. Alternatively, variability can be reduced by restricting the range of visitors sampled, but as we have seen this reduces generalisability. However, generalisability can be approached from another standpoint in educational evaluation. For example, if we restrict our sample of visitors to those with qualifications in the subject being displayed (these constitute a minority at the British Museum (Natural History)), and we discover that their performance is *below* an acceptable level, we can be reasonably sure that visitors without qualifications will do no better. Thus the results would be generalisable to a group of visitors not studied.

A further basic principle of good experimentation is concerned with the local control of variability. For example, if it is suspected that prior knowledge affects performance, then random allocation of visitors with prior knowledge should be carried out separately from the allocation of visitors without knowledge.

We can summarise the requirements for a true experimental design in four statements. There must be:

(a) at least two groups, one being the control;
(b) the manipulation of at least one *independent* variable, i.e. exposure to one or more mock-up exhibits or 'no-exposure';
(c) the random assignment of visitors to groups;
(d) when more than one mock-up is being tested, the random assignment of the different mock-ups to the groups.

Finally, it is also worth noting that many of the principles applied in the experimental approach to formative evaluation can be employed to considerable advantage in the design of summative evaluations.

Methods of data collection

Throughout our discussions about the 'tools of the trade' that the professional evaluator brings to bear on his work, we have implicitly assumed there is an ostensible problem to be solved or substantive information to be collected. These problems or areas of ignorance will have been spelled out in some detail at the beginning of a project, or at any of the stages prior to an exhibition opening, and the evaluator will turn his mind to ways and means of tackling the problem or gathering the information. We can see that all evaluation must begin with a clearly defined purpose. This is a most important phase of the evaluation process since the evaluator who is not sure precisely what he wants to find out is almost certainly never going to know if he has found it!

Deciding upon what needs to be found out and from whom is only the first part of the whole exercise. The evaluator has to decide what sorts of data will shed light on the problems he is tackling and he has to decide how to obtain these data, not to mention how he is going to analyse them and whether he ought to report them!

We can think of the process of data collection and data preparation in the following manner. First, visitors are sampled for the evaluation exercise, then they are observed in an exhibition, or they are interviewed before, during and after their visit to the exhibition under evaluation. The visitor will, in these various situations, act in certain ways. To use the jargon, he will make a *response*.

This response is *recorded* in some way and the recordings are then coded in a manner amenable to analysis. This analysis, or process of *decoding* is not necessarily statistical, e.g. we might produce verbatim reports transcribed from tape recordings. In what follows we shall be dealing primarily with some of the methods of collecting and recording the responses.

Observation studies

Observation is the most direct method of securing information about visitors' behaviour. Apparently, it is also the oldest; Sir Francis Galton (1822–1911) reputedly followed visitors as they ambled through the dimly lit corridors of the museums in Victorian England. Since then it has been central to most summative evaluations with the indices of **attracting power** and **holding power**, calculated from observational data, reflecting in a fundamental way whether an exhibit has been successful. An exhibit that fails to attract visitors, or one that fails to hold them long enough to communicate the intended message, is deemed a manifest failure.

The first step in building up an observational *schedule* is to identify the *limited range of behaviour* relevant to the evaluation project; it is not enough to observe, you have to observe something. Obviously, these behaviours must relate to the problems to be solved.

Having decided upon the range of behaviour, the next step is to define and *categorise* it unequivocally. For example, 'stops' at an exhibit and 'does not stop' at an exhibit are the two behavioural categories necessary to provide the computational basis of attracting power. The question of what constitutes a 'stop' is a matter of definition. Is it to include only those occasions when visitors stop in their tracks in front of exhibits or will it also include occasions when visitors look at exhibits while they are walking? Whatever the decision, it must be made before the evaluation begins, otherwise it will present great difficulties in interpretation later if the categories and definitions have changed during the course of the study. In addition, each category will need a simple, yet meaningful method of recording. In our example one might code '1' for a stop and '0' for a 'non-stop'.

There are a number of problems to be borne in mind before embarking on an observational study. First, it is a long, slow, drawn-out process in which lots of data are collected. At the outset it is well worth considering, therefore, if an alternative approach would provide a good enough answer. Secondly, there is the question of invasion of privacy; the evaluator has to decide whether he is justified in being a fly on the wall and observing visitors without their knowledge – this he can do by following them at a distance or by using closed-circuit television. Before such a thing is used it should be carefully considered to see if it could be the cause of justifiable public complaint. This is an ethical question that should not be dismissed too lightly; after all the procedure is in principle not too far removed from phone tapping. If the ethical questions cannot be answered to everyone's satisfaction, the observer can make himself known by 'joining' the visitor, and becoming a *participant* observer. Obviously, there is a very real danger of the observer's presence affecting the visitor's behaviour in these circumstances but experience seems to indicate that this can be a much less significant problem than is often thought.

Interviewing

The interview is the most ubiquitous method of data collection in exhibition evaluations, and the literature is replete with studies using various forms of interviewing technique. Interviews càn be conveniently described as *unstructured, semistructured* or *fully structured*. These descriptions apply to the procedures of the interviews and not to any of the considerations that have to be taken into account prior to the interviews being carried out. Every interview, regardless of its type, must be preceded by a detailed intellectual analysis of the purpose of the study, the type of data germane to that purpose, sampling considerations and so on; indeed it must be preceded by all the considerations we would take into account before embarking on any evaluation exercise.

An unstructured interview is a non-directive interview of the sort we referred to in connection with qualitative versus quantitative approaches to evaluation. Here, the interviewer is prepared to let the informant take the lead, making only the occasional odd comment to follow up an interesting remark made by the informant. The approach is used extensively in counselling and clinical work and it does tend to be surrounded by the mysticism associated with the Viennese consulting couch. It is not generally appropriate to the evaluations we are trying to characterise.

The semi-structured interview is directly analogous to observational procedures in terms of the considerations we must bear in mind. All prior decisions of what to look for, how to categorise and record them are pretty much the same. The interviewer has a schedule before him for completion during the interview (or after the interview if it is tape-recorded). We have found semi-structured interviews useful in formative evaluations of mock-up exhibits. For example, after visitors have viewed a mock-up, they are invited to explain the main points of the mock-up in their own words. As they are doing so, the interviewer runs through a check-list of the major points we would be looking for as indicants that they had grasped what the exhibit was intended to communicate. Any points missed by the visitor can be prompted for in a standard way later. Definitions, categorisations and recording conventions are the major preoccupations in designing a semi-structured interview.

The structured interview is one where precise questions are asked in a form of wording that remains *fixed* during each and every interview among the selected sample of visitors. The interviewer has virtually no freedom to do anything other than nod and make neutral noises; the interviewer reads a *questionnaire*. Before we consider how to design a questionnaire, a few words are required about the *process* of the interview itself.

First, we can see that its very nature is one of a rather complicated social interaction between a representative of the exhibition team and a representative of the public, to which each brings his own expectations and personal experiences. In fact, as might be expected, psychologists have spent some effort in trying to understand just what goes on in this sort of situation, and the arguments run deep. There are a number of comments we might make here but we shall restrict ourselves to some very general remarks about the major weaknesses associated with interviewing museum visitors. When we have asked visitors at the British Museum (Natural History) to express a liking or preference for the exhibits we have been developing, the response has almost invariably been favourable; only very occasionally are visitors dismissive. This *response set*, as it is known, probably occurs because the visitor believes the evaluator wants to be told that his exhibits are attractive and he is, therefore, merely providing the evaluator with the information he

thinks the evaluator wants to hear. A related effect is the tendency of visitors consistently to overrate or underrate an exhibit because it deals with a subject they are interested in or uninterested in, respectively. This is known as the *halo effect* and an example would be of visitors responding favourably to an exhibition on dinosaurs, simply because they like dinosaurs; they are unable to inhibit their own interest in the topic as such when it comes to evaluating the way it is presented. Just because it is about dinosaurs, they evaluate it favourably.

The first task for an interviewer is to follow the sampling procedure religiously in selecting the visitors to be approached for interview. The importance of following the procedures exactly in the prescribed fashion cannot be overemphasised as this is the very first point at which bias can creep into the data-gathering process. There is sometimes a temptation to *avoid* approaching a person who looks aggressive, dirty, ugly or whatever and does not take your fancy. This temptation must always be avoided in any random or systematic sampling procedure. It is to be hoped that the section on sampling has made the reasons for this abundantly clear.

Having selected the visitor, the interviewer must now obtain an interview. The aim in approaching the visitor chosen for interview is to increase his interest in taking part in the survey, or put another way, to decrease the likelihood that, overall, we obtain a high refusal rate to reduce the chance of bias creeping into the data. The opening remarks made by the interviewer are crucial if those who are less willing to co-operate are going to be won over. The most obvious reason presented by visitors for refusing to be interviewed is lack of time. It is also the easiest excuse by somebody who does not wish to be bothered. Here it is the interviewer's attitude that counts. While the interviewer must realise that it *is* an intrusion to ask a visitor to forgo a visit and answer questions, the request for an interview does need justification. Experience has shown there is no need for excessive diffidence or apologies but the purpose of the survey and how the results will be used should be explained precisely yet briefly. There are many satisfactory ways of casting the introduction but first and foremost all introductory remarks must be honest; and if the interviewer is enthusiastic about the purpose and reasons lying behind the study, his conviction can often sway the visitor who is not sure one way or the other of whether he wants to be interviewed.

The aim in most interviews, certainly in semi-structured and structured ones, is to attain a *uniformity* in asking questions, without any variations in wording or emphasis on the part of the interviewer who might think he can make a question more understandable to (assumed) different sorts of visitors by different sorts of approaches. Although more could certainly be said about the art of asking questions, much does depend on the way the questions have been formulated by the person drawing them up. We shall now consider how to design a questionnaire.

Designing a questionnaire

There is the tale of the director of a museum who, not having an answer to a question about exhibition policy put to him by the manager of his museum, instructed his survey officer to find it out from the public. The survey officer dutifully put the question before 1000 visitors who not only did not know the answer but had never before thought about the question. Thus, we have here the vision of a director proposing to determine the truth on the basis of collective indifference and collective ignorance. All of us are familiar with the results of surveys that inform very few people about very few things. It is therefore timely that the evaluator is reminded to ask himself at the outset of what decisions will be informed by the results of the questionnaire he is about to administer. He will know that if people are asked a question, they have the habit of giving an answer, but is the question really necessary? Many questionnaires can be reduced in length considerably if the evaluator is prepared to apply ruthlessly the criterion of relevance to all the possible questions that are suggested once it is known that a questionnaire is being prepared. The evaluator must always resist the pressures to write the *Domesday book*. On many occasions he may well decide it is not even worth carrying out a survey at all if he cannot identify how the results will be used. He may still be asked to carry it out, however, if there are reasons for doing so other than collecting information for making decisions (see Ch. 15).

As with most skills we acquire in life, a great deal is learned by doing, and writing a good

questionnaire is no exception. However, there are a few general guidelines that have been developed at other peoples' expense which should prove useful in helping the tyro-evaluator avoid the more obvious errors. These guidelines can be grouped under the broad headings of question content, question wording, question order and response categories.

We have already talked about the need to avoid questions irrelevant to the expressed aims of the study, but there is also the other side of the coin to be considered. Once the purpose has been clearly stated, questions have to be developed that *are* relevant. Do the proposed questions need to be broken down into several more simple questions, and are additional or supplementary questions required to explore quite thoroughly the avowed objectives of the study? The evaluator must also consider whether the visitors can be expected to have the necessary information to answer the questions he is proposing; whether questions are too general or too abstract; whether too much emphasis is given to one aspect of the study at the expense of others so that bias might creep in, and so on.

The actual words used in a questionnaire are so obviously crucial that it is surprising how often they tend to be phrased in a technical language or assume a particular class-bound mode of expression. Question wording should be free from technical terms (unless, of course, it is written for technical people), unambiguous and to the point. Furthermore, questions should be written in a language that is acceptable and appropriate to the visitors being interviewed, but this does not mean visitors should be talked down to. The fundamental precept in writing questionnaires is to imagine the people who are going to be asked to answer, and develop questions that are understandable and appropriate to them.

Considerations of question order become apparent as soon as you begin to draft a questionnaire and they are largely a matter of common sense as, indeed, are most aspects of questionnaire design. Unfortunately, common sense is the most uncommon thing in the world, and quite avoidable mistakes are often made. For example, questions of opinion should *always* follow questions about facts whenever the two occur together, since an expressed opinion on a topic often influences the manner in which factual questions are answered. Familiar questions should precede less familiar ones and the whole sequence of questions should be ordered chronologically.

In considering the sorts of responses to questions, thought must be given ultimately to the form of analysis envisaged and we shall consider some of these issues shortly. At this point perhaps it is sufficient to remember the importance of categorisation. In most questionnaire studies, the responses to questions will finally be aggregated and tabulated according to the response categories used. Loose, sloppy or ambiguous categories induce nightmares when it comes to analysis and all categories must be defined with an absolute clarity beforehand.

Further issues of data collection: objective tests and rating scales

Frequently, as we have seen in the preceding sections on observational studies and questionnaire design, the measurements we are interested in are straightforward frequency counts, e.g. the number of visitors in our sample who stop at each exhibit. In these instances, the problem of obtaining reliable information is concerned with questions of definition and categorisation (e.g. what is a 'stop'?) and not with measurement as such. But in some studies we are interested in variables on which a measurement for each member of a sample of visitors is required. For example, we might be interested in how much different visitors have learned after viewing an exhibit or in discovering whether their attitudes have altered. In these two cases, we need a yardstick of 'learning' and one for 'attitudes'. Such yardsticks have to be invented and constructed, they do not already exist in nature. The same is true of yardsticks to measure variables such as height and weight, but these are so familiar and so standardised across countries that they present no problems, and we rather take for granted the issues involved. However, when we come to develop yardsticks for psychological variables such as 'learning' and 'attitudes', we are presented with special difficulties as regards measurement. For one thing they are often difficult to define – 'learning' and 'attitudes' are good examples – and even if they can be defined fairly precisely, it is not very often that they can be measured correctly. In these circumstances, it is essential that the measurement process is as objective as possible so

that at least others can repeat the process with a good chance of confirming the results already obtained.

The issues involved in developing what are known as *objective* tests are complicated conceptually and mathematically, and a very sophisticated technology (known as **psychometrics**) has arisen to cope with them. Nevertheless, some of the basic principles involved can be applied by the amateur evaluator to help him construct his own *informal* objective tests for use in exhibit evaluation. When carefully planned, these tests can be made to coincide very closely with the content covered by an exhibit and are extremely useful in measuring visitors' knowledge and understanding gained as a result of seeing an exhibit.

Informal objective tests come in a variety of different forms but we shall discuss just two examples – the *short-answer* form which measures recall and the *multiple-choice* form which measures recognition. The short-answer form includes questions, incomplete sentences or definitions and is particularly well suited to measuring factual recall, and unless it has been very poorly constructed the sample to whom it is administered cannot give the correct answer by guesswork. The following examples show the various short-answer forms.

Question. 'What is the largest flesh-eating dinosaur?'

. . . .

Incomplete sentence. 'The name of the largest flesh-eating dinosaur is'

. . . .

Definition. 'Define carnivore.'

. . . .

The major weakness of the short-answer form is that it is sometimes difficult to construct items that call for only one correct answer; and if too many clues are given in the item, many visitors will answer it correctly.

The multiple-choice form is considered by many test experts to be the best type of test for measuring learning performance. Multiple-choice items consist of an incomplete statement or question followed by several choices including one correct answer and several distracters and they have great versatility. An example of a question-type multiple choice is:

Which of the following dinosaurs is carnivorous?

(a) *Camptosaurus*
(b) *Stegosaurus*
(c) *Tyrannosaurus*
(d) *Diplodocus*
(e) *Brachiosaurus*

The weakest aspect of multiple-choice forms is the difficulty in constructing good items. Often the correct answer can be guessed fairly easily because the distracters are so obviously wrong. Writing good items is a creative task.

Usually, when constructing an objective test, a large list of items is produced initially and this is reduced by eliminating the items that are ambiguous and also those that do not discriminate between individuals. This is done by trying out the initial items on a sample of visitors for whom the test is intended. A good measure of the discriminative power of an item is the variance of the answers given to it by the members of the sample. Normally, an item is scored '1' for a correct answer and '0' for an incorrect answer. If p is the percentage in the sample that get an item correct, then the variance of the item is given by

$$pq, \text{ where } q = 100 - p$$

As we have seen before, the maximum value of the variance is when $p = q$, that is when 50 per cent of the sample get the item correct. For values of p in the range 20 per cent to 80 per cent the variance is still relatively large, but it decreases dramatically for values of p outside this range. Notice should be taken of this fact because at first sight it might appear that only difficult items should be included in a test if the idea is to differentiate between those individuals who have learned something from those that have not. However, in the extreme case, where $p = 0$ per cent or $p = 100$ per cent, we are given no information about the relative abilities of individuals being tested. In constructing an informal objective test, it is always good practice to place a few easy items at the beginning to at least get everybody started.

There are many occasions when the evaluator will be concerned about issues other than how well an exhibition communicates bits of information. For example, he might be concerned to discover what visitors think about the 'design' of an exhibition. The first problem in this example is to get a clear idea of the aspects of design he is interested in. While a fully adequate definition of 'design' would be very difficult to formulate, it is possible to begin to list the factors thought to be associated with the notion. The final list could be compiled after discussions with designers and visitors with a view to reaching a fair measure of agreement about the adequacy and relevance of the items or factors included. The outcome might be a list of statements such as:

(a) is well laid out;
(b) is brightly lit;
(c) makes the subject seem exciting;
(d) is designed with the ordinary visitor in mind.

Different visitors might believe that each of the statements applies to an exhibition in varying degrees and provision needs to be made to allow for differences when recording the results. This can be achieved by employing a rating scale. The scale does not need to be complex and generally a five-point scale, scored as follows, will do the job:

Scale	*Score*
strong agreement	5
agree	4
no strong opinion	3
disagree	2
strong disagreement	1

A person's total score is easily computed by adding together the individual scores obtained for each statement.

Validity and reliability

Once the measuring instruments – the questionnaire, the observation schedule, the multiple-choice questions or whatever – have been developed, it is timely for the evaluator to ask if they are *valid* and *reliable*.

A *valid* instrument is often somewhat circularly defined in evaluation research as the extent to which it measures what it purports to measure. In fact, validity is a rather complex and difficult notion to come to grips with; indeed, in the absence of a sound theoretical background to underpin the variables one attempts to operationalise and measure in any research enterprise, it is not possible to talk about their validity in a meaningful way. Often, therefore, in evaluation research, which is usually concerned with practical issues independent of theory, the best one can do is to find an outside criterion against which the measuring instrument can be verified. For example, if an instrument has been designed to measure the extent to which different exhibits are able to increase learning on a given topic among visitors, an idea of its validity would be gained by the extent to which 'expert' teachers independently agreed with the instrument's assessment of 'successful' and 'unsuccessful' exhibits.

On the other hand, *reliability* is not so philosophically intractable. Any sort of measuring instrument is said to be reliable if it gives similar results when applied on more than one occasion under the same conditions. However, most of the measuring instruments we are brought up with (e.g. rulers, compasses, tape-measures) are so extremely precise, usually irrespective of who uses them and the objects he measures, it is not surprising that we are not accustomed to think about the idea of reliability; we take it for granted. But in evaluation research, the instruments used are much less reliable. Constructing a reliable instrument is not easy, *precisely* because there are few established standards of measurement. Consider, by analogy, the problem of measuring distance. It is not so very long ago that distance was measured in terms of the number of 'paces' or 'strides' taken by an individual; and even today (in England at any rate) the height of a horse is sometimes measured in 'hands'. It is easy for us *now* to see how when distance is measured in 'paces', its estimation varies from measurer to measurer. Furthermore, if we think about the problems involved a little more deeply, we can see that even the measures taken by a single individual will vary from occasion to occasion. His 'paces' might vary from one day to the next when measuring the same 'distance' and will certainly vary according to the terrain he is measuring. For example, when measuring uphill, we might notice that an individual measurer takes shorter paces than when he is measuring on the level. Consequently, in measuring distance by the number of 'paces' taken by an individual, it would be extremely advisable to have an estimation of the amount of variation in measurement from individual to individual according to the terrain being measured. In other words, it would

be advisable to get an estimation of the amount of *error* involved. Establishing the reliability of the instruments used in evaluation research is usually concerned with estimating the error involved in using them, and some very elegant and sophisticated statistical techniques have been developed for the purpose. All that really needs to be said here, however, is that reliability is increased greatly when there are few ambiguities in the way recording schedules are drawn up or in the way questions or statements are understood by visitors, and when there is little variability in the way in which they are presented by interviewers and subsequently analysed. These considerations serve to emphasise the importance we have already placed on establishing standard practices in carrying out evaluation projects.

Finally, it needs to be said that validity and reliability are not unrelated concepts. If an instrument is unreliable, it is likely to affect its validity. On the other hand, good reliability does not ensure good validity, and vice versa. It is quite possible to have a valid but unreliable measuring instrument (for instance, a broken thermometer) and a reliable but invalid measuring instrument (a working thermometer purporting to measure barometric pressure).

Coding the data

Ultimately, no matter what sort of data we collect, they usually have to be coded as marks on a piece of paper. The coding process needs to be conceived and developed at the beginning of a project so that when the data have been collected they can be manipulated with the minimum of effort, irrespective of whether the analysis is to be carried out 'by hand' or with the assistance of a computer. Even if the intention is not to use a computer, it is as well to think of the coding process in the framework of the computer punch card.

The standard punch card is rectangular in shape with 80 columns, each containing 10 cells numbered 0 to 9. When information from a questionnaire is to be punched on a card, each question or variable is allocated to a column (or adjacent columns) on the card and each of the possible answers (which are usually determined in advance) to that question is assigned to a specific cell in the column. The procedure is best

VISITOR SURVEY - BRITISH MUSEUM (NATURAL HISTORY)

For office use only							
(1)	(2)	(3)	(4)	(5)	(6)	(7)	(8)

SECTION 1 - CLASSIFICATION

1. SEX

	(9)
Male	1
Female	2

2. AGE

	(10)
11 - 16 yrs	1
17 - 20 yrs	2
21 - 24 yrs	3
25 - 34 yrs	4
35 - 44 yrs	5
45 - 54 yrs	6
55 - 64 yrs	7
65+ yrs	8

Figure 16.5 Part of the questionnaire used for the annual visitor survey, British Museum (Natural History).

illustrated by an example and here we shall refer to questionnaires we have used in carrying out the annual visitor surveys at the British Museum (Natural History). Figure 16.5 shows the first 10 columns of the questionnaire.

The first piece of information recorded is the 'number' of the survey (since the survey is repeated annually, each year has to be identified). It is a three-digit number, and the first three columns of the card are allocated to it. For example, the first year was 001, the second year 002, and so on. Thus cell 0 is punched in column 1, cell 0 in column 2 and the appropriate cell in column 3, that is, a '1' or '2' or '3' or '4' or '5' or '6'. (To date we have conducted eight surveys. In allocating three columns for this purpose we are assuming a maximum of 999 surveys will be carried out!) Column 4 is used to code whether the interview is taking place with a visitor entering the Museum (in which case cell 1 is punched) or with one leaving the Museum (a punch in cell 2). In this example, the actual cells used are arbitrary; all that matters is that they are mutually exclusive. In column 5 we code the place at which the interview takes place. At the Museum there are two entrance *cum* exits and we allocate two cells accordingly. Columns 6, 7 and 8 are used for coding the serial number of the

interview ($001 - n$, where n is the sample size).

The interviewer simply circles the appropriate numbers in columns 9 and 10. There are different punching conventions according to the computer program to be used for the analysis and the evaluator should be fully aware of these conventions before drawing up the code frame. For example, many programs are written so that a '0' punch is interpreted as a blank in non-numerical data fields (e.g. columns 9 and 10 in Fig. 16.5). Therefore, it is as well to avoid the cell and this is the reason we used 1 and 2 for sex instead of 0 and 1. The reader should note the difference between these recording conventions and those for deriving the standard error of an attribute discussed earlier in this chapter.

It is also important to make provision for missing information when data are to be transferred to punch cards. For instance, on many questionnaires certain questions are only asked of certain types of visitors and, therefore, a 'not applicable' code needs to be allocated. Usually, cell 9 is used for this purpose, so that at the analysis stage, a single instruction such as 'ignore numbers greater than 8', automatically ensures that only those visitors to whom the question was appropriate are included in the analysis. Where numerical variables are concerned visitors for whom the information is missing or inapplicable can also be picked out by using some coding device.

Trivial though all this might seem, a failure to follow simple rules can cause considerable problems at the analysis stage. All questionnaires or observational schedules must be designed to comply with the rules and until the evaluator has gained experience in designing questionnaires and drawing up code frames, he is well advised to have his work checked by the appropriate computer personnel *before* he begins to collect any data.

Analysing the data

We have now reached the stage where all the data have been collected and coded ready for analysis. The purpose of analysis is to reduce the data to an intelligible and interpretable form to answer the questions the study was designed to answer. However, it is wrong to think of the analysis stage as simply being tacked on the end of the other stages of the evaluation study. In fact, the evaluator begins to think about the kinds of analyses he is going to carry out at the outset of a study, just as soon as he begins to think about how he is going to tackle the problem that has been posed or collect the required information. The purpose of the study, the method of data collection, the type of data collected and the analysis of the data are inextricably interwoven.

Tables and graphs

Often in observational and questionnaire studies, we are interested in simply *tabulating* the data to see the proportion or percentage of persons falling in each of the pre-defined categories we have already coded. Tabulations are extremely easy to perform and they give a good summary of categorical data. Tables can be constructed very easily 'by hand', by sorting questionnaires into piles on the basis of the responses to the question under consideration and simply counting the numbers in each pile; and there are many computer programs available that print tabular data routinely by counting the 'cells' in each column and printing out the results in terms of percentages. If a computer is available, then it is straightforward to construct *cross breaks* which

are numerical tabular presentations of the data, in which variables are cross partitioned to describe the relations between the variables. A typical cross tabulation is shown in Table 16.8.

A very powerful tool of analysis is the graph. The *graph* is a two-dimensional representation of a relation or relations between variables. A graph shows pictorially sets of ordered pairs in a direct, visual manner that no other method can. If a relation exists in a set of data, then a graph will not just show it, it will also show its nature, whether it is positive or negative, linear or quadratic, and so on. Graphs are plotted on two axes and it is customary to plot the independent variable on the horizontal or x-axis and the dependent variable on the vertical or y-axis. Graphs are so familiar that there is no need for an example here.

Measures of central tendency and variability

Earlier in this chapter we described the mean and the standard deviation and how to compute them. There can be little doubt that when we are dealing with numerical data, these are extremely important statistics. However, there are many occasions when it is not appropriate to use the mean as a measure of *central tendency*, as it is called. The mean should be used whenever the underlying distribution being represented is normal or approximately normal. However, when the distribution deviates significantly from normal, the *median* or *mode* should be used for descriptive and other purposes. The median of a distribution is the middle value of a series when

Table 16.8   Cross tabulation in which age is broken down by sex, and the results represented as percentages.

| | Sex | |
Age (years)	Male (%)	Female (%)
under 11	20	16
11–16	3	5
17–20	11	9
21–24	15	20
25–34	23	21
35–44	13	17
45–54	8	5
55–64	5	6
65+	2	1

the various values are placed in order of magnitude. In a grouped frequency distribution (e.g. Fig. 16.1), it is always the value above and below which 50 per cent of all measures lie. Sometimes the mode – the value in a series occurring most frequently – is more useful. For example, in designing an interactive exhibit to allow more than one visitor to interact with it simultaneously, it would be sensible to design the exhibit to cater for the modal group size of visitors. Unless you know that a variable is normally distributed, it often pays to calculate the median value and the mode as well as the mean. (In a normal distribution the mean = the median = the mode.) The arithmetic mean is often used inappropriately in many fields of study and a good example from the field of exhibition evaluation is the computation of the holding power of exhibits. Typically, the distribution of viewing times of an exhibit is positively skewed and looks something like that shown in Figure 16.6, where the mean, which describes relatively few visitors, is quite a lot larger than the median, which gives a much better description of the data.

In fact, in many instances we find that time data are *positively skewed*, and to talk of the average (arithmetic mean) of data in this form is very misleading. It so happens that the distribution shown in Figure 16.6 is roughly log-normal (that is, the logarithmic transformation of a variable which is normally distributed) and, therefore, it can be transformed into a normal distribution by taking logarithms (to any base) of the raw data. When this is done, the arithmetic mean calculated on logarithmic data and then converted back to raw scores is much closer to the median value.

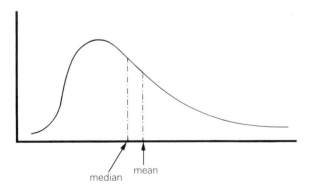

Figure 16.6 Skewed curve showing the mean and median.

It should be noted that there is no trickery involved in transforming scores in this manner; it is a perfectly legitimate thing to do. There are many instances in everyday life when we are required to convert scores or measurements in one system of measurement into scores or measures in another system, e.g. centimetres into inches.

There is another way in which averages can be misused. Suppose we start off with a few statistical facts:

The average holding power of exhibits is 30 seconds. The average attracting power of exhibits is 0.32.

The next thing you know, a subtle semantic transmogrification takes place and we hear:

The average exhibit has an attracting power of 0.32 and an average holding power of 30 seconds.

The notion of an average exhibit is quite meaningless. Having one attribute that is average does *not* mean that the exhibit *is* average.

We have already noted that the principal measure of variability is the standard deviation, which is especially useful when the variable is normally distributed. Means should never be reported without standard deviations and standard errors because an adequate interpretation is virtually impossible without variability indices. Another measure of variability that is useful is the *range*, which is the difference between the highest and lowest measures of a set of measures. The range can be very useful when the distribution of the variable under consideration is not normal.

Measures of relations or correlations

Often we are concerned to discover whether pairs of 'events' arising from a single source go together. We might wish to discover, for example, whether there is a relationship between the holding power of an exhibit and its attracting power. There are a number of coefficients of relation, or *correlation* as they are known which, no matter how different they appear, do essentially the same thing. In effect, they tell the evaluator the magnitude and usually the direction of the relation. Some vary in value from −1 to +1, which indicate perfect negative and positive relations respectively, and 0 indicates no relation whatsoever.

Measures of correlation are themselves subject to extensive and elaborate forms of analysis such as multiple regression and factor analysis and thus they are very useful and powerful tools of analysis. Nevertheless, the temptation to interpret causation from correlation must be resisted always.

Analysis of differences

To conclude this part of the book, at least a few words are necessary about the analysis of differences. The analysis of differences, particularly between means and percentages, occupies an important part of evaluation research. For example, we noted in the section on experimental designs in formative evaluation that the purpose of randomisation is to equate groups on certain 'already manipulated' or 'God-given' variables. If this is done satisfactorily, then any difference between the groups that have been exposed to different mock-up exhibits and those that have not may be attributed to the effect of the mock-up exhibits. But in any analysis of differences it is not just the statistical significance of the differences themselves which is of interest, for it is possible to discover differences that are statistically significant but that are very small and, therefore, of no *practical* significance. Indeed, in an early section of this chapter, we showed that by drawing large enough samples it is possible to detect relatively small differences which are statistically significant. Often in evaluation studies, we are interested only in comparatively large differences as a basis for action. Consider again our hypothetical example in Chapter 15 in which we compared two mock-ups of two different treatments to explain the notion of homeostasis. We denoted these two treatments *A* and *B*. In the real world, where there are constraints of time and money, it will almost certainly be more realistic to state beforehand the *magnitude* of the differences we are looking for and not simply *any* difference that is statistically significant as a basis for making a decision between *A* and *B*. If *A* takes twice as long to develop as *B*, and costs four times as much as *B* to produce, we might decide beforehand that *A* has to perform much better than *B* on our tests before we would adopt *A* as a solution. Thus, we

would not be simply interested in measuring whether $A > B$ on our tests but whether $A > B + D$, where D is the difference whose magnitude is determined by weighing practical considerations of production against some supposed educational benefit which, incidentally, are extremely difficult to operationalise – just to make everything that much more difficult!

For many purposes in the rough and ready environment of exhibition evaluation, there is a rule of thumb to tell you whether two scores are significantly different (statistically speaking, that is) from one another and it involves calculating the standard error associated with each score. First, calculate the difference between the two scores by simple subtraction and if this is less than twice the larger of the two standard errors, you can conclude that there is not much chance (only about 1 in 20, or 5 per cent) that there is any difference between the two scores. We did, of course, approach this question from a different direction earlier, when we discussed how to determine the sample sizes required for comparing differences between variables at an acceptable level of precision.

Reporting the data: writing the report

The final step in evaluation is to bring everything together in a report – upon which the whole evaluation exercise rests or fails. Contrary to popular belief, data do not speak for themselves and their acceptability depends in part – but only in part – upon the persuasive powers of the evaluator in representing them in his report. Whether or not the evaluator is successful in getting his recommendations accepted will depend upon a number of factors which include:

(a) the intelligence and breadth of knowledge the evaluator has brought to bear in solving the problems in hand;
(b) the technical ability of the evaluator in defining the problem and designing the study competently;
(c) the sensitivity of the evaluator in understanding the issues involved and the implications of the data collected;
(d) the chance occurrence of making everybody happy at the same time;
(e) luck – the good fortune that the conclusions

and recommendations coincide with the opinions of the decision-makers.

At one point or another throughout these two chapters dealing with evaluation, we have discussed these issues and it should be clear that the acceptability of evaluation findings depends upon a large number of variables including facts, fiction, pride and prejudice in varying proportion at different times. We shall not repeat these discussions now but instead concentrate on the issues involved in reporting the findings of an evaluation study. However, we remark in passing that evaluation is not unique in these respects, and many human endeavours including what is conventionally understood by 'scientific enquiry' are similarly open to the subjective appraisal of individuals with different value-systems and beliefs. Systematic evaluations – the sort we have tried to characterise throughout this chapter – are no less objective than many so-called scientific disciplines.

The good evaluation report should tell a story and, like a good exhibition, it should first of all be written for a well defined audience. The scientific report for a learned journal, a book like this one, a paper for a conference or a general article for a lay audience all demand different approaches although each may be based on the same data. The report should aim at communicating the *essential* elements only; it should never give minute descriptions of each and every detail for the sake of an outmoded pedantry. Every concession must be made to the reader to help him understand the major issues involved. The good report should be to the point and easily readable by those for whom it is intended.

Each report should have a clearly defined structure from beginning to end so that any reader who is at any point in the report should be able to understand clearly what is happening at that point in terms of what has come before. Everything that follows from that point must follow naturally from it and any digressions should be clearly signalled. The general rule is that the reader should know where he is, he should know where he has been and he should know where he is going.

The actual nature of the subdivisions of a report (e.g. Introduction, Method, Conclusions) will depend upon the audience, but generally speaking they should include at least the following.

(a) *Introduction, purpose or aims of the study.* 'The purpose of this study is . . .', although somewhat hackneyed is always a good opening shot. There is nothing worse than wading through a report with increasing agitation as the purpose becomes increasingly obscure. The *introduction* should always set the scene for what is to follow. This section might also include the background to the study; explain how the problems arose which the evaluation aims to solve and how it relates to other work in the field.

(b) *Method.* This section should contain sufficient detail concerning the design of the study, the way variables were operationalised and the method of data collection including details of the target sample and the sampling method.

(c) *Results.* Here there should be a clear statement of the results in summary form. In statistical terms, where appropriate, tabulations, frequencies, means, standard deviations, and so on should be presented. These results should tell the story of what actually emerged from the study and they should be put forward with clarity and purpose. If appropriate, significance tests and all the other analyses concerned with statistical *evaluations* of the summary statistics should be reported here.

(d) *Discussion of results, conclusions and implications.* It is at this point in the report that the evaluator requires all the knowledge and sensitivity he can muster. He has to go beyond the data, as it were, and interpret their significance in the light of the stated aims of the study. It is at this point that he must have the strength of his convictions and put his head on the block. However, he should always be careful not to make stronger claims than can be reasonably justified and whenever he is speculating this should be made clear. There is nothing wrong with speculation but it is wrong to misrepresent it as 'fact'.

(e) *Bibliographies.* In academic or professional reports it is customary to give complete descriptions of any references made in the text. Conventions vary from journal to journal and the evaluator should be guided by editorial dictates.

(f) *Appendices*. Separate appendices should be provided for all the material that was used but which was not required in detail in the main body of the text. For many purposes, appendices can be omitted but the evaluator should always be able to provide detailed information if he is asked to do so.

The evaluator should always remember that it is *after* he has submitted his report that the arguments begin. This should be a salutary reminder for him to be circumspect in the manner in which he represents his arguments. It does not mean his report should be boring to read; unfortunately, so many are.

17 Replacement and renewal

No exhibit lasts for ever, though some may have a longer life than others. This poses rather more of a problem to exhibitors who set out to communicate ideas than to those whose sole object is to display objects regardless of the fact that there is more to seeing than meets the eyeball. Ideas proliferate and old ones are supplanted by new ones, so the message which an exhibitor seeks to convey, be it explicit or implicit, is continually evolving, as are the media employed. Relatively little is known about communicating ideas effectively through exhibits. Sometimes an exhibit is barely set up when it becomes obvious that there is more than a grain of truth in the old adage, 'If it works it's out of date'. Exhibits can always be improved, but only if the necessary money and people are available. We make the fundamental assumption that there is always a shortage of money and the right people to develop and produce exhibits, so the best possible use must be made of their time. Our concern in this chapter is, therefore, with the problem of matching the size of the team to the exhibition area for which it is responsible, in the light of its *modus operandi*.

The simple model

Apart from the continual *replacement* of exhibits that have been rendered obsolete by new ideas or subsequent research, or have failed to come up to expectation in one way or another, there sometimes arises a need to produce *entirely new* exhibits, such as when extra exhibition space becomes available or when the scope of an exhibition is broadened to cover entirely new ground. Less frequently, but more traumatically for the exhibition team, it may become necessary to *renew* the whole set of exhibits.

Once it has been decided to expand, the team is faced with a task that is quite different from that of continual replacement; it has to provide entirely new exhibits where previously there were none at all. When there occurs a shift in policy and it is decided to produce new exhibits quite different in conception from the old ones, the task is more

akin to that of expanding the set of exhibitions than to the one of replacing individual exhibits. It is, of course, possible for both things to happen at once, for a change of approach to be accompanied by a decision to expand. All such situations involve what it is convenient to call 'once-and-for-all change'.

It is completely unrealistic to assume that an exhibition team can renew the exhibits on a routine basis, ploughing on without dealing with any exhibit for the second time before all have been dealt with for the first time. This is particularly so because of the growing tendency for museums to make objective evaluations of their exhibition activities (Chs 2 & 15), which lead in turn to the modification or replacement of exhibits. The medium and the message are both subject to change, and changes must be made where developments dictate, not according to a rigid sequential plan. It is easier to predict and evaluate the consequences of diverse courses of action under the various circumstances outlined above if we devise a simple model of the sort described in Chapter 4 to deal with secondment. Like its predecessor, the present model identifies the factors or variables that control the situation and links them together in a quantitative mathematical relationship which may be depicted graphically. Once again this makes it possible to bear all the factors in mind instead of arbitrarily fixing one or more of them at the outset; and the manipulation of the model gives a feel for the situation which would otherwise be difficult to acquire except in the hard school of practical experience, i.e. by making mistakes and having to correct them. It is better to avoid making mistakes in the first place.

The 'steady replacement' regime

In order to develop the model we may for the moment set aside all consideration of once-and-for-all change and concentrate on continual replacement. Suppose then, that the exhibition team consists of N groups jointly responsible for an exhibition area amounting to A m² (Fig. 17.1); for all practical purposes we can think of a group as one development partnership plus the number of other people necessary to cope with the partnership's output (Ch. 5). Suppose further that each group has on average an output amounting to r m² a year. If we use P to denote the length of time it would take the team to work steadily right through the exhibition area from one end to the other without at any time going back on themselves, it follows that

$$P = \frac{A}{Nr}$$

This equation is the constraint that dominates the situation. Once again we have four variables, but only three degrees of freedom (Ch. 4). Once values have been given to any three of the variables, the value of the fourth is determined too because it may be calculated from the equation. It is, therefore, referred to as the dependent variable, and the other three as the independent variables. Which of the four is the dependent variable is purely a matter of choice, but since we can easily depict three variables on our graph the choice that really

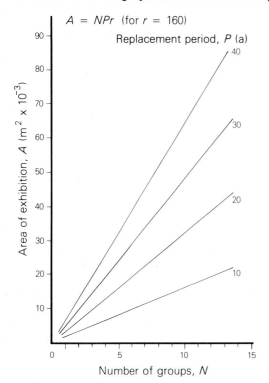

$A = NPr$ (for $r = 160$)

Replacement period, P (a)

Figure 17.1 The factors determining the rate at which exhibits can be replaced, and how they are related.

faces us is that of selecting one of the four as a sort of 'super parameter' and one of the remaining three as a 'lower order' one. A diagram can then be drawn for a constant value of the former, with a separate line for each of a series of values of the latter. Which of the other two variables is treated as x and which as y is purely a matter of convenience. The important thing is to regard the set of factors as one in which all elements are variable but some more variable than others. This hierarchy determines which are treated as parameters and which are not.

Once a team has been set up to deal with a specific exhibition area, A, N and r are fixed and thus effectively determine P. However, it may be that this value of P is unacceptable, that the exhibition becomes out of date in less time than it takes to replace it. Possible ways of reducing P then need to be considered, and in these circumstances it is appropriate to regard r as the most constant of the variables and P as the next most constant. The value chosen for P will then determine the number of groups needed to deal with a given area, or alternatively the area which can be handled by a team of given size. A graph like that in Figure 17.1 makes it easier to keep all the variables in mind when deciding what to do. In this diagram P is treated as a parameter and r as a 'super parameter'.

The 'constant proportion' regime

Whatever the status accorded to the variable P, whether it be regarded as dependent (as in the beginning of the preceding paragraph), or more or less independent (as at the end of the same paragraph), once the restriction imposed by the unrealistic assumption of steady replacement is relaxed, P acquires an importance that sets it apart from all the other variables. This is because it is a measure of the rate at which the team deals with its task in relation to the size of that task. Let us now replace the previous supposition of steady replacement by the less restricting assumption that we are going to replace a fixed proportion (by area) of the exhibits each year without letting what has gone before influence our choice of exhibits for replacement. This leaves us free to replace some of the exhibits two or more times before others have been replaced for the first time. More formally, let us assume that for all exhibits the probability of replacement at any given instant is constant and small.

Since it takes P years to change an area equivalent to that of all the exhibitions, the fraction changed in any one year will be $1/P$. After the first year the fraction unchanged will be $(1 - 1/P)$. In the second year the total amount changed will be the sum of two quantities. It will be a fraction $1/P$ of the fraction $(1 - 1/P)$ unchanged in the first year plus the same fraction of the part changed in the first year, which will be changed for the second time. Together these amount to $1/P$, the same amount as in the first year, but the amount unchanged at the end of the second year will be a fraction $(1 - 1/P)$ of that which was unchanged after the first year, i.e. $(1-1/P)(1-1/P)=(1-1/P)^2$.

The fraction unchanged continues to diminish by the factor $(1 - 1/P)$ each year, so that after t years it is $(1 - 1/P)^t$.

Replacement under these conditions is a process akin to the growth or decline of a biological population, the depreciation of a capital asset such as industrial plant or machinery by a constant percentage each year, the decay of a source of radioactivity, or the depreciation of a currency in times of inflation. Such processes are called exponential because time – the variable t – is the exponent in the expression which characterises them, as above. The declining population, the value of the asset, the strength of the source of radioactivity, or the value of the currency, as the case may be, never falls quite to zero, but after a long enough time it will be negligible for all practical purposes. In the same way, virtually all of the exhibits will eventually have been replaced.

The fraction unchanged after several years is naturally greater under a 'constant proportion' regime than under a 'steady replacement' one, because part of the effort is devoted to changing some of the exhibits for the second, third . . . n^{th} time before others have been changed the first time. Under 'steady replacement' the fraction unchanged after t years would be $(1 - t/P)$, which is less than the $(1 - 1/P)^t$ of the other regime by an amount which increases year by year.

The 'half-life' concept

There are various ways of evaluating the expression $(1 - 1/P)^t$ which characterises the 'constant proportion' regime, from using log tables to working it out on a pocket calculator of the scientific or financial type, with log and antilog functions. Rather than working it out each time, it may be worthwhile to plot a graph of $(1 - 1/P)^t$ against t for various values of P, but a better procedure is described below based on Figure 17.3.

The important thing to bear in mind is that it is easy to be over-optimistic about the age of the exhibits in a set by assuming that the operational regime is the 'steady replacement' one when in practice it amounts to the 'constant proportion' one or something very similar. This tendency is encouraged if the rate of working is characterised by P because this does not distinguish between the two regimes. The best way of guarding against it is to transform the variable P by expressing the rate of change of the exhibits as a half-life. The latter is a very convenient variable for expressing the precise nature of an exponential process and is widely used for this purpose. It is the period in which the dependent variable – the size of the population, the value of the asset, the strength of the source of radioactivity, the value of the currency, or the unchanged fraction of the exhibits – falls to half of what it was at the start of the period. Thus in a set of exhibits with a half-life of 10 years, half of the total area will be replaced in the first decade. Half of this – a quarter of the total – will be replaced again the second decade, along with half of the remainder – which is another quarter of the whole. Since $\frac{1}{4} + \frac{1}{4} = \frac{1}{2}$, the total output in the second decade will be the same as that in the first. The fraction unchanged at the end of the second decade will be $(1 - \frac{1}{2})^2 = \frac{1}{4}$. That is to say, half the exhibits will be unchanged after one half-life has elapsed, a quarter after two, an eighth after three and so on. If expectations are based on the 'steady replacement' assumption but the reality corresponds to the 'constant proportion' regime, and $P = 15$ (which corresponds to a half-life of 10 years), the team that sets out to replace the whole of the exhibits will find that after 15 years, instead of having finished the replacement work, it still has 35 per cent of it to do.

The half-life, h, is the value of t obtained by putting $(1 - 1/P)^t$ equal to 0.5. To evaluate this it is necessary once again to resort to logarithms, using either calculator or tables, but over the range $P=0$ to $P=50$ it is accurate enough for most purposes to use the approximation $h = 2P/3$, as may be seen from Figure 17.2. The line in this figure corresponds to $h = 2P/3$, the crosses show the

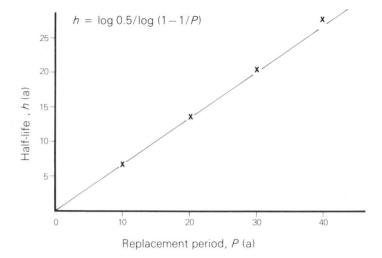

Figure 17.2 Half-life and replacement period.

more accurate values obtained by using logarithms:

$$(1 - 1/P)^h = 0.5.$$

Therefore,

$$h = \frac{\log 0.5}{(1 - 1/P)}.$$

The suggestion was made above that $(1 - 1/P)^t$ might be plotted against t for various values of P, but because of the danger of self-deception already mentioned it is better to plot it for various values of h instead of P. Such a plot, in conjunction with Figure 17.2, provides a convenient procedure for deciding what half-life to work to and how to match the size of the exhibition team to the area of the exhibition space. One is provided later (Fig. 17.3), but before considering its use we need to elaborate the model a little more.

Balancing replacement and renewal

The model must be elaborated to take account of once-and-for-all changes resulting from increased exhibition space or shifts in policy. In these circumstances one possibility is to stop all replacement work until the new exhibitions are complete, but this again might take too long for it to be a practicable proposition. Another possibility is to devote a constant proportion of all the available effort to replacement, either limiting this to the new exhibits or dividing it between the

new and the old, perhaps in proportion to their respective areas. A third possibility is the more balanced one of devoting more and more effort to replacement, and therefore less and less to renewal, as the new exhibits grow in number, until all the new space has been occupied or all the old exhibits have been replaced, as the case may be, and all the effort can be devoted to replacement under a regime such as the 'constant

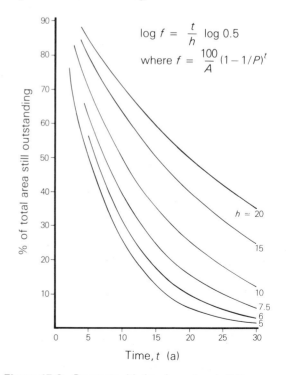

Figure 17.3 Progress with time for various half-lives.

proportion' one. Whatever the course of action decided upon, the fact remains that in any major project involving both initial work (renewal) and replacement, the balance between the two must be kept under careful control if the new exhibitions are to be completed in a reasonable time and the entire set of exhibits kept up to date. Let us therefore consider what happens if the effort devoted to replacement is the same proportion of the total effort available as the new area produced to date is of the total area, the remainder of the effort being allocated to further initial work (renewal). We can do this in a way that makes it possible to forecast how things will evolve if the variables on which h and P depend do not change their values, but at the same time is sufficiently flexible to enable us to cope with changes in these values that result from changes in political and economic circumstances.

To deal with this situation we introduce two further variables, both of which are time dependent. One is the number of groups in the exhibition team working on entirely new exhibits (renewal): call it n, in which case the number of groups on replacement will be $(N - n)$. The other is the area for which initial production is still necessary, the area outstanding: call it a, in which case the area of new exhibits at the particular time will be $(A - a)$. The other variables are as before:

N is total number of groups
r is rate of output, square metres per group per year
P is period of renewal or replacement, years
A is total exhibition area, square metres

with the constraint that $P = A/Nr$.

Suppose that the effort is reallocated at yearly intervals, and let the value of n (number of groups on renewal) during year t, i.e. after $(t-1)$ years, be denoted by n_t, where $t = 1, 2, 3 \dots$ Similarly, let the area outstanding, i.e. that needing renewal after t years, be denoted by a_t. Successive values of n_t and a_t may then be calculated from a pair of equations that are derived as follows.

In general, $N = A/Pr$. The starting conditions are

$a_0 = A$ (no new exhibits yet produced)

$n_1 = N$ (all groups on renewal)

and at the end of the first year the area outstanding is

$$a_1 = A - Nr = A(1 - 1/P).$$

During the second year we have

$$n_2 = \frac{A(1 - 1/P)}{Pr}$$

$$= N(1 - 1/P)$$

since $A/Pr = N$, and when it ends

$$\begin{aligned} a_2 &= A(1 - 1/P) - N(1 - 1/P)r \\ &= A(1 - 1/P) - A(1 - 1/P)/P \text{ since } Nr = A/P \\ &= A(1 - 1/P)(1 - 1/P) \\ &= A(1 - 1/P)^2. \end{aligned}$$

Repeating the process, deriving n_3, a_3, n_4, a_4 etc. leads to the pair of equations

$$\left. \begin{aligned} n_t &= N(1 - 1/P)^{t-1} \\ a_t &= A(1 - 1/P)^t \end{aligned} \right\}$$

The area outstanding at the end of year t is, it will be seen, the same as that calculated under the somewhat simpler conditions of the 'constant proportion' regime – the expression just derived for a_t is the same as that deduced more simply in the previous section of this chapter. However, it is not immediately obvious that the two regimes are equivalent in this respect. The equivalence arises from the emphasis on P as the determinant of the situation. It measures the capacity of the team, be it for renewal or replacement.

Given the values of a_t and n_t, it is easy to derive expressions that enable other variables to be calculated, all involving the factor $f = (1 - 1/P)^t$, which it is convenient to express as a percentage, $100f$. After t years.

(a)   Number of groups on replacement during the coming year

$$\begin{aligned} &= N - n_{t+1} \\ &= N\left[1 - (1 - 1/P)^t\right] = N(1 - f). \end{aligned}$$

(b)   Area to be replaced during the coming year

$$= Nr\left[1-(1-1/P)^t\right]=Nr(1-f).$$

(c) New area produced during last year

$$= Nr(1-1/P)^{t-1}$$

(d) Total new area produced by the end of last year

$$= A - a_t$$
$$= A\left[1-(1-1/P)^t\right]=A(1-f).$$

(e) Time from year t to complete renewal at the then current rate of working, i.e. without transferring any more groups from renewal to replacement:

$$= \frac{a_t}{n_t r}$$

$$= P(1-1/P) = P-1.$$

Once again, though it is convenient to derive these expressions in terms of P, in order to avoid over-optimism it is better to transform them to expressions in terms of the half-life, h.

Two things need to be borne in mind during a phase of expansion. First, any expansion in the space available for exhibits must be matched by a proportionate expansion of the exhibition team or the half-life will be increased in virtually the same proportion, being an approximately linear function of P, which will go up in exact proportion to the increase in area. Secondly, a half-life that is acceptable in more static circumstances may well be too long when ideas are changing rapidly, and this also applies when there is a shift in policy, irrespective of whether or not there is a concomitant expansion.

Whatever the change, when contemplating an increase or decrease in either the exhibition space or the size of the team (or a simultaneous change in both, not necessarily in the same direction), the easiest way to examine the consequences is by exploiting the characteristics of the half-life. An increase in A or a decrease in N will cause a proportionate increase in h. Change in the opposite direction is less of a concern because it actually decreases the half-life.

For any given values of A, N and r, and therefore of P and h, the effect of changing the half-life will be as shown in Figure 17.4, which summarises the way in which an entirely new

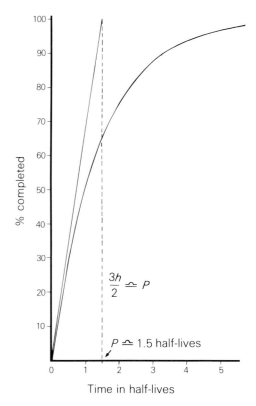

Figure 17.4 Rate of progress when time is measured in multiples of the half-life.

exhibition progresses towards completion under the assumed conditions. The timescale in this diagram is graduated in units of one half-life; the vertical dotted line marks 1.5 units on this scale and corresponds to the renewal period (cf. the line in Fig. 17.2). The curved line shows how the percentage completion, i.e. $100f = 100a_t/A$ approaches the horizontal 100 per cent line at the top, while the straight line shows for comparison how the work would progress if all replacement were eliminated. The curve shows that after P years have elapsed, instead of renewal being finished, only 65 per cent of the area will have been dealt with. That is to say, there will still be 35 per cent of the renewal work to do, so some of the exhibits will be somewhat long in the tooth (cf. previous section, with the particular case of $h=10$ and $P = 15$). Whereas it may be possible at this stage to accept that 35 per cent of the exhibits are antiquated, it is less likely that it will be acceptable for only 65 per cent of the new exhibits to have been produced if the original expectation was that they would all have been produced in P years.

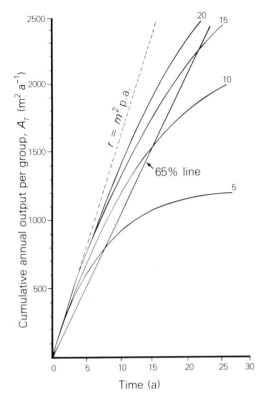

Figure 17.5 How renewing exhibits reduces the rate at which they can be replaced.

The model so far elaborated assumes that the effort to be devoted to initial work in the coming year is such that the rate of completion matches that corresponding to the half-life or renewal period. Under these conditions, the proportion of the groups on initial work may be deduced from Figure 17.3:

$$\frac{n_t}{N} = (1 - 1/P)^{t-1}$$

$$= \frac{a_{t-1}}{A}.$$

Thus all that is necessary to determine n_t/N for year t is to read off the ordinate for year $(t-1)$ and the appropriate curve. However, alternative ways of allocating the available effort between renewal and replacement may be preferred, especially in changing economic and political circumstances. One obvious possibility is to divide the team into two sections, one working exclusively on renewal and the other exclusively on replacement. If the new exhibits are not intended to displace the old, but merely to occupy an extension of the exhibition space, it might be possible to increase the overall size of the team temporarily, say until the entirely new exhibits are completed. This period then corresponds to the P of Figure 17.1, which serves as a guide to fixing the size of this section of the team. Assuming replacement takes place under the 'constant proportion' regime, the relation between the capacity and size of the replacement section of the team can be studied from this figure. Alternatively, Figure 17.5 can be used. It shows the cumulative output per group, denoted by A_t, as a function of t for various half-lives:

$$A_t = A\left[1 - (1 - 1/P)^t\right]$$

$$= Pr\left[1 - (1 - 1/P)^t\right] \text{ if } N = 1$$

which is for all practical purposes the same as

$$A_t = \frac{3}{2}hr\left[1 - (1 - \frac{2h}{3})^t\right]$$

(The purist who owns a suitable pocket calculator may choose to evaluate the expression more precisely.)

The dotted line in Figure 17.5 shows the output corresponding to the assumed rate of working, in this instance 160 m^2 a year. The actual capacity falls short of this because of the 'constant proportion' replacement policy, the more so the shorter the half-life.

One convenient stratagem in setting up the exhibition team is to base the number of groups on what one group can achieve in one and a half half-lives (i.e. one replacement period), 65 per cent of the amount given by the rate of working. The 65 per cent line on Figure 17.5 shows that at the particular rate of working for which the diagram was drawn (160 m^2 a year) there should be one group per 800 m^2 of exhibition space at a half-life of five years, one per 1550 m^2 at 10 years, or one per 2300 m^2 at 15 years. These are, of course, the equivalent of working for the same period at 65 per cent of the nominal rate, and the capacities given by the formula $A = P/Nr$ would be over 50 per cent bigger – 1200, 2400 and 3600 m^2 respectively, as shown by the dotted line in Figure 17.6.

To summarise, when following a policy of continual replacement of exhibits, and providing the specified assumptions are acceptable, the most convenient measure of the situation is the half-life of the exhibitions. Overemphasis on the

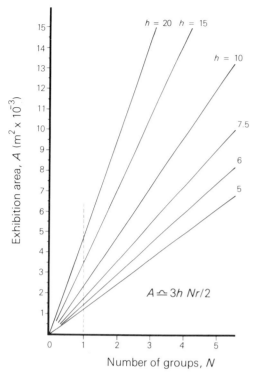

Figure 17.6   Team size, area and half-life.

renewal period may be misleading. The model developed in the preceding pages, which is represented in graphical form (Fig. 17.5), provides a useful basis for management decisions concerning the team responsible for producing and replacing exhibits.

Two types of output

As we pointed out earlier, the quantity P is a very useful measure of the capacity of the exhibition team in relation to the area for which it is responsible. The expression

$$P = \frac{A}{Nr}$$

where A is the exhibition area,
$\quad N$ is the total number of partnerships, and
$\quad P$ was defined as the replacement period,

may be rewritten to take account of a multiplicity of activities. The first job that we considered for the exhibition team was renewal, to which we subsequently added a second one, that of replacement.

To examine the allocation of the available resources between these two activities it is convenient to rewrite the formula as

$$p_i = \frac{a_i}{n_i r_i}$$

which may be interpreted by defining p_i as the number of years it takes n_i partnerships, each with an output of r_i m² a year, to produce a_i m² of exhibition. For renewal ($i = 1$), a_i becomes a_1, which becomes equal to A once any additional new exhibition space has been filled: p_1 is the time it would take n_1 partnerships to produce the a_1 m² at a rate of r_1 per partnership per year. For replacement ($i = 2$), once any new space has been filled $a_2 = a_1 = A$, but for present purposes we assume r_2 to be different from r_1, i.e. that the rates of output are different for renewal and replacement. Furthermore, p_2 is not necessarily the time it will take the n_2 groups to replace all of the exhibits. It is, in fact, the time it will take to produce replacement exhibits that *in toto* would cover an area equal to that of all the exhibits. The two are the same only if no exhibit is replaced for the mth time before all exhibits have been replaced for the $(m-1)$th time. In other words, the significance of p_2 depends on the way the exhibits are selected for replacement, i.e. on what is conveniently labelled the selection regime. Until all the exhibits have been renewed after a shift in policy, and any new space filled, the selection regime is only a part of the replacement regime, the other part being the allocation of resources, i.e. the giving of a value to n_2. Even if conditions are such that n_2 does not affect the total cost, it is an important control variable because of its influence on the replacment period p_2 which is the chief parameter of the replacement regime.

The relationship

$$p_2 = \frac{a_2}{n_2 r_2}$$

holds whether or not $a_2 = a_1$ and/or $r_2 = r_1$. The selection regime is not readily expressed in a generalised form, but useful guidance in allocating resources may be drawn from the capacity formula. This one, the generalised steady-state formula

$$p_i = \frac{a_i}{n_i r_i}$$

may be used to express N in terms of the p_i:

$$N = n_1 + n_2$$

$$= \frac{a_1}{r_1 p_i} + \frac{a_2}{r_2 p_2}.$$

If the a_i and r_i are regarded as given, this constraint leaves only one degree of freedom in selecting p_1 and p_2, i.e. in determining:

(a) the time it will take to complete the new exhibitions;
(b) how old the exhibits will be before they are replaced, which is some function of p_2 but is not necessarily identical with it.

The replacement regime may then be characterised by the ratio of p_2 to p_1 and this ratio expressed in terms of the decision variable n_2:

$$\frac{p_2}{p_1} = \frac{a_2}{n_2 r_2} \times \frac{n_1 r_1}{a_1}$$

$$= \frac{a_2}{a_1} \times \frac{r_1}{r_2} \left(\frac{N}{n_2} - 1 \right)$$

since $n_1 = N - n_2$. In slightly more general terms

$$\frac{p_2}{p_1} = \frac{a_2}{a_1} \times \frac{r_1}{r_2} \left(\frac{1}{f_2} - 1 \right)$$

where f_2 is the fraction of partnerships engaged on replacement.

The situation thus involves three controllable variables, n_2 (or equivalently f_2), p_1 and p_2, but only two degrees of freedom. It can be represented by a plot of, say, p_1 against p_2 for various values of f_2. If in the first instance we let $a_2 = a_1$ and $r_2 = r_1$, the plot will be as in Figure 17.7 which shows lines of constant P and others of constant f_2 plotted with axes of p_1 and p_2. More generally, it will have the same form but with lines of different slopes.

The interpretation of p_2 depends on the selection regime. As already noted, if no exhibit is replaced for the mth time until all have been replaced for the $(m-1)$th time, it is the time taken to replace all of the exhibits, and hence the life of an exhibit or the age of the oldest exhibit on display (assuming that it takes a negligible time to substitute the replacement exhibit for its predecessor).

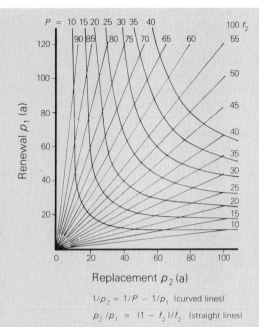

Figure 17.7 Balancing p_1 and p_2.

Under any other selection regime, the oldest exhibit will be older than this. If the exhibits to be replaced are selected at random, p_2 is some transform of the half-life of the set of exhibitions. 'At random' in this instance has its usual statistical meaning (Ch. 16), that each exhibit is as likely to be selected as any other, or more precisely that the probability of replacement is constant and the same for all exhibits. The characteristics of random processes are well established. They include a Poisson distribution of the number of events per unit time (in present circumstances an event is selection for replacement) and a negative exponential distribution of the interval between successive events. They have been studied extensively in connection with telephone systems where, under specified simple conditions, there is also a negative exponential distribution of waiting time, which enables the average waiting time to be calculated and also makes it possible to say what the chances are of having to wait more than a particular time before getting through. The life of an exhibit corresponds roughly to the waiting time, but as we shall see there is little point in pursuing this line of analysis.

The random model came into the picture as a necessary consequence of the suggestion that resources might be switched from renewal to replacement as the renewed exhibitions grew, a constant proportion of the growing exhibitions being replaced each year. Though an improvement on the 'replacement by age' model, it is still very much an idealisation. It allows for the possibility of replacing some exhibits for the mth time before all have been replaced for the $(m − 1)$th time, by allocating a greater proportion of the available resources to replacement than would otherwise be the case. In a sense it goes to the other extreme, in that it implies an over-long life for a small proportion of the exhibits instead of the same life for all of them. The most likely situation in practice is that the probability of selection for replacement will be less than the implied random value $(1/p_2)$ for some of the exhibits and more than this for some others, so that the age distribution of the exhibits will not follow the negative exponential one exactly. Given the diverse criteria that tend to influence the decision to change parts of an exhibition (not always the exhibits as such, sometimes signposting or other linking material has to be altered), especially if the exhibition is at all controversial, and also the uncertainty that is liable to exist about the future availability of manpower and other resources (including additional space), it would be unprofitable to engage in a more complex analysis with the aim of providing a more accurate specification of the age distribution of exhibits. There are other and better ways of looking at the future situation.

Looking forward

However unsystematic the allocation of resources, it is still simple to take a forward look at the growth of a new exhibition year by year, by iterative calculation of the amount outstanding.

$$a_t = a_{t-1} - (N - n_t)r$$

where a_t is area outstanding (i.e. not developed for the first time) after t years,
N is total number of partnerships,
n_t is number of partnerships on renewal during year t, and
r is output rate, area per partnership,

in which a_t may be regarded as the dependent and

n_t as the independent variable, N and r as parameters. An example of such a calculation is shown in Table 17.1, which also includes the replacement output year by year on the basis that the renewal and replacement rates are the same.

The value of a_t may actually increase from time to time, e.g. as additional space becomes available. Similarly N may vary from time to time, but not necessarily in step with a_t.

The value of n_t may be decided on an *ad-hoc* basis, but in the 'constant proportion' model it is calculated from the equation

$$n_t = \frac{(A - a_t)}{Pr}$$

where A, as usual, is the total exhibition space and P the renewal/replacement period – two further parameters. From this and the equation for a_t, formulae may be derived for calculating a series of variables such as annual renewal output, area completed to date, and so on. These all have the form

$$x_{t+1} = x_t(1 - 1/P) + k$$

where k is a constant differing from one variable to another.

The same expression leads to the transformation of the 'constant proportion' model into the random one. If the fraction of the exhibition space replaced each year is $1/p_2$,

the proportion still not replaced after t years = $(1 - 1/p_2)^t$,
so the proportion replaced $= 1 - (1 - 1/p_2)^t$.

Putting $t = h$, where h is the half-life, gives

$$1 - (1 - 1/p_2)^h = 0.5$$

whence

$$(1 - 1/p_2)^h = 0.5$$

or

$$h = \frac{\log 0.5}{\log(1 - 1/p_2)}$$

which is the same formula as that given in the first section of this chapter.

Table 17.1 Growth of a new exhibition year by year, assuming replacement and renewal rates are the same.

	Year									
	74/75	75/76	76/77	77/78	78/79	79/80	80/81	81/82	82/83	83/84
N = no. of development partnerships available	6			7	10					
r = output, m² per per annum partnership	160									
P = renewal period, yr	15									
Pr	2 400									
A = area available, m²	24 000									
a = area outstanding, m²	24 000	23 040	22 080	21 120	20 160	18 880	17 600	16 400	15 280	14 240
$A-a$ = area completed, m²	0	960	1 920	2 880	3 840	5 120	6 400	7 600	8 720	9 760
Renewal										
n = no. of development partnerships	0	0	0	1	2	2	2.5	3	3.5	4
nr = output per year, m²	0	0	0	160	320	320	400	480	560	640
Initial development										
$(N-n)$ = development partnerships	6	6	6	6	8	8	7.5	7	6.5	6
$(N-n)r$ = output for year, m²	960	960	960	960	1 280	1 280	1 200	1 120	1 040	960
$a/(N-n)r$ = time to completion, yr, from start of year at the year's rate of output	25	24	23	22	15.8	14.8	14.6	14.6	14.7	14.8

To make a realistic comparison between the effects of the two regimes, we can take a specific example. If $h = 15$ years, then $P = 22.5$ from Figure 17.2. The first regime requires that no exhibit is replaced until all the partnerships have finished the renewal work, which will take 22 years. They then all switch to replacement and work steadily through from start to finish again and again, taking 22 years for each cycle. The average age of the exhibits is 11 years, there is always about 20 per cent of the exhibitions that is over 20 years old, and no exhibit is replaced until it is 22 years old.

The other regime results in the replacement each year of about 4.5 per cent of the growing amount of the new exhibitions, but instead of renewal being complete after the 22-year period only 65 per cent will have been done, and even after half a century there will still be 10 per cent of

the space to do.

Both these scenarios correspond to seven groups, each producing 160 m² a year, and an exhibition of 25 000 m². Different figures would give different times and ages: this is the long-term aspect of looking ahead – propounding an argument to support claims by the exhibition team in the competition for resources. The strength of the argument lies in the fact that it starts from explicit assumptions. It enables the team to say to the authorities, 'You give us N groups to deal with an area of A m². We do our best, but we cannot produce more than r m² per group per year, so it will take P years to work steadily through the exhibitions from one end to the other as an absolute minimum. If we replace any exhibits before we have finished even after $2P$ years we shall still not be finished, and the average age of the exhibits will be over the $\frac{1}{2}P$ which represents the best that can possibly be done. Some exhibits are going to be more than $2P$ years old before they are replaced'.

The short-term situation

Whereas in the long term the values of A and N, and therefore of P, may be variable, in the short term they are fixed. Complete flexibility in the short term is possible only by ignoring the long-term implications of whatever is decided – A and N are effectively fixed. We take the view that neither of the two extremes discussed in the previous section is practicable. The essence of what follows is that in the short term the allocation of the resources available for exhibition work between the twin activities of renewal and replacement may be varied from time to time to suit the exigencies of the situation, provided that the long-term balance is maintained. A cumulative chart can be used to keep the long-term situation in view while allocating resources according to the requirements of the immediate circumstances.

Planning is dominated by the constraint

$$p_i \geq \frac{A}{Nr_i}$$

which is effectively the same as the function plotted in Figure 17.1, since the P and r of that figure may be replaced by p_1 and r_1 or p_2 and r_2 as the case may be. The overall value P is one of a pair of parameters that govern the allocation of resources between renewal and replacement. The individual values p_1 and p_2 characterise the rates of progress in renewal and replacement respectively; they are related to one another and to P. Since

$$n_i = \frac{A}{p_i r_i} \text{ and } N = \sum_i n_i = \frac{A}{Pr}$$

it follows that

$$\frac{A}{Pr} = A \sum_i \frac{1}{p_i r_i}.$$

If $i = 1$ or 2 and $r_i = r_2 = r$, this becomes

$$\frac{1}{P} = \frac{1}{p_1} + \frac{1}{p_2}.$$

The graph of p_2 against p_1 for any given value of P and constant r will therefore be a curve asymptotic to $p_1 = P$ and $p_2 = P$.

The other parameter is f_2, the proportion of the partnerships working on replacement: this also links p_1 and p_2 since

$$\frac{p_2}{p_1} = \frac{1}{f_2} - 1$$

or equivalently

$$f_2 = \frac{p_1}{(p_1 + p_2)}$$

The graph of p_2 against p_1 for any given value of f_2 is therefore a straight line, as in Figure 17.7.

In the long term, the essence of planning is the mutual adjustment of A and N, i.e. of defining a value of P; and also of striking a balance between p_1 and p_2, i.e. of defining a long-term value of f_2. In the short term it is a matter of deciding a short-term value for f_2 according to the exigencies of the situation without making it impossible to maintain the long-term balance by later adjustment of the short-term value of f_2.

The tools for long-term planning are the graph of $P = A/Nr$ and Figure 17.7. The former has been redrawn in Figure 17.8 to cover a wider range of values for P, A and N. For short-term planning they need to be supplemented by a cumulative chart that allows the amount of new exhibition produced to date to be compared with what should have been produced according to the long-term value of f_2. An example of such a chart is provided in Figure 17.9. This assumes $P = 15$, which corresponds to $A = 12\,000$ and $N = 5$, also that $f_2 = 25$ per cent, which corresponds to $p_1 = 20$ and $p_2 = 60$. The graph is one of A_t against t, where t is the time from start and A_t is the cumulative area, i.e.

$$A_t = \sum_{t=0}^{t=T} a_{1,t}$$

where $a_{1,t}$ is the renewal output ($i = 1$) in the year t.

The central line shows progress according to the long-term value of p_1, in this case the 20 years it takes to renew the entire area of $12\,000$ m². The other two lines correspond to $p_1 = P = 15$ years, i.e. to the fastest progress possible with the given values for P and N, which would mean all renewal and no replacement. They define the limits that must not be crossed if the long-term plan is to succeed. Future changes in A or N or both (i.e. in P), or in the long-term f_2 (i.e. in p_1) can be anticipated by altering the slopes of the lines as appropriate at the corresponding value of t.

The progress chart (Fig. 17.9) may be updated annually. For deciding the short-term value of f_2 at the beginning of the year the graph of Figure 17.10 may be used. This shows the replacement output for the year, a_2, plotted against the renewal output, a_1, where

$$a_2 = f_2 Nr$$

$$a_1 = (1 - f_2)Nr$$

and therefore

$$\frac{a_2}{a_1} = \frac{f_2}{(1 - f_2)}.$$

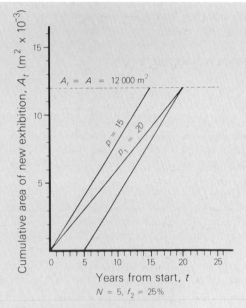

Figure 17.9   Progress chart.

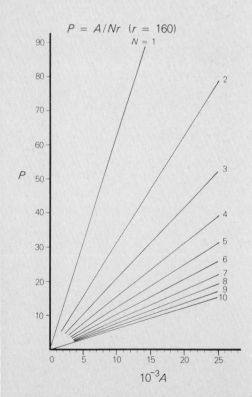

Figure 17.8   How the replacement period depends on the size of the exhibition area and that of the exhibition team.

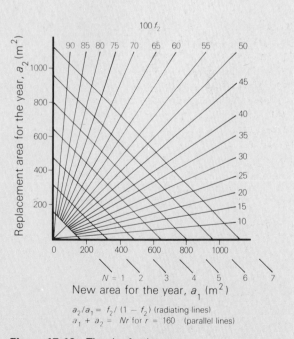

Figure 17.10   The plan for the year.

The lines radiating from the origin correspond to this equation for values of f_2 at intervals of 5 per cent. The parallel lines running down from left to right correspond to the constraint

$$a_1 + a_2 = Nr$$

with $r = 160$ and N varying from 1 to 7. The long-term situation is represented by the point of intersection of the f_2-line corresponding to the long-term value of f_2 with the line corresponding to the current value of N.

The latter line, together with the two axes, defines the area within which it is feasible to operate during the year. Output will be maximised as long as conditions correspond to a point on the N-line, but any point on this line may be chosen, according to prevailing considerations. The short-term value of f_2 may then be ascertained from the appropriate radiating line (or by interpolation between two adjacent lines). The use of f_2 rather than n_2 on the graph allows for the very real possibility of N changing at short notice, which merely shifts the position of the Nr boundary of the feasible area.

A graph similar to Figure 17.9 may be drawn for replacement projects, the line representing the long-term plan being in this instance based on p_2 in place of p_1. Both graphs may be elaborated by listing new sections of exhibitions or replacement projects as the case may be, in priority order, determining the cumulative areas, and marking the y-axis accordingly.

For the purposes of illustration it has been assumed throughout that $r_1 = r_2$, which accords with our experience in the British Museum (Natural History), but the possibility of different values should always be borne in mind and the planning graphs modified if new assumptions are justified.

Glossary

Statistical and computing terms are not included. For the former see Kendall, M. G. and W. R. Buckland 1957. *A dictionary of statistical terms*. Edinburgh: Oliver & Boyd. For the latter, see Chandor, A., J. Graham and R. Williamson 1977. *A dictionary of computers*. London: Penguin.

a. c. lacquer An acid catalyst lacquer, a hard-wearing varnish.

adaption The action or process by which the eye adapts to changes in brightness or colour in the field of vision.

airbrush A small, pen-shaped spray gun working on compressed air, which is used to obtain a smooth gradation of tones on **original** or retouched illustration work.

algorithm As used in educational technology, a name given to a problem-solving procedure which is both (a) readily communicable and (b) strongly guaranteed to give the right sorts of results under real-life conditions of usage.

arris A sharp edge formed by the intersection of two surfaces.

artwork Original material intended as a source of reproduction. It comprises typesetting, illustrations or photographs, or any combination of these.

ascender The stroke which ascends above the main body of a character such as 'h'.

'A' sizes The international standard range of paper sizes which range from A0 to A7. The ratio between the long and short sides is the same throughout the range: any 'A' series sheet folded in half across the long dimension and cut along the fold produces two sheets of the next smallest size.

attraction power The ratio of visitors stopping at an **exhibit** to the total number passing it.

A/W Artwork.

axonometric (of drawings) A three-dimensional representation based on two axes at 45° to the vertical but at right angles to one another (cf. **isometric**).

baffle A deliberate obstruction, especially one used in sequentially lit **displays** to stop light seeping from one section to another.

balancer A sheet of paper or laminate applied to the back of a photographic or laminated panel to prevent buckling.

bead A narrow strip, usually wooden, used, for example, to fix glass into a frame.

behavioural objectives Explicit formulations about what a successful learner will be able to do at the end of an educative experience.

bleach out The conversion of a continuous tone photograph to a line image, disposing of the middle tone range.

blow up A photographic enlargement.

body copy Block of text as opposed to single line **displays**.

bold face A heavy looking type used to emphasise headings.

bromide A particular type of photographic paper, nowadays used as a general name for a black and white photographic print.

butt To join edge to edge.

B/W Black and white.

Camera-ready artwork The final **artwork** for photographic reproduction.

cap-height The height of a capital letter, usually given in millimetres, used in specifying the size of type to be used.

caps A contraction of 'capital letters'.

caption A brief explanation that accompanies a photograph, illustration or diagram.

carcase The box-like main part of a structure.

case schedule A list of packing cases and their contents.

chamfer The surface produced by bevelling a sharp edge or corner.

Cibachrome A specific type of full-colour photographic positive, a print or **transparency**. It fades less than an ordinary colour photograph.

Cinemoid A semi-rigid sheet colour filter.

cladding Panels applied to a **carcase** or frame.

compromise exhibit An **exhibit** that attempts to reconcile conflicting objectives, e.g. to appeal both to specialist and layman.

continuous tone Having a complete range of tones from black to white (usually of photographs) (c.f. **halftone**).

copy Written material to be set in type.

cut See **halftone**.

cut-line A caption used with a **halftone** photograph.

cut-out A photograph from which the background has been cut away leaving only the outline of the subject.

descender The stroke that descends below the main body of a character such as 'p'.

diffuser A translucent material such as opal **Perspex**, multifaceted glass sheet or open plastic grid that is fitted between light fittings and a display to distribute light evenly.

display A general term which can refer to an individual **exhibit**, groups of exhibits or an entire **exhibition**.

dissolve A term used in audio-visual work to describe the gradual change from one projected image to another without leaving the screen blank in between. Two projectors are needed.

drayage Temporary storage for a travelling **exhibition**.

duotone A set of two-colour **halftones** produced from a single colour **original**.

duplicate A copy taken from a master or from another duplicate.

dyechrome A full colour photographic product that looks like a **transparency** when it is illuminated and a print when it is not. It contains a built-in diffuser.

dyeline printing A method of photographic reproduction from a transparent **original** on to paper or film impregnated or coated with a diazo compound.

dye transfer A colour print usually taken from a colour **transparency** when additional work or correction is needed before reproduction.

estimate A cost figure that is not binding when included in a contract (cf. quotation or **tender**).

exhibit A single unit within an **exhibition**, e.g. a display case or an audio-visual. (In North America the term would have the meaning of 'exhibition'.)

exhibition The series of displays dealing with a particular theme, e.g. Impressionist Art or Human Biology. (In North America it is the collective term for the totality of items displayed in a particular institution.)

fascia A horizontal strip above eye level.

F.F. Fluorescent fitting.

film positive A line image on a film base that reads normally.

filmsetting An optical method of setting type, the end-product being an image on film or photographic paper.

finishes Materials such as felt, paint or laminate applied to **cladding** to complete the basic structure of the **display**.

F.L. Floor level.

formative evaluation Evaluation that takes place during development and production. The results are used to improve the quality of the final product, which may be an **exhibit**, book, television show, curriculum, etc.

former A frame on to which sheet material can be moulded and fixed.

F.S. Full-size.

gallery A long passage; also a building housing an **exhibition**.

glare Dazzling or oppressive light, especially when reflected. It can be caused by an excess of light in one particular direction.

GRP Glass-reinforced polyester (fibreglass).

groundwork The modelled surface of a diorama.

halftone A print in which small dots of various sizes are used to give the optical illusion of **continuous tone**.

heat-sealing A plastic film coating applied to photographs for protection.

holding power The time spent at an **exhibit** given that the visitor has stopped.

information mapping A form of programmed instruction invented by Robert Horn.

isometric (of drawings) A three-dimensional representation in which all the angles between the axes equal 60° (cf. **axonometric**).

justification The arrangement of type and word spaces to give lines of equal length.

keylines Lines on a drawing that serve as a guide for further work to be carried out at the reproduction stage, tint areas to be laid by printer or photographs to be overmounted by graphic contractor.

keystoning A distortion of the projected image when two projectors are focused on the same screen.

landscape Having the longer dimension horizontal (of a photograph, image or panel).

layout A plan of the elements of a design without the detail.

leading (pronounced 'ledding') The spaces between the lines of typesetting; they are a major factor influencing the 'readability' of long sequences of text.

learning station One unit in a series of **exhibits** that is designed to present a coherent theme or body of information.

LED Light-emitting diode, a semiconductor light source much used in electronic devices such as watches and calculators.

Letraset The trade name for a dry transfer lettering system with an extensive range of type faces, textures and miscellaneous aids used in preparing **artwork**.

light-box A container housing light fittings behind a **transparency**.

linework An image, usually an illustration, drawn in black ink without any grey tones. It can be reproduced in any one colour.

line/tone combine An effect usually obtained by a printer or graphic contractor by combining two separate elements into one image.

lipping A strip of timber or other material used to finish the edge of a panel.

lumen The SI unit for measuring the amounts of light (cf. **lux**).

lux A measure of intensity of illumination; one lux is equal to one **lumen** per square metre.

mask An opaque, cut-out overlay that conceals the

unwanted portion of a photograph or **transparency** in a display.

mask mount   A projection slide made to cover parts of the image.

master   The **artwork** or **original transparency** from which copies are made.

mathetics   A form of programmed instruction invented by T. S. Gilbert.

measure   The width of the type area, the maximum length of a line of text.

medium   The agency of communication, e.g. graphic panels, audio-visuals.

misinterpretive exhibit   An **exhibit** that is over-designed so that the message to be conveyed is hidden or distorted.

mock-up   A roughly constructed approximation to a finished **exhibit**, usually produced for purposes of evaluation. The word is also used in the design of book covers, posters, and so on.

mode   The way in which the medium of communication is used, e.g. a model may be used in either the static or the dynamic mode.

monochrome   An **original** varying in intensity but not in colour.

negative   A photographic image in which the lights and shades are reversed and from which positive prints are made.

negative film transparency   This can be thought of as a negative that reads normally; used in back-lit displays requiring white or coloured lettering on black ground.

node   One of the two types of element in a network (e.g. a concept in a concept hierarchy). Nodes are joined to one another by arcs.

offset mount   A slide mount in which the film aperture is off-centre; used to avoid distortion when two projectors are focused on the same screen.

orientation   Informing visitors, by way of signposts and maps, where they are, where they are going and what they can expect to learn.

original   A photograph, drawing or piece of **artwork** intended for reproduction.

overlay   A flap over an original photograph, drawing or **artwork** giving special instructions to the printer or graphic contractor.

pacing   Controlling the diversity and contrast between **exhibits** so that the visitor is not given too much of the same thing or too much of everything.

Pantone colour system   A standard colour reference system identifying by code some 560 colours. It allows unambiguous colour specifications to be passed to a graphic contractor or printer.

paste-up   A preliminary assembly of elements in their correct positions, prepared for approval prior to commencing work on the final **artwork** stage.

Pepper's ghost   A reflection of an object above and in front of a semi-silvered glass screen that appears to merge with, or change into, a second object placed behind the screen. The effect depends on the way in which the two objects are illuminated.

performance cone   The area of effective illumination from a light fitting.

Perspex   The trade name for a rigid acrylic plastic, clear or coloured, used in colour filters or as an alternative to glass.

Plexiglass   Another trade name, equivalent to **Perspex**.

PMT   Photomechanical transfer. Generally limited to the photographic enlargement and reduction of **line-work**.

portrait   A photograph, image or graphic panel having the longer dimension vertical.

programmed instruction   A way of teaching that exercises careful and continuous control over the learning of the student.

proof   In printing, a trial impression that is supplied for correction, comment and approval prior to production of the final item.

pulse   A short electrical signal, e.g. on an audio-visual tape for controlling slide changes.

psychometric theory   A branch of psychology dealing with the measurement of psychological character-istics concerned with aspects of cognition and personality.

ranged left (or right)   A term used to describe type that is aligned on the left (or the right).

rebate   A rectangular recess along the edge of a piece of timber or a panel.

register   The exact correspondence of two or more printed images, achieved by associating a registering symbol with each of the images.

register mount   A slide mount with sprockets for locating the film.

reverse left-to-right   To make a photographic image face in the opposite direction by turning the negative over.

reversed-out (of wording)   White against a dark back-ground or a photographic image.

rods   Full-size construction drawings produced by exhibition contractors.

Rosco cine   An acetate filter for reducing daylight, used in **displays** where the image is seen only when the back lighting is triggered.

Roscolux   Another trade name, equivalent to **Rosco cine**.

rough   A sketch giving a general idea of the size and position of the various elements of the design.

sandwich   A composite structure used for back-lit displays. Graphics are sealed between sheets of glass or clear **Perspex** with an opal diffuser.

scribing   The cutting of a constructional material to fit around a moulded or irregular shape.

separations The transparent or semi-transparent overlay sheets on **artwork** carrying sections of whole image which are to be reproduced in different colours or by different processes.

set-up drawings Instructions for erecting a travelling **exhibition**.

show-rules Regulations for designing and building **exhibits** in a commercial exhibition site.

site-line A single, uninterrupted view.

silk-screen printing A method of printing using a squeegee to force ink through a stencil of fine mesh cloth or metal.

snap-change An immediate change from one projected image to another in an audio-visual programme.

split batten A horizontal piece of timber cut in two at 45°. One half is fixed to the back of a panel, the other to a wall. The panel is then hung on the wall so that one half of the timber fits over the other.

spot Spotlight.

S/S (a) In exhibition work, an abbreviation that means 'sight size' and refers to the visible *area* of the image, e.g. with a framed picture. The area including that hidden by the frame is the 'actual size' or 'site size'. (b) In graphic work, an abbreviation generally accepted as meaning 'same size', i.e. **artwork** that is to be reproduced at the same size as it is presented to the printer.

stand An individual exhibition area in a commercial **exhibition**.

stat A photographic enlargement.

story-board A series of key images for a proposed **exhibit**, etc. with **copy** and directions beneath.

summative evaluation Evaluation that is carried out to assess the effectiveness of an **exhibit**, book, television show, curriculum, etc., after it has been produced.

system build An **exhibition** built with a proprietary display system.

talking head A manikin on to which a film is projected to give the impression of someone talking.

target audience or population The group for which an **exhibit**, book, television show, curriculum, etc. is eventually intended.

technamation A technique for producing back-lit diagrams in which a spinning polarised disc and specially textured surfaces create the illusion of movement.

tender A final price submitted by an exhibition contractor usually in competition with others.

tone An image containing all grey values between black and white, or to a specific value of grey.

transparency A full-colour photographic positive intended to be viewed by transmitted light.

ultra-violet Radiation just beyond the visible violet end of the visible spectrum.

underinterpretive exhibit An **exhibit** that is visually unattractive and technically too complicated.

unjustified The arrangement of type where spaces between words are constant and as a result all lines are of a different length.

visual A perspective drawing or a plan of the basic elements of a design.

visual acuity The ability of a person to see detail.

voice-over The commentary accompanying an audio-visual or display.

wash drawing A monochrome drawing in which the middle tones are formed by washes of grey and black.

working drawings The drawings produced as a structural specification for the exhibition contractor.

wrap-around The mounting of the edges of a photograph print around the edges of a display panel.

X-height The height of a lower-case character without ascenders or descenders.

Bibliography

1 Introduction

Bayer, H. 1961. Aspects of design of exhibitions and museums. *Curator* **4**, 257–87.

Benton, T., C. Benton and A. Scharf 1975. *Design 1920s. German design and the Bauhaus 1925–32. Modernism in the decorative arts: Paris 1910–30.* Course A305, units 15–16. Milton Keynes: Open University Press.

Bloom, J. N., E. A. Powell *et al.* 1984. *Museums for a new century.* Washington: American Association of Museums.

Brown Goode, G. 1891. The museums of the future. *Annual report of the Board of Regents of the Smithsonian Institution for the year ending June 30, 1889,* sect. 3, 427–45.

Danilov, V. J. 1982. *Science and Technology Centres.* Cambridge, Mass.: MIT Press.

Engström, K. 1973. Aims of the exhibition and educational activities at the museum of natural history. In K. Engström and A. G. Johnels, op. cit.

Engström, K. and A. G. Johnels (eds) 1973. *The natural history museum and the community.* Oslo: Scandinavian University Books.

Finlay, I. 1977. *Priceless heritage: the future of museums.* London: Faber and Faber.

Günther, A. 1880. Presidential address to section D – biology. *Report of the British Association for the Advancement of Science,* 1880, 591–8.

Hudson, K. 1975. *A social history of museums.* London: Macmillan.

Hudson, K. 1977. *Museums for the 1980s. A survey of world trends.* London: Macmillan.

Levin, M. E. 1976. On the ascription of functions to objects, with special reference to inference in archaeology. *Phil. Soc. Sci.* **6**, 227–34.

Lewis, B. N. 1980. The museum as an educational facility. *Museums J.* **80**, 151–5.

Miles, R. S. 1986. Museum audiences. *Int. J. Mus. Management, Curatorship* **5**, 73–80.

Miles, R. S. 1986. Lessons in 'Human Biology': testing a theory of exhibition design. *Int. J. Mus. Management, Curatorship* **5**, 227–40.

Miles, R. S. and A. F. Tout 1978. Human biology and the new exhibition scheme in the British Museum (Natural History). *Curator* **21**, 36-50.

Neurath, M. 1974. Isotype. *Instruct. Sci.* **3**, 127–50.

Neurath, M. and R. S. Cohen (eds) 1973. *Empiricism and sociology: the life and work of Otto Neurath.* Boston, Mass.: Reidel.

Popper, K. 1972. *Objective knowledge.* Oxford: Oxford University Press.

Thompson, J. M. A. (ed.) 1984. *Manual of curatorship.* London: Butterworth.

Wittlin, A. 1970. *Museums: in search of a usable future.* Cambridge, Mass.: MIT Press.

2 The general framework

Eason, L. P. and M. C. Linn 1976. Evaluation of the effectiveness of participatory exhibits. *Curator* **19**, 45–62.

Etzioni, A. 1968. *The active society: a theory of societal and political processes.* London: Collier-Macmillan.

Friedman, A. J., L. P. Eason and C. I. Sneider 1979. Star games: a participatory astronomy exhibit. *Planetarian* **8**, 3–7.

Griggs, S. A. 1981. Formative evaluation of exhibits at the British Museum (Natural History). *Curator* **24**, 189–202.

Griggs, S. A. and J. Manning 1983. The predictive validity of formative evaluation of exhibits. *Museums Studies Journal* **1**, 31–41.

Lord, B. and G. D. Lord (eds) 1983. *Planning our museums.* Ottawa: National Museums of Canada.

Macdonald-Ross, M. and R. H. W. Waller 1975. Criticism, alternatives and tests: a conceptual framework for improving typography. *Prog. learning educ. tech.* **12**, 75–83.

Miles, R. S. 1985. Exhibitions: management, for a change. In *The management of change in museums,* N. Cossons (ed.), 31–4. London: National Maritime Museum.

Nicol, E. 1969. *The development of validated museum exhibits.* Project 5-0245, OEC1-6-050245-1015 Washington, DC: Eric Reports for US Dept of Health, Education and Welfare.

Royal Institute of British Architects 1980. *Handbook of architectural practice and management,* 4th edn. London: RIBA Publications.

Royal Ontario Museum 1976. *Communicating with the museum visitor. Guidelines for planning.* Toronto: Royal Ontario Museum.

Screven, C. G. 1976. Exhibit evaluation – a goal-referenced approach. *Curator* **19**, 271–90.

Screven, C. G. 1984. Educational evaluation and research in museums and public exhibits: a bibliography. *Curator* **27**, 147–65.

Screven, C. G. 1986. Exhibitions and information centers: some principles and approaches. *Curator* **29**, 109–37.

Shettel, H. H. 1968. An evaluation of existing criteria for judging the quality of science exhibits. *Curator* **11**, 137–53.

Waddington, C. H. 1977. *Tools for thought*. London: Cape.

3 Psychological and educational aspects of exhibition design

Deci, E. L. 1975. *Intrinsic motivation*. New York: Plenum Press.

Gagné, R. M. and L. J. Briggs 1979. *Principles of instructional design*. New York: Holt, Rinehart and Winston.

Gilbert, T. F. 1969. *Mathetics: an explicit theory for the design of teaching programs, 1962*. London: Longmac.

Glaser, R. 1965. *Teaching machines and programed learning, 2: data and direction*. Washington, DC: National Education Association.

Harlow, H. F. 1959. Learning set and error factor theory. In *Psychology: a study of science*, vol. 2, S. Koch (ed.), 492–537. New York: McGraw-Hill.

Horn, R. E. 1976–80. *Developing instructional materials and procedures: an information mapping course*. Massachusetts: Information Resources.

Lepper, M. R. and D. Greene (eds) 1978. *The hidden costs of reward*. New York: Erlbaum.

Lewis, B. N. and I. S. Horabin 1977. Algorithmics 1967. *Improv. Human Perf. Q.* **6**, 55–85.

McClelland, D. C., J. W. Atkinson, R. A. Clark and E. L. Lowell 1953. *The achievement motive*. New York: Appleton–Century–Crofts.

Pask, G. 1966. Comments on the cybernetics of ethical, psychological and sociological systems. In *Progress in bio-cybernetics*, vol. 3 (Weiner Memorial Volume), J. P. Schade (ed.), 158–250. Amsterdam: Elsevier.

Rowntree, D. 1974. *Educational technology in curriculum development*. London: Harper & Row.

Rowntree, D. 1981. *Developing courses for students*. New York: McGraw-Hill.

Seligman, M. E. P. 1975. *Helplessness*. San Francisco: W. H. Freeman.

Tarpy, R. M. 1975. *Basic principles of learning*. Illinois: Scott, Foresman.

Tresemer, D. W. 1977. *Fear of success*. New York: Plenum Press.

4 and 5 Planning the work and The exhibition team

Battersby, A. 1967. *Network analysis for planning and scheduling*, 2nd edn. London: Macmillan.

Battersby, A. 1975. *Mathematics in management*. London: Penguin.

Howell, D. B. 1971. A network system for the planning, designing, construction and installation of exhibits. *Curator* **14**, 100–8.

Lord, B. and G. D. Lord (eds) 1983. See Chapter 2 list.

Miles, R. S. 1985. See Chapter 2 list.

Royal Ontario Museum 1976. See Chapter 2 list.

6 Organising the intellectual content

Beer, S. 1959. *Cybernetics in management*. London: English Universities Press.

von Bertalanffy, L. 1973. *General system theory*. London: Penguin.

Gagné, R. M. 1970. *The conditions of learning*, 2nd edn. New York: Holt, Rinehart and Winston.

Klir, J. and M. Valach 1967. *Cybernetic modelling*. London: Illiffe.

Pask, G. 1975. *The cybernetics of human learning and performance*. London: Hutchinson.

Screven, C. G. 1986. See Chapter 2 list.

The UK Post Office 1975. *Handbook of data communications*. Manchester: NCC Publications.

7 Laying out the exhibition

Bayer, H. 1961. See Chapter 1 list.

Brawne, M. 1965. *The new museum: architecture and display*. London: Architectural Press.

British Standards Institution 1979. *Code of practice for access for the disabled to buildings*. BS no. 5810. London: British Standards Institution.

Clarke, G. C. S. 1981. Evolving an exhibition on evolution. *Museums J.* **81**, 147–51.

Coleman, L. V. 1950. *Museum buildings*. Vol. 1: *a planning study*. Washington, DC: The American Association of Museums.

Fairweather, L. and J. Sliwa 1977. *AJ metric handbook*, 3rd edn. London: Architectural Press.

Gardner, J. and C. Heller 1960. *Exhibition and display*. London: Batsford.

Goldsmith, S. 1967. *Designing for the disabled*, 2nd edn. New York: McGraw-Hill.

Lakota, R. A. 1975. *The National Museum of Natural History as a behavioural environment. Part 1: An environmental analysis of behavioural performance*. Washington, DC: Office of Museum Programs, Smithsonian Institution.

Lakota, R. A. and J. A. Kantner 1976. *The National Museum of Natural History as a behavioural environment. Part 2: Summary and recommendations*. Washington, DC: Office of Museum Programs, Smithsonian Institution.

Lehmbruck, M. 1974. Museum architecture. *Museum* **26**, 129–280.

Lord, B. and G. D. Lord (eds) 1983. See Chapter 2 list.

Melton, A. 1935. Problems of installation in museums

of art. *Publ. Am. Assoc. Museums* N.S. **14**, 1–269.

Miles, R. S. 1986. See Chapter 1 list.

Royal Ontario Museum 1976. See Chapter 2 list.

Witteborg, L. P. 1958. Design standards in museum exhibits. *Curator* **1**, 29–41.

8 The individual exhibits

Alexander, C. 1964. *Notes on the synthesis of form.* Cambridge, Mass.: Harvard.

Alt, M. B. and K. M. Shaw 1984. Characteristics of ideal museum exhibits. *Br. J. Psychol.* **75**, 25–36.

Chapanis, A. 1965. *Man–machine engineering.* London: Tavistock Publications.

Chartered Institution of Building Services (Lighting Division) 1980. *CIBS lighting guide – museums and art galleries.* Lighting guide no. 14. London: CIBS.

Cohen, M. S., G. H. Wintel, R. Olsen and F. Wheeler 1977. Orientation in a museum – an experimental visitor study. *Curator* **20**, 85–97.

Danilov, V. J. 1978. *Traveling exhibitions. An overview of not-for-profit traveling exhibitions services.* Washington, DC: Association of Science–Technology Centers.

Fairweather, L. and J. Sliwa 1977. See Chapter 7 list.

Gardner, J. and C. Heller 1960. See Chapter 7 list.

Gleadowe, T. 1979. *Organising exhibitions: a manual outlining the methods used to organise temporary exhibitions of works of art*, 2nd edn. London: Arts Council of Great Britain.

Grandjean, E. 1969. *Fitting the task to the man.* London: Taylor and Francis.

Griggs, S. A. 1983. Orienting visitors within a thematic display. *Int. J. Mus. Management, Curatorship* **2**, 119–34.

Hjorth, J. 1977. How to make a rotten exhibition. *Curator* **20**, 185–204.

Hodge, R. and W. D'Souza 1979. The museum as a communicator. *Museum* **31**, 251–67.

Macdonald-Ross, M. and R. H. W. Waller 1976. The transformer. *Penrose Annual* **69**, 141–52.

McCormick, E. J. 1976. *Human factors in engineering and design.* New York: McGraw-Hill.

Melton, A. 1935. See Chapter 7 list.

Miller, G. A. 1970. The magical number seven, plus or minus two: some limits on our capacity for processing information. In *The psychology of communication.* London: Penguin.

Neal, A. 1976. *Exhibits for the small museum: a handbook.* Nashville, Tenn.: American Association for State and Local History.

Neal, A. 1987. *Help! for the small museum: a handbook of exhibit ideas and methods*, 3rd edn. Boulder, Colorado: Pruett Publishing.

Pugh, F. 1978. *Handling and packing works of art: a manual outlining the methods used to pack and handle works of art.* London: Arts Council of Great Britain.

Singleton, W. J., R. S. Easterby and D. Whitfield 1971. *The human operator in complex systems.* London: Taylor and Francis.

Tyler, B. and V. Dickenson 1977. *A handbook for the travelling exhibitionist.* Ottawa: Canadian Museums Association.

Witteborg, L. P. 1981. *Good show, a practical guide for temporary exhibitions.* Washington: Smithsonian Institution Travelling Exhibition Service.

Wittlin, A. S. 1971. Hazards of communication by exhibits. *Curator* **14**, 138–50.

9 Choosing media and their modes of use

Alt, M. B. 1979. Improving audio-visual presentations. *Curator* **22**, 85–95.

Borun, M. 1977. *Measuring the immeasurable: a pilot study of museum effectiveness.* Washington, DC: Association of Science–Technology Centers.

Browne, M. 1896. *Artistic and scientific taxidermy and modelling: a manual of instruction in the methods of preserving and reproducing the correct form of all natural objects.* London: Black.

Bruman, R. 1984. *Exploratorium Cookbook I: a construction manual for Exploratorium exhibits.* Revised edn. San Francisco: Exploratorium.

Clark, R. E. 1983. Reconsidering research on learning from media. *Review of Educational Research* **53**, 445–59.

Gardner, J. and C. Heller 1960. See Chapter 7 list.

Grandjean, E. 1969. See Chapter 8 list.

Grantz, G. 1969. *Home book of taxidermy and tanning.* Harrisburg, Pa: Stackpole Books.

Hall, M. 1987. *On display. A design grammar for museum exhibitions.* London: Lund Humphries.

Hartley, J. 1978. *Designing instructional text.* London: Kogan Page.

Hipschman, R. 1980. *Exploratorium Cookbook II: a construction manual for Exploratorium exhibits.* San Francisco: Exploratorium.

Kapp, R. O. 1973. *The presentation of technical information*, 2nd edn. London: Constable.

Lakota, R. A. and J. A. Kantner 1976. See Chapter 7 list.

Lanteri, E. 1902–11. *Modelling: a guide for teachers and students*, vols 1–3. London: Chapman and Hall.

Lord, B. and G. D. Lord (eds) 1983. See Chapter 2 list.

Macdonald-Ross, M. 1977. Graphics in texts. In *Review of research in education*, vol. 5, L. S. Shulman (ed.). Itasca, Ill.: Peacock.

Macdonald-Ross, M. 1977. How numbers are shown: a review of reasearch on the presentation of quantitative data in texts. *Audio-Visual Commun. Rev.* **25**, 359–409.

Macdonald-Ross, M. 1978. Language in text. In *Review of research in education*, vol. 6, L. S. Schulman (ed.). Itasca, Ill.: Peacock.

McFall, W. 1975. *Taxidermy step by step.* New York: Winchester Press.

Malone, T. W. 1981. What makes computer games fun? *Byte,* vol. 6, 258–75.

Metcalf, J. 1981. *Taxidermy.* London: Duckworth.

Neal, A. 1976. See Chapter 8 list.

Neal, A. 1987. See Chapter 8 list.

Neurath, O. 1939. *Modern man in the making.* London: Secker and Warburg.

Olschki, L. (ed.) 1977. *La ceroplastica nella scienza e nell'arte,* vol. 20, parts 1 and 2. Atti del i congresso internationale, Firenze 3–7 guigno 1975. Florence: Biblioteca della Rivista di Storia delle Scienze Mediche e Naturali.

Parsloe, E. (ed.) 1984. *Interactive video.* Wilmslow, Cheshire: Sigma Technical Press.

Reynolds, L. 1979. Teletext and viewdata: a new challenge for the designer. *Inform. Design J.* **11**, 2–14.

Romiszowski, `A. J. 1974. *The selection and use of instructional media: A systems approach.* London: Kogan Page.

Rowley, J. 1925. *Taxidermy and museum exhibition.* New York: D. Appleton.

Rowntree, D. 1974. See Chapter 3 list.

Screven, C. G. 1986. See Chapter 2 list.

Serrell, B. 1983. *Making exhibit labels: a step-by-step guide.* Nashville, Tenn.: American Association for State and Local History.

Shettel, H. S. 1973. Exhibits: art form or educational medium? *Museum News* **52**, 32–41.

Simlinger, P. 1980. Designing public information symbols. *Inform. Design J.* **1**, 182–90.

Swann, C. 1969. *Techniques of typography.* London: Lund Humphries.

Thier, H. D. and M. C. Linn 1976. The value of interactive learning experiences. *Curator* **19**, 233–45.

Toft, A. 1970. *Modelling and sculpture.* London: Seeley, Service.

Waller, R. H. W. 1979. Typographic access structures for educational texts. In *Processing of visible language,* vol. 1, P. A. Kolers, M. E. Wrolstad & H. Bauma (eds), 175–87. London: Plenum Press.

Washburne, R. F. and J. A. Wager 1972. Evaluating visitor response to exhibit content. *Curator* **15**, 248–54.

Wittlin, A. S. 1971. See Chapter 8 list.

Wright, A. 1970. *Designing for visual aids.* London: Studio Vista.

10 and 11   Disabled visitors and Conservation

Beechel, J. M. 1974. *Interpretation for handicapped persons.* Master's thesis, University of Washington, College of Forest Resources.

Bostick, W. A. 1977. *The guarding of cultural property.* Paris: Unesco.

British Standards Institution 1979. See Chapter 7 list.

Callow, K. B. 1974. Museums and the disabled. *Museums J.* **74**, 70–2.

Goldsmith, S. 1967. *Designing for the Disabled,* 2nd edn. New York: McGraw-Hill.

Kenney, A. P. 1979. *Hospitable heritage: the report of museum access.* Pennsylvania: Lehigh County Historical Society.

Revière, G. H. and H. F. E. Visser 1960. Museum showcases. *Museum* **13**, 1–55.

Royal Ontario Museum 1976. See Chapter 2 list.

Royal Ontario Museum 1979.` *In search of the black box. A report on the proceedings of a workshop on micro-climates.* Toronto: Royal Ontario Museum.

Snider, H. W. 1977. *Museums and handicapped students. Guidelines for educators.* Washington, DC: Smithsonian Institution.

Stolow, N. 1987. *Conservation and exhibitions.* London: Butterworth.

Thomson, G. 1970. *Conservation and museum lighting,* 2nd edn. London: The Museums Association.

Thomson, G. 1986. *The museum environment,* 2nd edn. London: Butterworth.

Tillotson, R. G. 1977. *Museum security.* Paris: International Council of Museums.

Turner, I. K. 1980. *Museum showcases. A design brief.* British Museum Occasional Papers, no. 29.

Welsh Office 1978. *Access for the disabled: Design guidance notes.* Cardiff: HMSO.

12 and 13   The specification and Scheduling, monitoring and controlling exhibit production

Lewis, B. N. 1971. Course production at the Open University. 1: Some basic problems. *Br. J. Educ. Tech.* **2**, 4–13.

Lewis, B. N. 1971. Course production at the Open University. 2: Activities and activity networks. *Br. J. Educ. Tech.* **2**, 111–23.

Lewis, B. N. 1971. Course production at the Open University. 3: Planning and scheduling. *Br. J. Educ. Tech.* **2**, 189–204.

Lord, B. and G. D. Lord (eds) 1983. See Chapter 2 list.

Royal Ontario Museum 1976. See Chapter 2 list.

14   Improving the performance

Barrass, R. 1978. *Scientists must write. A guide to better writing for scientists, engineers and students.* London: Chapman and Hall.

Evans, H. 1972. *Newsman's English. Book 1: Editing and design.* London: Heinemann.

Flesch, R. 1960. *How to write, speak and think more effectively.* London: Harper & Row.

Kapp, R. O. 1973. *The presentation of technical information,* 2nd edn (revised by A. Isaacs). London:

Constable.

Melton, A. 1935. See Chapter 7 list.

15 and 16   Evaluation – its nature and limitations and Designing and carrying out the evaluation study

Alt, M. B. 1980. Four years of visitor surveys at the British Museum (Natural History) 1976–79. *Museums J.* **80**, 10–19.

Anderson, S. B., S. Ball, R. T. Murphy *et al.* 1975. *Encyclopedia of educational evaluation. Concepts and techniques for evaluating education and training programs.* San Francisco: Jossey-Bass.

Beveridge, W. I. B. 1968. *The art of scientific investigations.* London: Heinemann.

Borun, M. 1977. See Chapter 9 list.

Brown, G. S. 1957. *Probability and scientific inference.* New York: Longmans, Green.

Campbell, D. T. and J. C. Stanley 1965. *Experimental and quasi-experimental design for research on teaching.* Chicago: Rand McNally.

Cranbach, L. J. 1960. *Essentials of psychological testing,* 2nd edn. New York: Harper & Row.

Educational Testing Science 1963. *Multiple choice questions: a close look.* Princeton: ETS.

Edwards, A. L. 1956. *Techniques of attitude scale construction.* New York: Appleton.

Elliott, P. and R. J. Loomis 1973. *Studies of visitor behaviour in museums and exhibitions: an annotated bibliography.* Washington, DC: Office of Museum Programs, Smithsonian Institution.

Ferguson, E. L. and J. D. Nason 1980. Human subject rights and museum research. *Museum News* **53**, 44–7.

Griggs, S. A. 1981. See Chapter 2 list.

Griggs, S. A. 1984. Evaluating exhibitions. In Thompson, J. M. A. See Chapter 1 list.

Griggs, S. A. and J. Manning 1983. See Chapter 2 list.

Guttentag, M. and E. L. Struening (eds) 1975. *Handbook of evaluation research,* vol. 2, Beverly Hills and London: Sage.

Harré, R. and P. F. Secord 1972. *The explanation of social behaviour.* Oxford: Blackwell.

Kerlinger, F. N. 1964. *Foundations of behavioural research.* New York: Holt, Rinehart and Winston.

Levine, M. 1974. Scientific method and the adversary model: some preliminary thoughts. *Am. Psychol.* **29**, 661–77.

Loomis, R. J. 1987. *Museum visitor evaluation: new tool for management.* Nashville, Tenn.: Am. Assoc. State and Local History.

Moser, C. A. 1958. *Survey methods in social investigations.* London: Heinemann.

Screven, C. G. 1984. See Chapter 2 list.

Shettel, H., Butcher, M. *et al.* 1968. *Strategies for determining exhibit effectiveness.* Washington DC: American Institutes for Research.

Struening, E. L. and M. Guttentag (eds) 1975. *Handbook of evaluation research,* vol. 1. Beverly Hills and London: Sage.

Index

Figures in italics refer to illustrations.

abstract expressionism 153
access, to show-cases 108
accountability
  new age of 133
  value placed on 132
African village, diorama 61
age, of exhibits 180
aims 11, 43, 106, 124
air conditioning 108
Alexander, C. 75
algorithms 32
American Association of Museums 101
American Museum of Natural History 9, 101
analogy, as way of coming to know 37, *3.6*
analysis
  of differences 168
  of evaluation data 166
animal diversity, as exhibition theme 55
arc, in a network 39, 51
art galleries 8
artwork 113, 117–18
astronomy exhibition, in Lawrence Hall of Science 16
attendance information 125
attention 24–6
attitude, as psychological variable 162
attracting power 15, 80, 145, 156, 159, 167
attributes 151
audio-visual
  aids 20, 28, 32
  maintenance 87, 110
  theatres 12, 17, 61, 88
audio-visuals 12, 13, 17, 78, 81, 86–9, 101, 104, 111–14, 117, 118, 120

back-lighting 69, 75, 90
back projection 88
back-tracking 28, 31, 33
bar charts 121, *13.3*
Barrass, R. 124
Battersby, A. 39
Bauhaus 6
Beechel, J. M. 105
Beer, S. 54
behaviour of visitors 25
belief systems 128, 131
Bertalanffy, L. von 54
bird gallery, in British Museum (Natural History) *8.1*
blind visitors 104
book-on-the-wall exhibits 66
booklets 122
books, and exhibitions 2, 9, 12, 66, 117, 118, 122–4
bookstalls 122, 124

Brachiosaurus 163
braille 104
breathers, in show-cases 108
briefs 12, 16, 43–5, 52, 56, 57, 76, 111, 115, 117, 126, *4.4*
British Museum (Natural History) 1, 3–7, 8, 16, 43, 47, 53, 56, 57–9, 85, 97, 104, 108, 113, 116–17, 120, 145, 156, 158, 160, 165, 184, *1.1, 1.2, 1.3, 2.1, 2.4, 2.5, 3.2, 3.3, 3.4, 3.5, 3.6, 6.3, 6.4, 7.1, 7.5, 8.1, 8.2, 8.5, 8.15, 9.4, 9.5, 9.6, 9.8, 9.12, 9.14, 9.16–9.19, 9.20, 9.22*
Brown Goode, G. 3, 5
Browne, M. 101
Bruman, R. 100
buffers 108
Building Workers' Union exhibition 17, *1.7*

Cage, John 153
Callow, K. B. 102
Camptosaurus 163
captions 14
catalogues 12, 40
categorisation 159, 160, 162
census 151
Central Services Department, of British Museum (Natural History) 117, 118, 120
central tendency, measure of in statistics 166
Change Agents 142
chiff-chaffs 104
Children's Museum, Boston 16
circulation, around exhibits 6, 7, 57, 59, 61, *7.6, 7.7, 7.8*
codification, of feedback 125
coding, of evaluation data 164–6
cognitive fixity 38
cognitive obstacles to learning 20
colour
  to evoke exhibit theme 63
  in graphics 91–2
communication 7, 122
competitive tender 117, 118
compromise exhibits 66
computers
  printed output 99
  programs 96, 110
computer-aided learning 32, 80
computer-based exhibits 66, 79, 80, 95–101, Table 9.1, *3.5, 9.16–9.19*
computer-generated graphics 99
concept hierarchies 44, 51–3, 54, 57, 115, 119, *6.1, 6.3, 6.4*
concepts 50–1, 54, 56, 60–1, 72, 124, 131
conceptual frameworks 21, 28, 31, 56, 65, 72
confidence limits, in statistics 151
conservation 2, 13, 75, 106–9, 111
contract size 119
contracts group, in British Museum (Natural History) 117
control groups, in evaluation 145, 146–7

conviviality
  conditions of 23
  in learning environments 38
coordination of dimensions 75
copyright 88, 90, 101, 110
correlation, coefficient of 167
cost control 45
cost effectiveness 22, 132
criteria, for judging exhibits 17, 163, Table 2.1
critical path analysis 39–41, 120
cross breaks, in tables 166
Curator 101
curators 3, 7, 66, 102
cybernetics 54

Danilov, V. J. 76
data, in evaluation
  collection of 158–63
  preparation of 158
deadlines 116, 121
deaf visitors 104
defining the mission 11
definition, as way of coming to know 34, *3.2*
demonstration, as way of coming to know 34, *3.3*
demountability 74, 75–6
department stores, planning data 60, Table 7.1
design
  as a process 56, 63
  drawings, in specification document 113–14, 117
  from the gallery downwards 4, 7, 8, 54
  from the message upwards 4, 8
  goal referenced approach 15
designers
  introduction into museums 7
  relations with curators 7
  role in exhibit design 7
Deutscher Werkbund exhibition 7
development
  partnerships 47, 49, 117, 118, 125, 172, 178–84
  process 11, 43, 46, 47, 52, 102, 111, 113, 116, 120
  team, matched to number of draughtsmen 47–9
Development Section, in British Museum (Natural History) 116–18
development cycle, for exhibits 15, *2.3*
diagrams 88, 91–2, 113, 117
dials 97
Dickenson, V. 76
diffusers 194
dinosaurs 9, 160, 162
'Dinosaurs and their Living Relatives' exhibition, in the British Museum (Natural History) *9.17*
dioramas 61, 85, 111, 113, 117, *9.5*
Diplodocus carnegii 108, 163
disabled visitors 102–5
discovery rooms 96
disjointed incrementalism 17

dispersion, statistics of 148–50, Table 13.3
displacement sensors 110
Disraeli, B. 127
dissolves, in audio-visuals 87, 112
Domesday book 161
dormouse 111
drawing office 47–9, 117, 118, 119
dressing, of exhibits 12, 117, 118, 120
dummy activities 40
dust 13, 107–9, 110
dynamic exhibits 9, 13, 78–101, 117

Eason, L. P. 16
ecology, as exhibition theme 53–5
Editorial Section, in British Museum (Natural History) 117, 118
education
    and exhibits 1–3, 20–38
    materials 118
    programmes 12
    staff 124
educational
    exhibits, things that go wrong 21
    museums, Brown Goode's definition 3
educationalists
    in museums 7
    rôle in design of exhibits 20–1
effectiveness
    of audio-visuals 86
    of exhibits 17, 18, 22, 47, 111
electronic
    circuitry 74
elephants 28, 32, 120
emotional
    impact 2
    obstacles to learning 20
empathy 26–7
emphasis, given by
    colour 70, 8.10
    isolation 70, 8.9
    italics 94, 9.15
    light 71, 8.14
    position 70, 8.11
    shape 70–1, 8.12
    size 70, 8.8
    texture 71, 8.13
enactment, as way of coming to know 37, 3.5
Encyclopaedia Britannica 98, 99
Engström, K. 10
entry knowledge 27, 44
ergonomics
    and disabled persons 10.1
    lighting 67–9, 8.6
    standardisation 74
    viewing space 61, 7.9
error elimination, in trial and error cycle 15
errors, sensitivity to 33
Etzioni, A. 18, 19
evaluation 12–14, 16, 23, 33, 43, 49, 74, 76, 127–70, 171
    atomistic 144

criteria of success 136–7
    formative 134, 139–41, 144, 147, 156–8, 168, 2.4, 2.5, 8.5
    holistic 144
    methodological limitations of 135–41
    political limitations of 135, 141–3
    prospective studies in 146
    psycho-dynamics of 130, 141, 143
    qualitative approaches 144, 159
    quantitative approaches 144, 159
    retrospective studies in 146
    scientific 127
    summative 134–5, 139, 140, 144, 145–6, 156
    ways in which data can be received 141
evaluators, professional 127–8, 129, 130, 131, 132, 133, 134, 135–7, 141, 142–3, 158
Evans, H. 124
evolution and diversity, as exhibition theme 53–4
Evolution Gallery, in Royal Scottish Museum 8.4
evolutionary theory 153
exhibits
    categories of 17–18, Table 2.1
exhibitions
    definition of 1–2
    educative component of secondary importance 1
    indices of success 33
    natural 2
    part visitors expected to play 34
    reasons for visiting 25–6
    self-congratulatory 1
exit gradient effect 57
experiential information 125–6
experimental information 125
exponential processes 173, 179
extraneous variation 157

fabrication, of exhibits 117, 119, 120
factor analysis, in statistics 168
families, as visitors to exhibitions 60
fatigue effects 20
feedback
    from travelling exhibitions 77
    in exhibit development 15, 16
    to visitors 82–3
Festival of Britain 7
films 78, 86–8, 112
filters, for light 106
Finnegans wake 153
flashback, in audio-visuals 87
Flip panels 91, 9.12
Flesch, R. 124
flexibility 74-5
floor
    area 47, 119
    plan 56, 64
format 32
forms of life, as exhibition theme 55
frequency distributions, in statistics 147–50, 167, Tables 16.1, 16.2

front-end analysis 45, 134
function, as a factor in design 56, 66–9
fungi 55

Gagné, R. M. 51
gallery 4, 15, 40, 54, 56–9, 71, 76, 122
Gallery of British Zoology, in British Museum (Natural History) 3
Galton, Sir Francis 159
gambler's fallacy 154
Gardner, J. 68, 101
gemstones 63
general systems theory 54
generalisability, of evaluation results 15, 137, 138–9, 140, 146, 147, 158
Geological Museum, London 98
Gilbert, T. F. 32
glare 67–9, 8.6
Gleadowe, T. 76
Goethe, J. W. von 29
graffiti 110
Grandjean, E. 80
Grantz, G. 101
graphic
    design, publications on 101
    panels 69, 79, 104, 140
    sandwiches 74, 75
graphics 59, 67, 75, 88–92, 111–14
Graphics Section, in British Museum (Natural History) 117, 118
graphs 166
Great Teachers 27
grids, as aid to design 67, 8.2
Gropius, W. 6–8
Gross National Product 131, Table 15.1
group, as a unit in the exhibition team 172, 175–7, 181
guessing 38
Günther, A. 4
Guttentag, M. 133

habitat groups 85
half-life, of exhibits 173–4, 176–7, 179
halo effect 160
Hartley, J. 101
Health and Safety at Work Etc. Act 1974 101
heat, as conservation factor 107, 109
Heller, C. 68, 101
Hipschman, R. 100
histograms 147, 150, 16.1
holding power 15, 81, 145, 156, 159, 167
homeopathic medicines 37
homeostasis 97, 139
hope, in motivation of visitors 26
Horabin, I. S. 32
Horn, R. E. 32
how life works, as exhibition theme 55
Howell, D. B. 40
Hudson, K. 2, 3
'Human biology' exhibition, in British Museum (Natural History) 53, 2.1, 2.5, 3.4, 3.6, 9.4, 9.12, 9.18, 9.19, 9.20, 9.22
human joints, models of 81, 83

humanisation of knowledge 8
humidity
    absolute 107
    relative 13, 106, 107
hypothesis testing, in evaluation 145–6

ignorance, tests of 27
illumination levels Table 11.1
illustrations 72, 88–91, 110, 113–14, 117–18, 124, 144
implementation stage, of mounting an exhibition 11–13, 126, 127, 134
importance, as a factor in design 56, 64
improvability, of humans 22
index collection, in British Museum (Natural History) 3
information mapping 32
initial problem, of trial and error cycle 15
insect pests 107
installation 114, 117, 118
    of travelling exhibits 77
installation and dressing stage, of mounting an exhibition 11, 12
instructions, with exhibits 56, 69, 75, 99, 100
interaction, as way of coming to know 34, *3.4*
interactive exhibits 32, 69, 72, 95–101, 140, 167, *9.20*
International Council of Museums (ICOM) 9, 109
    definition of museum 9
International Journal of Museum Management and Curatorship 101
interviewing 159, 161
interviews
    fully-structured 159–60
    open ended 144
    semi-structured 159–60, 161
    unstructured 159
'Introducing ecology' exhibition, in British Museum (Natural History) *3.2, 3.5, 7.1, 9.5, 9.16*
island displays 61
Isotype 8, 88, 91, *9.10*

Joyce, James 163

Kantner, J. A. 61, 80
Kapp, R. O. 124
Kenney, A. P. 102, 104
key
    drawings 66
    numbers 66
keyboards 99
Klir, J. 54
knowledge, compared with understanding 50–1

labels 4, 43, 49, 56, 67, 75
Lakota, R. A. 58, 61, 72
Lanteri, E. 101
Law of Diminishing Returns 22, 31, 151
Lawrence Hall of Science 16, 37
layouts 15, 67, 69

leaflets 210
learning 34, 74, 78, 129, 137, 162
    by looking 32
    from experience 14–15
    nature of 20, 21, 38, 50, 51, 52
lectures 2, 3, 122, 124
'Lepidoptera', exhibition in British Museum (Natural History) *8.3*
leisure 22
levels, of the intellectual structure of exhibits 24, 51, *6.2*
levers 99
Levin, M. E. 9
Lewis, B. N. 32
lichens 55
life processes and behaviour, as exhibition theme 53–4
light, as conservation factor 106
light-box 68
light sensor beams 110
lighting 12, 57, 67–9, 109, 113, *8.6*
Linn, M. C. 16
Lord, B. and G. D. 101
low-relief diagrams 104

machines 59, 117, 120
maintenance 49, 74, 76, 77, 87, 106, 108, 110, 118
maintenance stage, of mounting an exhibition 11, 13–14
Malone, T. W. 96
mammals 55
man, as exhibition theme 53–4
'Man's place in evolution' exhibition, in British Museum (Natural History) 85, *3.3, 9.6*
mapping, content onto space 55, 56
maps 59, 71, 72
mass media 13, 24, 142
mathetics 32
McFall, W. 101
McLuhan, M. 78
mean, arithmetic 147–54, 166–7, *16.6*
mechanical exhibits 17, 110, 111, 114, 117
media 56, 59, 64, 72, 74, 78–101, 122, 171
    functions of 80–3
    selection of 78–9
median, in statistics 166, *16.6*
Melton, A. 57, 122
memory, nature of 9
mental blindness 38
mentally disabled visitors 104–5
meta-evaluation 134, 135
metal foil tapes 110
Metcalf, J. 101
Metra Potential Method (MPM) 40, *4.2*
microclimates 106, 107–9
Miller, G. A. 65
minerals 63
misinterpretive exhibits 65, 66
mock-up exhibits 15, 134, 139–40, 147, 156–8, 160, 168, *2.5, 8.5*
mode
    in statistics 148, 166

of communication 28, 56, 64, 78–101
modelmaking 101
Modelmaking and Taxidermy Section, in British Museum (Natural History) 118
models 66, 81, 83–5, 106, 108, 111–14, 117–18, 120, *9.2, 9.3, 9.4*
modularity 74–5
modules 74–5
monitoring, of exhibit production 115
motivation 20
mould 107
mounted animals 84–5
multi-level structure, for an exhibition 51, *6.2*
multiple-choice tests 162
multiple regression, in statistics 168
Museum 101
Museum News 101
Museum of Housing and Town Planning, Vienna 7
Museum Studies Journal 101
museum technology 122–4, 126
museums
    of art 3, 8
    as centres of scholarship 2
    attempts to define 8–9
    and educational exhibits 2–10
    failure of educative purpose 3
    history of 2
    of history 3
    maritime 71
    as places in which to mount exhibitions 1, 4, 41–2, 49, 53
    as public institutions 2, 3, 58, 60, 124, 131, 152
    as repositories for objects 2
    as research institutions 2, 41
    of science and technology 2, 3, 55, 66
Museums Association in Britain 101
Museums Journal 101

nature trails 61
Neal, A. 101
negative transfer of knowledge 31
network analysis 39
Neurath, M. 8
Neurath, O. 7, 8
new problem, in trial and error cycle 15
Newton's Second Law of Motion 50
Nicol, E. 16
nodes 39, 51, 54, 115, 119
normal distribution in statistics 149–51, 167, *16.2, 16.3*
norms, in evaluation 137
novelty
    amount tolerated 24
    lure of 24
numbering of exhibits 73–4

objective tests
    in evaluation 162–3
    informal 162
objectives 2, 12, 15, 43, 56, 63, 74, 78, 87, 108, 110, 111, 112, 117, 125, 140

behavioural 18, 32–3, 52–3
objects, role as 'real things' in exhibitions 9, 65, 83–6, 106, 108
observation
  schedules 163, 166
  studies 159, 160
Olschki, L. 101
open storage, style of exhibits 4
organisation
  chart 126
  of exhibition team 46
organisational plan, of an exhibition 71–2
orientation 33, 72, 96, *8.15*
  area 71–2
  directional 58
'Origin of species' exhibition, in British Museum (Natural History) 53, 57–60, *6.3, 6.4, 7.5, 8.15, 9.14*
overall plan, for an exhibition 56, 64
overarching
  principles 33–4
  techniques 28
Owen, Sir Richard 3
ozone 107

pacing, of information 64, 79
parameter
  definition of 42
  super- 172
partially-sighted visitors 104
participant observers, in evaluation 159
Pask, G. 54, 55
perception, psychology of 9, 20, 25, 131
perceptual frame 67
performance standards, in evaluation 137, 139, 140
period rooms 85
phases, of work 54, 111, 125
photomicrography 88
Photographic Section, in British Museum (Natural History) 120
photographs, use in exhibits 7, 75, 88–9, 106, 110, 111, 113, 117
photosynthesis 30
physical convincers 37–8
physically disabled visitors 102–4, *10.1*
plan, long-term for exhibits 53–5, 120, 126
Plan of Creation, as basis for original arrangement of exhibits in British Museum (Natural History) 3
planning 43, 47, 49, 54, 55, 59, 120, 126
planning stage, of mounting an exhibition 11–12
plant diversity, as exhibition theme 55
Plato 137
play mode, pure 23
plinths 59, 66, 85
Poisson distribution in statistics 138, 179
Polaris Fleet Ballistic Missile project 39
policy 43, 45, 126, 144
politics 130, 143
pollution

acidic 107
air 107–8
oxidant 107
Popper, Sir Karl R. 9
population
  survey 155
  target 147, 155
positive transfer of knowledge 31
posters 118
post-test only control group 158
power, as a factor in exhibit design 18, 19
pre-planning and authorisation stage, of mounting an exhibition 11–12, 14, 18, 127, 135
presentation and evaluation stage, of mounting an exhibition 11, 12–13
press-buttons 81, *9.21*
pressure
  groups 142
  sensitive mats 110
pre-testing 157
procurement 117, 120
production
  and standardisation 74
  of exhibits 11, 12, 46, 74, 111, 113
Programme Evaluation and Review Technique (PERT) 39, 120, *4.1*
programmed text 28, 32
progress chart, of exhibition development 183, *17.9*
projectors 78
psychological factors, in exhibit design 18
psychologists, role in design of educational exhibits 20–1
psychometric theory 140, 162
public, as general visitors of exhibitions 2, 14, 20, 21
Public Services Department, in British Museum (Natural History) 117, 120
publications 122–4
Publications Section, in British Museum (Natural History) 117, 120
publicity 41, 60, 76
Pugh, F. 76
punch cards 164
push-buttons 81, *9.21*

quantum mechanics 153
questionnaires 138, 144, 145, 160, 161–2, 163, 165, *16.5*
questions, in exhibition text 81

random access 98–9
random numbers 153, Table 16.6
random processes, characteristics of 179
random sample 147, 150, 152–8, 160
randomisation 157, 158, 168
range, in statistics 167
rapid information transfer 37
rating scale, for exhibits 18, 163
reading speed 101
recruitment plan 126

Rehabilitation Act 1973, USA 102
relational
  networks 29, *3.1*
  thinking 29
reliability, in evaluation 140, 163–4
renewal of exhibits 39, 49, 171–84
repetition, in exhibits 24
replacement of exhibits 39, 49, 171–84
  constant proportion model 172–3, 174–5, 180
  random model 179–80, 180
  selection regimes 178–82
  steady replacement regime 171–2, 174–5
replicas 63, 85, 86, 104, 108
replication, in evaluation results 158
report, writing of in evaluation 168–70
representative sample 144
resources 11, 12, 39, 40, 43, 53, 87, 115
response set, in evaluation 301
reward 26
right turning tendency 57
Rowley, J. 101
Rowntree, D. 29
Royal Ontario Museum 106
Royal Scottish Museum *8.4*

sales information 125
sample size 151–2, 153, 168, *16.4*
sampling
  frame 155
  method 155–6, 160
  of visitors 147, 155–8
scatter 148
schedules, for travelling exhibits 77
scheduling 12, 39, 44, 76, 115–21
school visits 124, 125
science
  centres 2, 8, 95
  museums 95
Science Museum, London *9.3, 9.11*
screen-printing 75, 94, 118
Screven, C. G. 15, 91
searchlight theory of mind, Popper's 9
secondment 41–3, 171, *4.3*
security 77, 109–10
self-image 25–6
self-limitation 38
sequence, as a design factor 56, 64, 69–71
sequencing, of exhibit content 28, 31, 74
  epistemological 32
  logical 31, 50–5
  psychological 31
Shettel, H. H. 17, 18, 78, Table 2.1
short-answer tests, in evaluation 162
show-case museums 4
show-cases 4, 7, 12, 17, 43, 54, 60, 67, 68, 74, 77, 85, 108, 109
significant teaching 28
signposts 59, 72, 74, 90, 180
silica gel 108
Simlinger, P. 90
simplification, avoidance of distortive effects 31
site preparation 12, 40

skewness, in statistics 167
skills, as subject for educational exhibits 50
slip-clutches 110
slow-motion, in audio-visuals 87
snap-change, in audio-visuals 112
Snider, H. W. 102–3, 105
Social and Economic Museum, Vienna 7, 1.8
social scientists, and evaluation 127, 131
sociological factors, in exhibit design 18
sonograms 104
souvenirs 41
space, need to partition in gallery 58
space requirements, estimation of 60–1
sparrow 120
Special Effects Section, in British Museum (Natural History) 118
specification
    document 111–14, 117, 12.1
    process of 12, 15, 47, 75, 99, 111–14, 117, 118, 124
sponsors 12, 13, 14, 20, 32, 43, 129, 132, 135, 136, 142
stages in mounting an exhibition 11–14, 45
    implementation 11–13, 127, 134
    maintenance 11, 13
    planning 11–12
    pre-planning and authorisation 11–12, 14, 127, 135
    presentation and evaluation 11, 13
    updating and revision 11, 134
standard
    deviation, in statistics 147–53, 166–7
    error, in statistics 150–3, 167, 168, 16.4
    scores, in statistics 150
    sizes, of materials 74
standardisation, of exhibit components 74
standards
    for estimating space Table 7.1
    for the physically disabled 103, 10.1
static exhibits 9, 81
Statistical Bureau, EEC 131
statistical inference 132
statistics
    limitation of 137–41
    misuse of 132
Stegosaurus 163
stop-frames, in audio-visuals 87
story-lines 10, 43, 61, 78
story-boards 78, 87, 112
stratified sample, in evaluation 157

stress 23
Struening, E. L. 133
subject-matter 16, 27, 28–9, 43, 52, 56, 72–4
subject-matter experts 12, 43, 117
sulphur dioxide 107
sulphuric acid 107
survey population 145
Swann, C. 101
Swedish Museum of Natural History 9
symbols 90, 91

tabulation of data 166
take-away materials 22
target audience 10, 22, 31, 43, 44, 87, 136, 137
taxidermy 101
television
    as a medium 32, 95
    closed-circuit 159
temporary exhibits 9, 11
tentative theory, of trial and error cycle 15
tests
    of recall 137
    of recognition 137
text 66, 69, 75, 92–4, 104, 110, 112, 113, 117, 118, 124, 144
theme
    as starting point for design 10, 12, 56, 74
    expressed in the design 61, 63
theory, role in trial and error procedure 17, 18
Thomsom, G. 106, 107
three-level structure, for exhibitions 51–2, 6.2
Tillotson, R. G. 110
Toft, A. 101
topic maps 52
touch-sensitive plates 99, 9.21
trade exhibitions 1
Trade Union movement 132
'Treasures of the Earth' exhibition, in the Geological Museum, London 98
training plan 126
travelling exhibitions 11, 76–7
    installation of 77
    location of 11, 76–7
    transport of 77
tree rings, formation of 29, 3.1
trial and error 8, 15, 17–19
Tyler, B. 76
typography 94, 101
Tyrannosaurus 163

ultraviolet light 106, 108
underinterpretive exhibits 65
understanding, nature of 29, 50–1
updating and revision stage, of mounting an exhibition 11, 134

Valach, M. 54
validity, in evaluation 140, 163–4
value judgements, as factor in exhibit design 19, 65, 66, 169
variable
    'already manipulated' 156–7, 168
    dependent 48, 166, 172
    in mathematics and statistics 42, 167
    independent 48, 158, 166, 172
variance, in statistics 138, 149, 163
Victorian natural history 3
videodics 85, 98–9
videotape 85, 99, 110
Vienna method 8
viruses 55
visitor surveys 137
visitors
    and perception of objects 9
    as lay members of public 3, 14, 20, 21, 27
    as readers of books 9–10
    freedom 51, 58
    knowledge and interests 27, 44, 66
    numbers visiting exhibitions 60
    physiological and psychological needs 6, 20, 23–4, 57, 67, 74
visual
    fatigue 69
    noise 75
volunteers, for testing exhibits 30, 134

Waddington, C. H. 15
warders 109, 11.1
ways of knowing
    by analogy 37, 3.6
    definition 34, 3.2
    demonstration 34, 3.3
    enactment 37, 3.5
    interaction 34, 3.4
whole to part relationships 28
willow warblers 104
Wittlin, A. S. 2, 65, 66
work unit, in exhibit planning 115, 119
working drawings 47–9, 114, 117
world-view, of exhibition critics 131
Wright, A. 101

yardsticks, in evaluation 162